Still Practicing

Psychoanalysis in a New Key Book Series
Volume 15

PSYCHOANALYSIS IN A NEW KEY BOOK SERIES

DONNEL STERN
Series Editor

When music is played in a new key, the melody does not change, but the notes that make up the composition do change in the context of continuity, continuity that perseveres through change. "Psychoanalysis in a New Key" publishes books that share the aims psychoanalysts have always had but that approach them differently. The books in the series are not expected to advance any particular theoretical agenda, although to this date most have been written by analysts from the Interpersonal and Relational orientations.

The most important contribution of a psychoanalytic book is the communication of something that nudges the reader's grasp of clinical theory and practice in an unexpected direction. "Psychoanalysis in a New Key" creates a deliberate focus on innovative and unsettling clinical thinking. Because that kind of thinking is encouraged by exploration of the sometimes surprising contributions to psychoanalysis of ideas and findings from other fields, "Psychoanalysis in a New Key" particularly encourages interdisciplinary studies. Books in the series have married psychoanalysis with dissociation, trauma theory, sociology, and criminology. The series is open to the consideration of studies examining the relationship between psychoanalysis and any other field—for instance, biology, literary and art criticism, philosophy, systems theory, anthropology, and political theory.

But innovation also takes place within the boundaries of psychoanalysis, and "Psychoanalysis in a New Key" therefore also presents work that reformulates thought and practice without leaving the precincts of the field. Books in the series focus, for example, on the significance of personal values in psychoanalytic practice, on the complex interrelationship between the analyst's clinical work and personal life, on the consequences for the clinical situation when patient and analyst are from different cultures, and on the need for psychoanalysts to accept the degree to which they knowingly satisfy their own wishes during treatment hours, often to the patient's detriment.

PSYCHOANALYSIS IN A NEW KEY BOOK SERIES

DONNEL STERN
Series Editor

Vol. 15
Still Practicing
The Heartaches and Joys
of a Clinical Career
Sandra Buechler

Vol. 14
Dancing with the Unconscious:
The Art of Psychoanalysis
and the Psychoanalysis of Art
Danielle Knafo

Vol. 13
Money Talks:
In Therapy, Society, and Life
Brenda Berger & Stephanie Newman (eds.)

Vol. 12
Partners in Thought:
Working with Unformulated Experience,
Dissociation, and Enactment
Donnel B. Stern

Vol. 11
Heterosexual Masculinities:
Contemporary Perspectives from
Psychoanalytic Gender Theory
Bruce Reis & Robert Grossmark (eds.)

Vol. 10
Sex Changes:
Transformations in Society
and Psychoanalysis
Mark J. Blechner

Vol. 9
The Consulting Room and Beyond:
Psychoanalytic Work and Its
Reverberations in the Analyst's Life
Therese Ragen

Vol. 8
Making a Difference in Patients'
Lives: Emotional Experience
in the Therapeutic Setting
Sandra Buechler

Vol. 7
Coasting in the Countertransference:
Conflicts of Self Interest between
Analyst and Patient
Irwin Hirsch

Vol. 6
Wounded by Reality:
Understanding and Treating
Adult Onset Trauma
Ghislaine Boulanger

Vol. 5
Prologue to Violence:
Child Abuse, Dissociation, and Crime
Abby Stein

Vol. 4
Prelogical Experience:
An Inquiry into Dreams
and Other Creative Processes
Edward S. Tauber & Maurice R. Green

Vol. 3
The Fallacy of Understanding
and the Ambiguity of Change
Edgar A. Levenson

Vol. 2
What Do Mothers Want?
Contemporary Perspectives in
Psychoanalysis and Related Disciplines
Sheila F. Brown (ed.)

Vol. 1
Clinical Values:
Emotions That Guide
Psychoanalytic Treatment
Sandra Buechler

Still Practicing

The Heartaches and Joys of a Clinical Career

Sandra Buechler

Routledge
Taylor & Francis Group
New York   London

Routledge
Taylor & Francis Group
711 Third Avenue
New York, NY 10017

Routledge
Taylor & Francis Group
27 Church Road
Hove, East Sussex BN3 2FA

© 2012 by Taylor & Francis Group, LLC
Routledge is an imprint of Taylor & Francis Group, an Informa business

Version Date: 20111031

International Standard Book Number: 978-0-415-87912-5 (Hardback) 978-0-415-87913-2 (Paperback)

Library of Congress Cataloging-in-Publication Data

Buechler, Sandra.
    Still practicing : the heartaches and joys of a clinical career / Sandra Buechler.
        p. cm. -- (Psychoanalysis in new key ; no.15)
    Includes bibliographical references and index.
    ISBN 978-0-415-87912-5 (hardcover : alk. paper) -- ISBN 978-0-415-87913-2
    (pbk. : alk. paper) -- ISBN 978-0-203-85226-2 (e-book)
    1. Psychoanalysis. I. Title.

RC506.B838 2012
616.89'17--dc23   2011041331

Visit the Taylor & Francis Web site at
http://www.taylorandfrancis.com

and the Routledge Web site at
http://www.routledgementalhealth.com

For Daphne, Isaac, Eva, Phoebe, their parents, and George

Contents

Introduction: The Personal Impact of Lifelong Clinical Practice   xi

PART I
Hardships in Training

1 Failing to Cultivate Clinical Strengths   3

2 Emotional Hazards of Clinical Training   27

PART 2
Early Career Vicissitudes

3 Traumatically Overwhelming Professional Settings   57

4 Difficult Patients as First Cases   75

PART 3
Evolving Requirements

5 Ongoing Challenges to the Clinician's Sense of Self   97

6 Cocreated Dysfunctional Patterns of Relating   113

7 Bearing Isolation and Sorrow: Chronic Mourning in Clinicians   131

PART 4
Sustaining Practice

8 The Ordinary Tragedies of an Analytic Life   157

9 Transcending Shame and Sorrow   179

10 Analytic Resilience   201

Epilogue: Still Practicing   219
References   221
Index   227

Introduction: The Personal Impact of Lifelong Clinical Practice

We probably don't look much different from any other group of aging professionals determined to have "fun" at a cocktail party. Our smiles are a little forced; our eyes are just a little too shiny. But listen to what we say when we are alone with each other, when no nonclinicians are within earshot.

You will hear casual questions like "How is your practice going?" Anxiety will be evident round the edges of the questions. "How is your practice going?" can be code for "Have you lost as many hours as I have?" "Are you scared you won't make enough money to retire?" "Which of us will have to end our careers prematurely to spare ourselves the humiliation and tedium of a dwindling practice that barely covers the office rent?" "Will it be you or me?"

And just beneath the surface lurk more painful questions, like "Did I fail?" "Am I just not a good enough clinician?" "Do I get so few referrals because everyone knows I'm a lousy therapist?" Failure, the fear of failure, and the anticipation of it have a slightly sour smell. We become tentative, furtive, in our effort to hide our defeat from ourselves.

The insecurity of the aging clinician is probably no different from the insecurity of newly minted therapists, starting out in private practice, but the anxiety is somehow more unseemly. We feel we should have made it by now. We imagine others are thinking the same thing about us.

A career as a clinician has at least one similarity to an acting career. You never stop auditioning. You are always being measured by someone else. Increasingly, those sizing you up are less than half your age. This can get hard to bear. Patients never call back after the first consultation, leaving no clue about what went wrong. Insurance administrators assessing your work on the telephone suggest that your patient might do better with a more efficient treatment.

Clinicians can be fired at any time. There is no department of human resources to listen to an appeal. In fact, it can feel inappropriately self-concerned and defensive to protest at all.

The difficulties of long-term clinical practice go way beyond the working conditions. Among ourselves we may grouse that we get no (paid) sick days, vacations, personal time, or pensions and that even jury duty can be costly. But these are the concrete, surface problems. What about the impact on our personal security and our pride?

Egos aside, what about the effect of all the losses of patients, including those who leave abruptly and mysteriously and others who fade more gradually but, perhaps, equally painfully? Although pediatricians, teachers, and other professionals also eventually lose their "clients," our level of involvement often makes the experience of loss much more painful, in my view. At times we are akin to foster parents, deeply involved in a life for a circumscribed period of time and then thrust out of it. But, unlike foster parents, we can't casually telephone to find out how things are going (many of us, myself included, feel that initiating contact with a former patient is generally inappropriate and violates an important boundary).

These are just a few of the more obvious difficulties of a clinical career. I think there are other equally consequential aspects. Clinical work is likely to acquaint us with some of life's most painful tribulations, often from an early age in our own development. It focuses much of our concentrated attention on another person, for long stretches of time. It continuously confronts us with our own limitations, as clinicians and as human beings. No other career is so unceasingly revealing of the practitioners' psychological shortcomings. Our blind spots are stumbling blocks in our work, not just in our personal lives. Our character issues can determine our paychecks, as well as our private relationships.

Sooner or later, the clinician will confront his or her most frightening personal demons in the course of an otherwise ordinary day. The 9 o'clock patient puts us on familiar ground, going over troubling but bearable conflicts. And then the next patient arrives. It is necessary to be able to switch gears, emotionally, and let go of whatever we were experiencing with the 9 o'clock patient in order to be ready for whatever the next person brings. It might be some version of the clinician's most dreaded nightmare. Some of us may quake if we have to think about the ravages of dire illness. Some of us are cowed by the deprivations and humiliations of poverty. For some, the constant drum of losses that come with aging seems unbearable. What is the most terrifying ring of hell for *you*? What sends *me* to the depths of horror? The version of human suffering each of us most fears may be in the waiting room.

A woman I have treated for decades dissolves as she enters the session. The mother she forever fended off and dearly loved is dying. But opinion is divided as to whether to speed the death or let it run its course. Her mother is clearly suffering tremendously and says she wants nothing more than death. But some of the family, and the physicians, want to hold out hope for her recovery. My patient has been her mother's fiercest critic. Now, with all their battles over, would it be settling scores for the daughter to plead with the doctors for her mother's speedy death?

Faced with such questions frequently, we would like to believe we can be neutral. We don't make decisions for our patients. We just help them come to their own conclusions. From my perspective this simply isn't true. It is a version of the Nazis' excuse that they were "just following orders." Inevitably, my values will have an impact on my patient's decisions about her mother's treatment. What I ask her, what I assume, how I phrase it, and the feelings I express and the ones I try to keep to myself all may affect her decision. I will not tell her what to do. But, in some fashion, I believe I will inevitably tell her what I would do in her place. For example, if I allude to how their previous warfare may be complicating this moment for the patient, she may (correctly) hear that I believe it would be best if she could put their battles aside now and face this terrible decision on its own terms. Her mother is no longer her lifelong, beloved enemy. Now she is just an old woman in extreme pain, deserving release.

Or so I believe. But this particular horror, of being strung between tubes, is one of my own most terrifying versions of hell. In most walks of life I can avoid thinking about it, using well-practiced defenses. But in this session I think I owe it to my patient to help her squarely face her mother's situation. I can't afford my defenses right now. Or rather, *we* can't afford for *me* to have my defenses right now. Being clinically trained, I automatically check in with myself, looking for countertransferential blind spots. Unlike my patient's friend, or cousin, who can dodge the issue, I am on the lookout for my own (as well as my patient's) dodging. Long accustomed to self-examination, no matter what the pictures in my own mind elicit in me, I can't easily look away. Of course, I know that I still have defenses. I am a human being, and there are limits to what I can face. But more than most people, I have an obligation to be aware of how my psyche functions. I have to face my psychological limitations for the sake of my work, not just for the sake of my own personal growth.

How does it affect clinicians to try to be emotionally available to people in great distress? More generally, what is the impact of renting out our minds, for the better part of our days, all our lives? How does it affect us to postpone thinking about some of our own ongoing issues, because we feel it might detract from our ability to concentrate in a session? What is the impact, over the years, of our effort to fully face the dilemmas our patients present, while putting some personal concerns on hold? I believe it is necessary, and not just desirable, for us to let go of some potential distractions while we work. It would certainly overwhelm me to focus on my own ongoing personal issues at the same time as I think, along with my patient, about her dilemma with her mother. My circuitry, so to speak, would be overloaded. I have to let go of something. When I am with a patient, I try to hover between what I am hearing, what I am feeling, what I remember of the patient's early life, and what we have been experiencing together in recent sessions. Focusing on all these "channels" at once takes deep concentration. I can't keep hold of any more than that.

What can sustain me through so many hours of maintaining this deep concentration on my patients? In this book I first consider the foundation training can provide, to set the stage for a lifetime of practice. How can those learning to do treatment develop the emotional strengths they will need to pursue their careers? Those pursuing clinical training must learn how to sustain their own well-being as they dedicate themselves to helping others live richer lives. The first chapter spells out how training often fails to adequately prepare us for a life in clinical practice. The training process should strengthen us so we can bear the painful feelings that often accompany our work as clinicians. Clinicians need to live with the loneliness, sorrow, shame, guilt, regret, and other feelings likely to surface in a lifetime of practice. In particular, we must develop adequate confidence in ourselves as clinical instruments and the capacity to recover from the sorrows we are likely to face. How does training often fail to instill these capacities, and how can it better facilitate them?

The second chapter focuses on the potential lifelong legacy of the emotional pain that training can engender. I believe that it is crucial to consider the possible costs, as well as the benefits, of entering the field. How does some training exacerbate candidates' feelings of paralyzing anxiety and personal insufficiency, resulting in their long-lasting sense they are inadequately suited for their careers? More specifically, what are some of the ways that training not only fails to nurture clinical development but, at times, actually hinders it? This can leave clinicians vulnerable to an erosion of confidence in their clinical abilities. Inadequate training also paves the way for despair about one's professional future and other forms of burnout.

I think that what happens in our first professional experiences after training can have a tremendous impact on the subsequent course of our careers. In Chapters 3 and 4 I describe the fallout from working in extremely trying settings and from having initial encounters with "difficult" patients. These situations can leave lasting marks on our professional self-esteem and on our capacity to bear the tribulations that often accompany a clinical career.

Many of us started our careers working in extremely difficult circumstances, such as long-term care facilities that resembled warehouses for storing human beings. Some of us tried to participate in vastly underfunded projects, located in devastatingly poor neighborhood surroundings. What can be the impact of beginning one's career in these situations? How might such beginnings affect the therapist's emotional balance? What could be some long-term effects on the clinician's personal well-being and professional identity?

Beginning clinicians often encounter, along with inherently problematic settings, the most challenging patients, because more senior practitioners may not be willing to see these patients, so they frequently refer them to younger colleagues who are eager to build their practices. The literature contains many reports of the impact on the clinician of treating resistant patients. Freud's frustration with his patient Dora provided an example, and Ferenczi's diary is replete with descriptions of how his work with difficult patients caused him profound suffering. But what, I believe, has yet to be explored is the particular impact of painful clinical experiences in the *earliest* phase of a therapist's career. Does their impact tend to differ from painful experiences encountered later on? And are there some extremely challenging early career experiences that tend to strengthen clinicians and, perhaps, help define reasonable limits for our expectations of our impact on patients?

The fifth chapter describes challenges to the clinician's sense of personal worth and identity. No other work puts the practitioner in this position. Architects' feelings of *professional* competence may be at stake in every project (to some degree), but their core identity as human beings is not. What are some likely consequences of this lifelong challenge? How do our narcissistic injuries at the hands of our patients and managed care predispose us to assail each other in public forums and private skirmishes?

A career in practice poses ongoing challenges. Chapter 6 explores some problematic patterns of interaction between clinician and patient that, once established, could recur over the span of a clinician's career. It will be argued that our diagnostic terms still follow a "one-person" model rather than a "two-person" model. We write of obsessive, paranoid, schizoid, narcissistic, and borderline *patients* rather than of, for example, paranoid *interactions* or climates. Although in some situations one-person diagnostic terminology may still be appropriate and required, generally our thinking should keep pace with our theoretical understanding of every interpersonal interaction as the product of both individuals. This chapter illustrates the atmosphere in obsessive, paranoid, schizoid, narcissistic, and borderline interactions in treatment. What is gained, and what is lost, by describing these patterns as mutually created? With each pattern, what is the effect of its repetition in the career of the analyst?

Throughout their careers, clinicians are subject to an extraordinary array of losses, as described in the seventh chapter. Emotion theorists, clinicians, memoirists, and other writers have understood sadness as a normal human reaction to a significant loss. What are the inevitable losses clinicians regularly encounter? Obviously all therapists, regardless of orientation, eventually lose every patient they treat. What is likely to be the impact of these losses? What less obvious but perhaps equally significant losses do clinicians face?

Along with dealing with these regularly occurring losses, clinicians often find themselves temporarily, or even permanently, holding information that can't be shared with anyone outside the consulting room. What is the impact on the clinician of occupying this lone, and sometimes lonely, position?

Sustaining loneliness and loss can evoke mourning reactions, which can take a variety of forms, including an absence of positive feelings. How can we recognize the more subtle guises of mourning in clinicians? This chapter proposes that the clinician's mourning can be especially hard to read, because it so often remains unformulated, in Donnel Stern's (1997, 2005) terms. Powerful incentives hinder its formulation. What mitigates for, and against, our knowing about our own mourning? For example, if a clinician's mourning takes the shape of a profound cynicism about treatment, it may never be understood and helpfully addressed. It will be argued that undiagnosed mourning has played an important part in some of the theoretical and political battles that plague our field.

The clinician faces pervasive losses that may be harder to capture in words than the losses of sense of self and losses of relationships with patients that have been discussed so far. Chapter 8 describes some of these ongoing losses, many of which are inherent in treatment's frame. The frame is discussed most frequently as the source of frustrations for the patient. But what about the losses sustained by the clinician? What does it cost us to adhere to its prohibitions? In this chapter, I suggest some of the challenges posed by trying to be reasonable and reality oriented in our expectations from patients. In a sense, the frame tells us which of our fantasies of ideal connections are unrealizable in treatment. Clinicians dream of perfect unions, just as patients do. Often, it is our job to help patients accept the relationship's limitations. But, often, no one is helping us deal with these harsh realities. Where do we find the strength to bear all the disconfirmed dreams, hopes, passions, fantasies, and wishes imposed on us by treatment's necessities? Most especially, how can we learn to bear the loss of all the *selves* we might have become, if the treatment relationship had different parameters?

Chapter 9 addresses some of the potential wellsprings of the capacity to bear the shame and sorrow inherent in life as a clinician. Where can we look for the strength to bear our challenges without burning out in the latter stages of our careers? Asked in another way, we can wonder how the clinician can transcend his or her shame and sorrow. One answer I propose is that writing, reading, teaching, speaking, and having group membership can provide opportunities to balance our painful feelings with emotionally enriching experiences. Clearly, at least for some of us, writing can be therapeutic, as well as clarifying, but just what impact does it have on the clinician's overall emotional balance? My own experience offers some preliminary suggestions, but other clinicians have begun to address how writing can help us thrive. In recent contributions, Bernstein (2008) and Palmer (2008) examined this issue. This chapter looks at their work from an emotion theory perspective. How can writing help some clinicians thrive over the course of their careers?

Unfortunately, however, these activities don't always provide the nurturance we may be seeking but may, instead, only exacerbate our shame and sorrow. Some ideas about why this happens are suggested in this chapter.

Clinicians frequently have to be able to "bounce back" from a discouraging session, a fallow period in a particular treatment, or a time when the work with many patients seems to be going badly. Chapter 10 explores some sources of therapeutic resilience that clinical work, itself, can provide. Is our ability to bounce back any different from resilience in other walks of life? Is there a way to instill resilience in training? Can we restore resilience? We concern ourselves with the well-being of others, but we must pay adequate attention to our own capacity for renewal. At least for me, what lends me resilience differs in the face of my rage or sorrow or anxiety or any other fierce, painful feeling I am having. I need to be in touch with the strands of my feelings in order to attempt to have resilience.

Chapter 10 ends with a discussion of the seeds of burnout. In 1986, Arnold Cooper wrote an article on burnout in clinicians that I consider a landmark in the field. A central premise was that how we practice, from our first workday, affects the degree to which we suffer burnout toward the end of our careers. Cooper examined the goals and assumptions that he thinks result in an increased likelihood of significant burnout. This chapter looks at burnout as, often, a gradual loss of faith in clinical work. Like the theatre, the clinician's trade is often pronounced dead and, yet, survives. But individual clinicians suffer a loss of faith, as can be heard in casual conversations and supervision sessions that take a kind of despair about the future for granted. Aside from the erosion of faith that results from the impact of managed care and society's economic instability, what are other sources of our crises of faith in clinical work? This chapter looks at clinicians' experiences of patients' ingratitude as one factor.

Finally, in the epilogue, I describe how the meaning of the title of this book evolved for me as I wrote it. At first, "still practicing" was an affirmation that I am still "alive and kicking," despite the shameful and sorrowful experiences I have endured. But it also quickly came to signify that, despite having some 40 years of clinical experience, I am still preparing to become a better clinician in the future. Only toward the end of the process of writing this book did I come to understand that, for me, "still practicing" also means that I hope that my clinical encounters with shame and sorrow will strengthen me to bear the personal and professional losses my future holds.

Part I

Hardships in Training

Chapter 1

Failing to Cultivate Clinical Strengths

He has earned a Ph.D. in psychology and a postgraduate certificate in analytic treatment. In addition, he has decades of clinical experience. And yet, when a new patient challenges him to explain how treatment will help, he becomes tongue-tied. The patient notices and grows more reluctant. The analyst thinks to himself, "Here it comes. This patient knows that I am a fraud. He sees that I don't know what I am doing. I am not smart enough to be an analyst. I always knew that I wasn't good enough material. And, in training, I didn't really apply myself. I just got through it. I can't help people. Now it is out. What if word gets around? How will I make a living?"

Although this fictional self-reflection is an extreme, I believe that many graduates of advanced training programs feel anxiety, shame, and guilt about representing themselves to the public as competent professionals. Why should this be so?

Seeking advanced clinical training is a tremendous act of faith. Candidates trust that their investment of time, money, and effort will pay off in the long run. And faculty need to believe in the worth of the training or else we, too, might suffer crises of faith. Personally, I believe training *is* worthwhile, because it *can* cultivate the candidate's talents. I have often said that the violinist, painter, and surgeon take care of their instruments, and we do, too, but in analysis our instrument is our own psyche. Analytic training should optimize each candidate's potential as a clinical instrument.

I suggest that a major component of our effectiveness as clinicians is our faith in ourselves and our conviction about the meaningfulness of our work with patients. Therefore, nurturing this faith and conviction should be a training priority. But I believe that in training we often miss crucial opportunities to enhance faith and conviction. Even more problematic are aspects of training that I think are likely to damage the candidate's professional sense of self. In this chapter I explore some ways we frequently fail to nurture candidates' self-esteem and the long-term consequences that can result. In the next chapter I address ways we sometimes actually do harm to those in training.

Professional confidence is vital to the clinician for many reasons. For one thing, it is hard for me to imagine how we can inspire patients to engage in long-term intensive treatment if we don't truly believe in the process and in ourselves as its practitioners. I suggest in this chapter that in addition to these fundamental beliefs, of equal importance is the need for clinicians to be personally capable of non-narcissistic investments in their patients' life and growth. I argue that the goals of training should include enhancing the candidates' faith in their clinical competence and their capacity for non-narcissistic investments in their patients. I feel that without passionate conviction in treatment's effectiveness, our own effectiveness, and our ability to make primarily non-narcissistic investments in our patients, burnout is likely at some point in the clinician's career.

I would bet that anxiety accompanies the novice taking his or her first steps in training for most of the professions. It can't be easy to try on the role of a lawyer, ophthalmologist, or dentist. Inevitably, being judged while at the steep end of a learning curve could raise anyone's pulse. But I believe nothing matches the situation of the novice clinician, especially when being trained analytically. It is not merely a set of skills being acquired, tried out, and, at the same time, evaluated. It is a capacity ultimately inseparable from *who one is as a human being.*

Before I mention some of the ways we fail to nurture these strengths, or sometimes actually inhibit their development in the candidate, I would like to very briefly describe how I understand the clinician's main task. In other words what, exactly, are we trying to train candidates to do?

I begin with a sketch, drawn from my own clinical experience. It is early morning, and I am looking over my schedule for the day. What strengths do I need at that moment? How can they be cultivated? Who must I be to live the moment well? What does living it well mean?

For me, preparing for the day includes looking over my notes from the previous sessions with each patient or supervisee I will see. I am trying to surround myself with words relevant to our work. To be ready for a session requires that I begin to recreate, within myself, the ambience of working with that person. Once the session begins, the creation of that ambience is an overtly interpersonal process. But even before these people enter the office, they are exerting an influence on me. I have begun to tilt, in a sense, in their direction by remembering words and phrases from our work. These words may come from their last dream, or my own recent countertransference feelings, or a bit of the patient's life history, or a piece of theory that I have found helpful. If I know someone thoroughly, it may take only seconds to create a surround, an atmosphere of our words. I try to notice difficulties I have with this task. What do they mean about me, about the other person, and about us? In my own training, how well was I prepared to open myself to such close self-scrutiny?

In those first moments I am most likely to notice my own obstacles to fully entering the day. Is there someone or something I dread seeing?

Why? Do I feel that in the last session with someone I lacked sufficient courage to face a dilemma we are in? Can I really want to know why that happened? Will today be the day that I find the courage to openly address a tough question that has haunted me with my patient? If yesterday I didn't privilege truth over my own pride, can I explore why this happened and learn from it? If yesterday I defensively sidestepped a potentially difficult moment, can my patient and I revisit it, think about the meaning of what happened between us, and recapture an opportunity? If yesterday I felt utterly unhelpful, today can I find sufficient conviction in myself as a clinician to truly wonder why? In each of these situations, being willing to really explore *why* they happened can be very meaningful. But I think that to be curious about what these experiences mean, I have to come to work believing in analysis as a potentially effective therapeutic process, believing in myself as a well-trained, personally and professionally well-equipped, adequately courageous clinical instrument and believing in my own capacity for non-narcissistic investments in the well-being of my patients.

So, in my view, training must prepare us to face those first moments of the day, many thousands of times, over the course of a clinical career. Who must I be to fully face my day tomorrow morning? What courage, conviction, concentration, and passion will it take? How can training cultivate the strength to recognize the consequences of my limitations in yesterday's sessions and deal with them more forthrightly today?

Another way to say this is that in my view, clinical work requires a capacity to meet difficult moments head-on. This may or may not require speaking about them. But whatever happens, we then have to be able to meet the next moment head-on. And then do it again and again. I don't think it is possible to meet each moment fully. So along with this effort comes an awareness of various degrees of success and failure in meeting moments head-on. In every session, this experience has to become our most valued teacher. We have to be able to listen as this teacher spells out what each encounter means about us, about our patients, and about the interplay of the two of us.

A patient lies down on the couch to begin the third of her weekly hours. She tells me a dream she had just after our last session. Someone was stabbing her in the throat. I start thinking about the way I have been treating her lately. If I tell myself not to bring this up but rather to wait and see what emerges, am I avoiding really grappling? I can certainly justify waiting and, for example, inquiring about various aspects of the dream. But, at least as I see it, it is part of my job to ask myself how I would feel about commenting on the connection between my behavior in the last session and her dream. Fully meeting the moment often requires us to face hurt we are causing from the patient's point of view. What can I learn about myself, her, and us from these reflections? How can training prepare clinicians to face these mirrors over and over again, with each hour of every workday, for the decades of a career, without burning out?

Meeting moments head-on is only one of the many challenges for the clinician. In my book *Making a Difference in Patients' Lives* (Buechler, 2008), I divided analytic functioning into its cognitive, emotional, and interpersonal components so I could write about the challenges of each. I know it is really impossible to separate the cognitive, emotional, and interpersonal elements of treatment, but this is the only way I found to address the challenges clinical hours present. For brevity's sake, I will just mention some challenges I explored more fully in the book. As I do, I ask you to consider how you think training could prepare us to cope with each of these tasks.

Before I describe these components, I again suggest that one of the greatest overall challenges of clinical work is maintaining a primarily non-narcissistic investment in life and growth. I have tried to describe this investment several times. I feel the clearest expression came to me in my paper on "Searching for a Passionate Neutrality" (Buechler, 1999), so I quote from it here:

> One hopes that the experienced analyst already knows he is competent. He doesn't need a "success" with this patient to prove it to himself or anyone else. He is, therefore, from a narcissistic point of view not invested in whether the patient makes a good life for himself, or even whether the patient has a life at all. But from a human point of view this cannot be a matter of indifference. Passionate engagement in treatment is a genuine investment in life itself. It is communicated in the "music" of the treatment—in the analyst's tone, manner, directness, allegiance to the truth, and the deeply felt conviction about the meaningfulness of the work. (p. 226)

I will return to the subject of our non-narcissistic investments, but, for now, I would like to very briefly list just a few of the clinician's tasks, as I understand them. What will then follow is a discussion of how we might prepare candidates to fulfill these tasks.

THE RIGHT STUFF TO BE A CLINICIAN

We need the ability to make connections between previously unconnected aspects of the material and confidence in that ability. I refer to this as the capacity to connect "c" with "q" rather than just being able to connect "c" with "d." While listening, the analyst is hearing what the patient says, how it is said, how it feels to the analyst to hear it, and how it might connect with previous material.

What does doing this work require? First, I would say, we have to be able to concentrate for extended periods of time. Listening analytically takes great powers of concentration, because we are hearing multiple layers at once. We may, for example, hear a story, the patient's emotional tone telling the story, our own reactions, the parallels between this story and other events in the patient's life, similarities between this story and her last dream, connections with occurrences in the last session, likenesses between this story and episodes from the analyst's life experiences, and so on. Others may define analytic listening differently and would therefore understand its challenge in another way. This could be interesting to explore. From my point of view, listening analytically requires, simultaneously, an active, highly focused concentration and a much more passive receptivity. That is, the analyst who is listening to "c" and connecting it with "d" and with "q" is also, at the same moment, listening blankly "without memory or desire." Our minds are simultaneously well stocked with data and impressions about this patient *and* empty, waiting, ready for anything. We are, for example, primed to hear another instance of this patient's obsessive doubting and, at the very same time, open to hearing her story of proud decisiveness. Our minds are furnished with memories of this patient's interpersonal patterns and, at the very same time, devoid of all expectations. We rent out rooms that are simultaneously furnished and unfurnished. In other words, what we do is, in a sense, impossible. We can't hear analytically without remembering the patient, but we can't hear openly without forgetting the patient. If we remember too well, we are in danger of stereotyping, distorting, squeezing this moment into old patterns, failing to recognize what is new about it. But if we don't remember the patient well enough, we will miss opportunities to see repetitions that are old, transferential, character driven. I want to note here that I believe that to make our living by simultaneously remembering and forgetting, we have to be exceedingly comfortable experiencing our limitations. Unless we have solid confidence in ourselves as clinical instruments, I can't see how we could be comfortable making a living doing something so paradoxical and contradictory. Another way to say this is that the candidate has to become extremely secure that she has something of value to contribute to her patients' lives in order to face the complexities of doing clinical work.

We also need the capacity to hold on to conviction about the ultimate value of the treatment, despite evidence that, at the present moment, it seems to have no effect or a negative impact. This is the strength that I refer to as the analyst's "sense of purpose." The sense of purpose is not any particular goal but rather a conviction that the work can meaningfully enrich both participants' lives. The clearest expression of this belief is the analyst's willingness to work hard. Effort communicates the value I place on the treatment more clearly than any statement I could make. Transparently working hard is a nonverbalized statement that contrasts with schizoid tendencies to glide through the hour rather than live it fully. I believe that sometimes it is necessary for the analyst to contrast with schizoid functioning in order to point out the patient's schizoid quality and not just to counter it. Thus, relatively nonschizoid functioning in the analyst is an *interpretation* and not just a corrective emotional experience. Most of the time, I think, the most effective interpretations are embodied in *how* we work rather than expressed in the words we say. In contrast to the schizoid tendency to glide through sessions and, more generally, get through the hour, and the day, and a life, I believe that the analyst must demonstrate something palpably different. The way I have said this in the past is as follows:

> I believe it is largely through our effortfulness that the analyst comments on the schizoid dilemma. By obviously working hard we clearly say that expending effort is worthwhile. By bothering to try hard to understand and respond we make a statement about the meaningfulness of human communication. By searching for just the right word to describe an experience we vote that the right word matters and, more broadly, that clarity matters, truth matters, treatment matters, the quality of a life matters. (Buechler, 2002a, p. 494)

What gives us this conviction, determination, and abiding sense of purpose? How do we develop the capacity to fight for life, often seemingly without a partner in arms, for long, bleak stretches of time? The roots of this inclination must lie deep within our personal lives, but, I think, it can be nurtured in training. That is, a candidate should have some potential to work hard to help people live more fully. But training can bring out that potential, as I elaborate below.

So far, I have mentioned the analyst's capacity for making non-narcissistic investments in others, for forging new connections in the material, for embracing the contradictory injunctions of both remembering and forgetting the patient, and for embodying a sense of purpose about the treatment. A further requirement is the analyst's emotional resilience. I have tried to understand this quality in many different ways. What allows us to bounce back after a difficult moment, or session, or longer stretch of time? What helps us regain our emotional balance after we have been knocked off-kilter? Where do we find the strength to learn from our mistakes and move on?

Emotional resilience is at the heart of empathy, from my point of view. I differentiate empathy from sympathy. The sympathetic listener feels something similar to what she is hearing. But the empathic listener goes further. She feels in tune with the other person, recovers her balance, and learns something potentially useful from this process. To illustrate, it is generally not empathic to join a child having a tantrum by having one of your own. Empathy requires us to feel the edge of the tantrum, so we emotionally reverberate with it, but then right ourselves and, finally, understand something potentially useful about what happened so we can help ourselves and the child grow from the experience. Resilience comes from our own need to recover balance. Perhaps we have felt intense, contagious rage or anxiety or sorrow in a session. Being available for this mutual experience is the first stage of a healing empathy, but, by itself, it is not enough, in my judgment. Curative empathy requires us to dig deeper into ourselves than that. We need to call on all our emotional resources, to come *back* to a curious holding. Once we have done that, we can wonder about the whole journey and, we hope, learn something about ourselves and the patient. Sometimes in living through an unbearable sadness, we may better understand the patient's losses and our own. If the process stopped there, it might be comfortingly sympathetic and, therefore, alleviate loneliness in both people. Although this is certainly not a bad outcome, it is often not enough, in my judgment. I agree with conceptions of analysis as a process of structural change and not just amelioration of painful feelings. That is, analysis aims at changing how people function and how they process their experiences and not just what those experiences are. In analysis it is not enough to help people feel better today. We aim to help them know life differently, to take it in differently. Structural change means to me hearing with new ears and seeing with new eyes. We don't just help people hear or see something more positive today. We help them hear and see more life today and forever after. They no longer waste one ear and one eye in trying *not* to hear and see, that is, in defensiveness. They spend less of their resources defending *against* their experiences and more of their resources *having* their experiences. Through bearing something along with the patient, we feel how they take life in. And then we use whatever we have inside to regain the capacity to wonder and to connect. And then both of us stop, look back, learn, and maybe change. Engaging empathically takes tremendous emotional resources. Every positive feeling, from joy, to hope, to curiosity, to love, must be recruited, and it is necessary to have a capacity for bearing every negative feeling, from loneliness, to anger, to fear, to sorrow. This work requires us to be human beings who can think feelingfully and feel thoughtfully. Training must bring out our natural potential for resiliently regaining our empathic relatedness.

Elsewhere (Buechler, 2008) I have outlined three requirements for doing psychoanalytic work: the ability to serve as a contrast, relational challenge, and catalyst. Very briefly, I have already described the idea of contrast, in my example of the analyst's nonschizoid functioning. A relational challenge means, to me, that with the analyst it must be hard for the patient to do business as usual without self-reflection. That is, in the way we relate we make it difficult, for example, to be paranoid without becoming aware of the paranoia. Finally, being a catalyst means, to me, that our stance facilitates interpersonal experimentation both within the session and outside it. For example, we help people express anger even though they have spent many years avoiding it.

I will add just one more ability to this list of requirements for the budding analyst: the capacity to become a transitional object. As material to be molded, I, like the teddy bear or blanket, have limitations. I have a reality of my own that is not a product of the patient's fantasy. A teddy bear can probably be seen as a sweet baby bear or a jungle tyrant, but it is hard to make it into a convincing waterfall. Similarly there are limits in how I can be experienced. A blanket comes with its own contours, and so do I. But, within these boundaries, I believe I should be malleable enough for the patient to transform me into the analyst he or she most needs. In other words there are limits to reality, but within those limits, a great deal is still possible. I think that the patient should be able to transform the texture, but not the contours, of the analyst. Thus, the analyst is a transitional object, like the blanket or teddy bear, partially, but only partially, shaped by the patient's desires. Here is how I previously described this aspect of the analyst's role:

> Analysts as material for transitional relating must have their own prop-
> erties, so they seem real enough to the patient, but the feel of being with
> them should be, in large part, the patient's creation. More specifically
> I mean that patients affect the frequency of my interventions, the tone
> of my voice, the direction of my gaze, the posture of my body, the
> length of my sentences, the pace of the interchange (from rapid fire
> staccato to slow and measured), and the use I make of silence. I am
> calling these elements "textural" to emphasize their relationship to the
> feel of the experience of being with me. (Buechler, 1996, p. 67)

Thus, as an analyst, I need to be able to be both theme and variations. As theme I am always myself, with my particular signature style. I bring my whole history of experience with each of the fundamental emotions to every session. I have my own characteristic way of being angry, and afraid, and curious. I am always me, and part of how I know myself is that I know what I was like as an angry 2-year-old and as an angry teenager. Thus, I don't agree with some ways others understand projective identification, in that I don't believe people can project their way of feeling into me without it being shaped by my particular emotional history and profile.

But within these contours, it is my job as an analyst to be capable of being transformed and, therefore, transformative. The first experience of having an emotional impact is probably the facial exchange the baby has with a responsive adult. The baby smiles, and we smile back. And her face and our face have begun a lifelong dance, in which each partner has impact and responds to impact. By smiling I tell the baby that she has the power to change my face, that is, she is transformative. In making her transformative I transform her from just a passive recipient to a passive recipient who is also an active participant. I believe treatment has to do something very similar. By being texturally transformed, I give the patient the power to have an impact and shape, from out of me, something like the analyst she needs me to be. She transforms me, to some extent. But in the act of transforming me, she is also transformed into an active interpersonal subject.

Although this list of the analyst's requirements may be exhausting, it is not exhaustive. To briefly summarize, so far I have mentioned having the capacity for non-narcissistic investments; making new connections; embracing contradictory injunctions; embodying a sense of purpose; relating empathica; becoming a contrast, catalyst, and relational challenge; and being a transitional, transformative object. Generally, how well does training prepare us for this daunting task?

MISSED OPPORTUNITIES FOR NURTURING CANDIDATES' CONFIDENCE

I suggest there are many ways that our training procedures often fail to adequately prepare candidates to do their job. I discuss just a few of them below.

First of all, and perhaps most important, in training candidates we often fail to clearly describe our own experience of what doing analysis has required of us as human beings. This misses a crucial opportunity to adequately prepare candidates to do their jobs. Partially as a consequence of this, they often begin doing analytic treatment feeling at a loss. This, naturally, contributes to their lack of professional confidence. I suggest that this early career experience can have lasting deleterious consequences, paving the way for early burnout. I will return to this point shortly.

Why don't we teach more effectively and help candidates feel better equipped for their profession? Although it is genuinely hard to define the analytic task, and we have real differences of opinion about what it entails, I believe that this is not enough to explain how unprepared graduates frequently feel. Anna Freud listed and described the defenses in 1936. At least in my judgment, these defenses have not changed. A thorough understanding of them is an essential piece of equipment for anyone attempting to do analytically oriented treatment. And yet I believe we often fail to transmit this basic knowledge. Although it is certainly true that we may differ in how we approach dissociation, denial, projection, and the other defenses, I think it would be hard to argue with how useful it is for an analyst to understand them. For over 70 years, Anna Freud's description has provided us with a perfectly adequate starting point. What limits our capacity to transmit it?

Briefly, I would suggest that our own unmet narcissistic needs, as analytic educators, play a significant role in our limited effectiveness. I think we are afraid to speak clearly and simply about analysis. For one thing, we fear being accused of oversimplification. Having been accused of this many times, I can certainly attest to the sting of this criticism. It can be hard to be clear without reducing the process to an oversimplified formula. Yet I would rather oversimplify than obfuscate, if these were the only choices. At least, then, listeners would understand what I am saying and could disagree. But when we mystify the treatment process we may leave candidates dumbfounded, in several senses. They are struck dumb, in that they feel afraid to speak up and show how little they understand. But they also feel dumb or unintelligent, ignorant, and inadequate. Perhaps most important, unless we are clear about theory, we prevent candidates from comparing it with their own clinical and personal experience and determining for themselves whether they find our theories relevant to their work. Out of our own narcissism, do we need to seem as though we have mastered esoteric theory? Although many have promoted demystification for patients, I think we have not done enough to demystify the treatment process for candidates and graduate analysts as well. Are we afraid that, along with our mysteries, we would lose our status in the hierarchy of treatment forms? Or in the name of clarity, are we willing to drop unnecessary jargon and expose our own clinical work?

A related issue is our current fascination with uncertainty and the unknowable. In my judgment we are in love with the inscrutable. Of course, an appreciation of it is vital. Without sufficient attention to the limits of our knowledge, we are in danger of the hubris of our analytic ancestors. In brief, analysts don't have any special knowledge about whether someone should live in Westchester, have three children, or get a dog. We are not experts in that sense. But if we were not expert in something, why would people pay us? We do have a knowledge base. We know more than nonprofessionals about patterns of defense, character issues, and some of the ways people tend to cope with their emotions. Like dentists, lawyers, and other professionals, we are schooled in a kind of pattern recognition. The pediatrician has seen countless cases of chicken pox and so can usually diagnose it easily. Being able to recognize an example of a familiar pattern is a skill that contributes to her sense of professional competence. Having this skill helps her feel she earns her fee and helps her transmit to patients a sense that they are getting something valuable. In the long run, her knowledge of how chicken pox looks will contribute to her feeling useful. I believe that the analytic practitioner needs a similar base. But, almost by definition, those who train analytically are in a different generation from those who are being trained. Because in my generation the vogue is for dwelling on our uncertainties, I think as teachers we may emphasize what interests *us* most at the expense of transmitting what *candidates* most need in order to graduate with a fundamental confidence in their ability to function analytically. It is as though music teachers, themselves entranced by the atonal, forgot to help beginners learn chords. But the profound appreciation of the atonal is possible only after having an acquaintance with the musical traditions that preceded it. I think that our neglect of the basics is not accidental. It feeds our own self-esteem to identify ourselves with theories that we think have cache. In short I believe that our challenge *as teachers*, not unlike our challenge *as clinicians*, is to privilege a primarily non-narcissistic investment in candidates' growth.

Returning to the question of the ways analytic education fails to prepare practitioners, a second major problem is that we don't adequately help candidates bridge what they learn from practice with what they learn from other walks of life. Candidates may come for training already well-versed as parents, teachers, clinicians, supervisors, readers, dancers, musicians, and so on. Too often what we transmit tells candidates to isolate analysis from everything else. Not only does that cut off potential sources of wisdom, but it also encourages the attitude that they have nothing of value to contribute from their own previous and concurrent experience. I remember, very early in my own training, wondering if I would ever be able to integrate my research experience with what I was learning at the institute. I came to feel that I would have to wait until after training to try to form these bridges. Perhaps that was as it had to be for me, but I wonder if something valuable could have been gained if I had been encouraged to make these connections from the beginning. I think we encourage candidates to act as though they are blank pages, ready to be filled up. They bring nothing of value. What are the consequences of this fundamental attitude? Aside from fostering an isolation of analytic theory, I think this outlook can seriously compromise candidates' self-respect and the development of a sense of integrity or wholeness. We all need to bring everything we have ever learned about life to each analytic hour. Only then do we have any chance of feeling at all prepared.

A third gap is our frequent failure to clearly identify the basic human resources each candidate can bring to the analytic task. We don't adequately prepare candidates for an analyst's life, which inhibits their development of a sense of confidence. Although I deal with this issue more fully in my previous books, I will mention a few examples. As analysts, we have to be able to switch from involvement with one set of emotionally charged issues to another, many times each day. Sometimes the sound of a buzzer has to snap us out of a profound reverie. For example, on a particular day I might be talking with one patient about an unfathomable loss he has just suffered. Just as I am finding the strength to empathize, the buzzer rings, telling me the session is almost over, and the next patient has arrived. This moment asks me to function resiliently in a different sense from the replenishing confidence I described above. I have to be able to return to a kind of emotional baseline every 45 minutes. I think we all know this can be difficult. Although what this takes may be discussed in some supervisions, this is a rather haphazard way to address an extremely important part of the clinician's basic equipment. Of course, once again, I am arguing that it is hard for the ill-equipped analyst to practice with confidence for the rest of her career.

The analytic life also requires the practitioner to feel comfortable with the practical side of the work, including fees and referrals. Dealing with these issues draws on the analyst's healthy entitlement and conviction that what she offers has value. I think it is meaningful that, long after graduation, these are issues that can continue to challenge us. They are inherently difficult, but, I suggest, they are made even more problematic when we, as educators, miss opportunities to inculcate a fundamentally sound sense of professional worth in those we train.

Related to this omission is our insufficient focus on what I have called clinical values (Buechler, 2004). That is, I don't think we pay enough attention to the courage, hopefulness, love for the truth, and basic kindness that doing treatment requires, at least from my point of view. Theoretical preparation is only a small part of our equipment. We must be highly emotionally resilient, and a ready courage is tremendously important in our work. But how could those qualities be nurtured in training? I believe people learn most through modeling. The courageous supervisor teaches clinical courage best.

I would also like to mention our insufficient preparation, in my judgment, for what it is like to age as an analyst. (Of course it says much about me that I am thinking about this issue!) Personally, I can't recall any mention of it in my own training. I think it might be incredibly helpful to talk about how dealing with erotic transference and countertransference, for example, changes as we age. I am sure these issues have somewhat different meanings for me now than they did when I was in my 30s. And yet, most often, transference and countertransference are discussed in training, at conferences, and in our literature as though we were ageless. What it is like to be desired and to desire, or not to be desired and not to desire, must surely have a different coloring at various points in life. No matter how much we emphasize that in fantasy everything is possible, in reality we are all members of a culture that sees each phase of life as having its own set of privileges. I think it takes a fairly sturdy sense of self to bear what the wider culture communicates to us about how we should see ourselves at each age. But it is even more complicated for me, as an analyst. In the transference, some patients may see me as 30 or 70, and my countertransferential wishes may match or greatly differ with these perceptions. What if my countertransference leads me to misperceive how old I seem to the patient? How might discovering this affect my own self-esteem? Once again, although some training analysts and supervisors may address these issues, I feel when we graduate we are often left insufficiently equipped to deal with them. Training can't prepare us for everything we will face in our careers, but it should aim for a sturdy enough professional and personal self-confidence to stay the course.

SOME SPECIFIC ISSUES THAT AFFECT PROFESSIONAL CONFIDENCE

So far, I have discussed a number of gaps in preparedness for an analytic practice. In this section I extend this discussion, whereas in the next chapter I address aspects of training that not only fail to prepare the candidate but actually damage his or her self-esteem. I am suggesting that all of these failures of omission and commission can contribute to the hardships of the clinician's subsequent career.

First, all too often the training process unnecessarily mystifies aspects of the analyst's role (such as recognizing defenses) so that trainees are likely to feel deficient. I am not suggesting that there is a recipe for the analysis of defense (or any other aspect of the analyst's task). But I think that some basic ideas and approaches can be conveyed. To the extent that we fail to equip clinicians with potentially available skills, we are adding to narcissistic vulnerabilities they may carry forevermore. Of course trainees bring to training their particular character, with its strengths and deficits. Those who have an especially strong sense of self-esteem may be less affected by these practices.

Second, as already mentioned, we do not actively enough cultivate the candidate's "non-narcissistic investment" (Szalita, quoted in Issacharoff, 1997) in the work. If nurtured, this investment could be a tremendous bulwark against burnout. I return to this vital issue shortly.

Third, we do not adequately prepare trainees for a career that involves a lifetime of losses of patients. Even worse, we frequently inculcate the feeling that losing patients is automatically a sign of profound personal and professional inadequacy. Even without our influence, trainees tend to take patients' terminations as narcissistic injuries, but I think we often exacerbate the problem. No doubt some supervisors usefully explore this issue and its personal meanings for an individual candidate. But all too often programs lack an organized approach to make sure it is constructively addressed.

Fourth, by passing on a legacy of discomfort around patient's and clinician's love for each other, we fail to prepare therapists to deal with this issue. This has enormous consequences, including the loss of the full benefits of a potential safeguard against early burnout.

Fifth, we often fail to nurture candidates' trust in themselves and their patients and faith, in various senses. We sometimes communicate an attitude that candidates, and their patients, are likely to be avoiding the "real" issues, out of cowardice or stubborn willfulness. Thus we inculcate suspicion rather than faith. We teach clinicians to suspect something naughty is afoot, in their patients and in themselves. The attitude we communicate is that the analyst should look for what is "really" going on, under the surface. The surface cannot be trusted. This can enhance obsessive self-doubting and, perhaps even more important, fails to infuse trainees with a core of faith in their own clinical intuition.

Sixth, humility is not sufficiently stressed in the curriculum. That is, we don't adequately communicate the attitude that the therapist is helping the patient with just one piece of the work the patient may accomplish in a lifetime.

Seventh, I don't think we focus enough on transitions, including the hourly transition from one patient to another. Some supervisors may direct attention to this issue, but it is a haphazard process. This leaves many clinicians feeling inadequate to deal with their daily experience.

Eighth, and more generally, I don't think we adequately address helping trainees develop the physical and psychological stamina a clinical life requires. Very little, if any, organized attention is paid to helping therapists find personal solutions for the practical hardships of practice. These can include many frequently occurring forms of impact of the work on the analyst's body. These are implicitly considered too trivial to study in training. But neglecting them misses an opportunity to strengthen candidates against one source of burnout. In addition, I think it subtly communicates contempt toward very consequential issues and toward those who suffer from them.

And finally, also as already suggested, perhaps the most consequential deficit in training is the absence of concerted effort to help clinicians connect their work with the wellsprings of strength and wisdom they have achieved through their other life experiences. There is no organized attempt to help candidates clinically integrate lessons learned as readers, parents, and dancers. Personal analysis and supervision may address these issues, but, once again, this is a haphazard approach. I think this *idealizes isolating* (from the rest of one's life experience) a body of analytic knowledge, with its own language and procedures. This does not adequately facilitate the development of a soulful, sustainable approach to practice.

NURTURING THE CAPACITY FOR NON-NARCISSISTIC THERAPEUTIC INVESTMENT

To summarize, to my way of thinking, most of our failures of omission in training spring from two sources: our inability to convey basic skills clearly enough, and our relative neglect of the spiritual and emotional needs of candidates. In brief, we don't pay adequate attention to the development of the trainee's confidence in his or her professional preparedness, sense of purpose, faith in the healing potential of psychoanalysis, clinical stamina, capacity for non-narcissistic investment in others, and connection with inner wellsprings of strength and wisdom. We inculcate skepticism (about the process and the motives of its participants) more than faith. We teach candidates to fear their loving feelings rather than mine them as a vital therapeutic resource. We leave them with little to sustain them physically, emotionally, and spiritually. In subsequent chapters I further explore the consequences of this failure.

As mentioned above the capacity for non-narcissistic investments is a vital piece of equipment for the clinician. To further explore these investments, I refer to an interview of Alberta Szalita, conducted and published in a paper by Amnon Issacharoff in 1997. Dr. Issacharoff asked Dr. Szalita to reflect on her many years of practice and how she changed as a clinician over time. Here is what she said.

> It's not that I considered myself not good before, but now I feel that I am more what I am supposed to be, including the way I see neutrality as part of my work. It is clear that one cannot be completely neutral. But now I am much more responsive and less involved. (p. 617)

When I first read this I kept replaying these words in my head, for I felt they held something important for me to understand. But what could "more responsive and less involved" mean?

In the same interview, when asked what frees her to speak her mind openly, Dr. Szalita answered, "It boils down to one thing: to what degree you are concerned with yourself and to what degree you are, as a therapist, concerned with the other person" (p. 627).

It was through my own writing that I came to a personal understanding of these words. I took them to mean that the analyst should aim for a non-narcissistic investment in the work. "More responsive and less involved" means to me that we should be responsive to the needs and feelings of the patient, but we should not have a personal stake in the patient's life-style choices. We should not be narcissistically invested, that is, worried about how the treatment makes us look to ourselves. We shouldn't need a "success" with this patient to prove ourselves as clinicians. So, from a narcissistic point of view, we are neutral and not dependent on any particular outcome. But, from a human point of view, the outcome cannot be a matter of indifference to us. Passionate engagement in treatment is a genuine investment in life itself.

Here is the conclusion I came to in the paper on passionate neutrality that evolved from these thoughts. It still seems right to me.

> I think this is how we can understand the changes over time that Szalita notes in her analytic stance. She has, and knows she has, "an intention to be useful to the patient" (p. 626). Her secure knowledge of this non-narcissistic intention lends conviction to her tone. This allows her to *embody* passionate engagement, while still conveying a neutral invitation to the patient to reveal all that lies within him. (Buechler, 1999, p. 226, emphasis in original)

But how can this non-narcissistic investment be nurtured in training? Surely it can't be taught, in the same way that mathematics is taught. But can it be *conveyed*?

First of all, it certainly can be demonstrated in supervision. Many moments of a supervisory session provide opportunities for the supervisor to choose between narcissistic gratifications and non-narcissistic investments. For example, the supervisee reports an unwitting enactment. Let's say the patient is involved in some obsessive power struggles with his boss. The patient comes to the supervisee for some help dealing with this boss, and the supervisee comes to me for supervision. I can see how the supervisee and the patient are enacting a power struggle as they talk about the patient's work situation. I can also see the potential for similar enactments of obsessive issues in the supervision. So obsessive tendencies exist in the patient, his boss, the supervisee, and his supervisor (me). We all have the potential to get entangled in vague verbal battles, where, in a short time, the point of it all becomes unclear, but everyone is unaccountably disturbed by the interchange.

What are my choices as the supervisor? If I point out the supervisee's unwitting enactments, I am bound to elicit his shame. It is like showing people they didn't know they were only partially dressed. Publicly displaying defenses without knowing it is like being psychically naked without realizing it. Of course it would present another set of problems for me to ignore the situation and say nothing about the enactment. I would be failing to carry out my responsibilities to the supervisee and, possibly, losing an opportunity to enhance the supervisee's work with his patient. But this situation also presents opportunities for narcissistic gratifications or non-narcissistic investments for me. My timing and my tone are likely to reveal whether I relish a chance to show how smart I am, at the supervisee's expense. *How* I talk about the enactments is at least as meaningful as what I say. For example, if I include myself as part of the enactments, I will probably have a very different impact than if I focus the spotlight solely on the supervisee. I have a choice whether to prioritize making my point, without considering the timing of it and its likely impact on the supervisee's self-esteem. I might consciously think I am doing my duty, but in *how* I do it I could be enacting my own desire to narcissistically benefit from the supervisee's difficulties. Is my tone gleeful? In my timing do I show consideration for the impact I am having? If the supervisee is clearly becoming anxious or embarrassed, do I show concern about that, or do I just jump on the opportunity to make my point? My tone, my timing, and my inclusion of myself can convey that we are all human, and self-confrontation is worth its price, because it allows us to know ourselves better and do better clinical work. This can express more clearly than any words the value of a non-narcissistic investment in life and growth. Or, as previously quoted, in Dr. Szalita's characteristically blunt and succinct words, "It boils down to one thing: to what degree you are concerned with yourself and to what degree you are, as a therapist, concerned with the other person" (Issacharoff, 1997, p. 627). I would add that, in supervision, it boils down to the same question of priorities.

The consequences of the supervisor's failure to foster non-narcissistic investing are potentially profound and wide-ranging. Without this investment, doing treatment can become a sterile exercise. The clinician whose sense of purpose has not been sufficiently nurtured in training can more easily become cynical about treatment's power to effect change. Worn down by repeatedly going through the motions, yet feeling compelled to keep practicing for practical reasons, the clinician is in position to burn out long before retirement is an option.

TRAINING CANDIDATES IN THE BUSINESS OF TREATMENT

Let's consider how a mythical candidate, Joan, might experience her training. She has chosen as her training analyst someone with whom she is uncomfortable enough to believe her defenses will be fully confronted. In supervision she is seeing how her needs to be liked and her difficulties with anger and aggression are truncating her work. Classes are acquainting her with how little she really understands theoretically. She is feeling more and more inadequate, but that itself is too shameful to reveal (and she worries whether revealing her feelings of inadequacy could, somehow, threaten her career).

Joan has one analytic patient that she has persuaded to come three times a week, by giving him a very modest fee. John, Joan's patient, is entering middle age, plagued by ambivalence in every area of his life. In relationships with women and in his career, he continually stands poised at the brink of firm commitments. John and his girlfriend have lived together for 5 years, and she is getting impatient to get married and face the issue of whether to have children. In his work as a consultant, John is clearly capable and earns a decent living but has never fully taken advantage of his talents.

When Joan first raised the possibility of his becoming an analytic patient and coming to treatment three times a week, for less money than he was paying for twice weekly psychotherapy, John agreed to it. Consciously, he told himself he would be getting a good deal, so why not take advantage of it? Even though he didn't think he needed a third session, it would be hard to pass up such a bargain. But he could sense the spike in his contempt for Joan. How good could she be if she is willing to work for so little? And he felt some disgust for his own greedy bargain hunting. Was he really getting anything from the treatment? After all, three times zero is no more than two times zero. Maybe the whole thing was just for suckers. Maybe Joan isn't very smart. She doesn't seem to get most of his jokes. She is earnest but might not be bright enough.

Dutifully, John shares these thoughts, because he is supposed to say anything that comes to mind. He wonders, aloud, whether Joan knows what she is doing. You get what you pay for. Maybe bargain-basement treatment is no bargain. Feeling he has let himself be hoodwinked, John decides to be more forceful. He asks Joan what he is supposed to be getting from the treatment now, how he should feel helped by the end, and how long the whole thing will take. Joan gulps, audibly. John is furious and contemptuous. What kind of business is this? He asks whether Joan is just using him to clock enough hours to get through her training. Is that what this is really about?

Joan summons all her strength, trying not to cry. She searches frantically for what to say. She has to think of something she can tell John that will persuade him to stay in treatment. She can't lose her only analytic patient, just months into the work. What will she tell her supervisor? What will the training committee think of her? How will she ever graduate?

Joan reflects on the "deals" she has made so far in training. She is practically seeing her patient, John, for free. Most of the money she is paying her analyst and supervisor is coming out of savings. She is in class during prime-time evening hours, so she isn't making much money in her practice. She feels so demoralized that when she senses someone might want to refer a patient to her, she can't get any words out. Of course she should sound confident and eager to have the referral. She sure could use the money. But does she have any idea how to help people? John is right. This is bullshit. She is a fraud. Maybe he will sue her. Maybe she should just return all the money he has paid so far and withdraw from the program. Oh, what a relief that would be! But then what would she do? Still practice but without any hope that training will make her a better clinician? Start all over again in a new field? What new field?

Suddenly it occurs to Joan that what she is going through is not very different from John's dilemmas. Joan, too, is poised on the brink and awash in ambivalence. Hmm. What could this mean? What would happen if she brought this into supervision?

Elsewhere I have written about the concept of integrity in training (Buechler, 2003). Related to the word *integer*, integrity is a kind of wholeness. I think the financial "deal" candidates are often forced to make with their patients can cost them some of their sense of professional and personal integrity. This can exacerbate feelings of fraudulence that may arise for various reasons in treatments they conduct later in their careers.

The financial aspects of training receive little formal attention (for an exception, see *The Candidate Journal*, 2009, Vol. 3). I think they can play a major role in its more demoralizing aspects. Patients aren't the only ones who can feel they have been "suckers." Candidates, too, can feel they have let themselves be taken for a ride. They often work for very little money, pay huge amounts for training, and emerge with a very murky sense of what they were supposed to have learned. Of course, the candidate's character plays a major role in how the situation is experienced and lived. But over the years I have found that serious challenges to the candidate's feelings of integrity, purpose, and adequacy are common.

The failure to fully examine the economic aspects of training, the kinds of "deals" candidates have to make to complete the requirements, and the pressure to hold on to patients can have many unfortunate legacies in a clinician's subsequent career. I think the most devastating consequence is that an opportunity is lost to cultivate and validate the clinician's professional integrity. Difficulties bearing patients' terminations, problems dealing with setting and collecting fees, ambivalence about practice, and feelings of distaste and incompetence about the "business" are all potential results of our failure to address money's role, and the need to keep patients for required lengths of time, when we are in training. As I have already suggested, we inculcate a vulnerability to shame when we communicate that clinicians must have somehow failed if their patients leave prematurely. This message in training makes every subsequent termination into a potentially traumatic event for the analyst. And, in one way or another, because every patient eventually terminates, not helping candidates deal with it without undue anxiety, shame, or guilt is a crucial omission. If, while the candidate is still in training, we don't address the financial and educational meanings of patients terminating and the meaning of the "deals" the candidate is making to keep enough patients to graduate, we make money and termination into taboo subjects that easily recruit secrecy and shame. I would say that we are "teaching" the very opposite of the clinical values (Buechler, 2004) that we aspire to. Instead of inculcating that "the truth sets you free," we are communicating that some truths (like the financial deals that candidates feel pressed to make) must remain unexamined. This affects candidates differently, depending, in part, on their character styles. Some, more schizoid individuals, develop hard shells. They learn how to present their work in an acceptable fashion, honing their professional false selves. Others, with more depressive or narcissistically vulnerable characters, feel intense shame and guilt. They take upon themselves the blame for being unable to keep patients in analysis without, in a sense, bribing them. Those of a more paranoid cast spend their training years anxious they will be found out. They fear being exposed as having done something wrong clinically or in supervision.

All of these outcomes are tragic, in my view. In a way they are failures of commission and omission. The commission is the damaging message that money and termination are too trivial to discuss or issues only for the untalented. The omission is the lost opportunity to help candidates deal with these aspects of the work and retain their self-respect, commitment, and love for the profession.

What would rescue our mythical candidate, Joan? We left her facing her sole analytic patient, John, just as he was about to lower the boom, so to speak. Let's say he was deciding whether to cut back to twice a week. Joan was deciding whether it was right to try to talk him into retaining their current schedule. What if he took this as evidence of her self-interest? Would he be right? What does that mean about their work? What if his cynicism and suspiciousness got reinforced? What if he quits treatment altogether?

And, on a practical level, what should Joan charge for twice a week? If she goes back to the higher fee he paid for twice a week initially, would that be experienced by John as a kind of punishment for cutting down? But it wouldn't be fair to give him the reduced fee she set for him as an analytic training case. Something was making this extremely uncomfortable. Who could she talk to? Her training analyst probably would answer a question with another question. Her supervisor might evaluate her negatively for being inept with frame issues. Her peers might not see her as someone to whom to refer patients. Friends outside the field wouldn't really understand the issues.

It is Tuesday, and John's session is at the end of the day. Joan is filled with more dread than she can understand. Somehow, this has all taken on great significance. Her adequacy as a human being, the value of her life, seems to be at stake. What if John picks that up? What if he (rightly?) feels even greater contempt for her than he has shown in the past? What does it mean about her, as a clinician and as a human being, that she is willing to make these deals, that she feels so much dread about her patient, and that she has not been able to inspire his willingness to stay in analysis? Is there any way to learn how to have the qualities she lacks, or is she just hopeless, permanently deficient in the "right stuff" to become a competent analyst? Should she try to hide her problems from her supervisors and peers? But wouldn't that be totally spineless? And what if they were discovered?

Obviously it would be helpful if all who participate in training had a more matter-of-fact approach to talking about the "deals" candidates make. It may not be possible, or even desirable, to eradicate the deals themselves. After all, in a sense, they are good deals for everyone. The patient gets a better fee, more intensive treatment, and the benefit of the supervisor's insights about him. Joan gets further training and credit toward graduating as an analyst. Her supervisor gets to pass on a tradition that is personally and professionally meaningful. Is anything wrong with all this? Not necessarily. It may depend on how much Joan is helped to think about the meaning of these deals in each treatment she conducts.

But surely Joan won't be well prepared for dealing with a lifetime of losses of patients unless she develops enough of a sense of purpose and integrity to weather these losses. Faced with some patients terminating abruptly and others more slowly and deliberately but, perhaps, no less painfully, the clinician needs, to alter a line from Yeats, a center that *can* hold. There is a strength that can carry us through potentially demoralizing experiences. This resilience will be the subject of the final section of this book. For now, I just suggest that the experiences that create doubts in candidates, about their sense of integrity and purpose, will certainly fail to instill the needed ballast.

Let's save Joan. Let's say she somewhat evasively refers to her dread about the session with John, as she describes the week to her supervisor.

And her supervisor reads between the lines enough to perceive that Joan is very anxious, feels inadequate, and is having trouble keeping John in analysis. The supervisor brings this up, giving Joan a chance to experience how freeing the truth *can* actually be. Joan is helped to see John's behavior as primarily reflecting his issues and not (mainly) hers. She learns that terminations are not, necessarily, the clinician's failures. She is helped to face whatever made her so vulnerable with this patient. She begins to really feel that the more intensive treatment could substantially improve his life and is worth fighting for. If John cuts down or leaves entirely, she will feel loss but not, also, intense shame, anxiety, and guilt. She will be willing to examine what his termination does say, that she might do differently in the future, and what she can learn about herself from this experience. But it will no longer feel like life or death, swim or sink, worthy or unworthy. In the future her belief in her value as a clinician will be stronger. Her sense of clinical purpose and integrity will accompany her to work. When patients challenge her she will more clearly know what she is fighting for.

This more fortunate outcome does happen, sometimes. It is all a matter of degree. But in the next chapter we will look at more of the perils of training and the emotional imbalances they can yield. For now, I ask you to consider how training affected (or how it would affect) *your* overall emotional balance and your ability to weather the challenges of a clinical career. Did it leave you more vulnerable to the narcissistic injuries inevitable in practice? Or were you left fortified against unbearably intense shame, guilt, and regret? Did training help you bear the sorrows of losing each of your patients in one way or another? Was your resilience strengthened, so that even if shame, sorrow, or other feelings overtake you, you are able to bounce back? Were you guided in developing a bedrock of positive feelings about your work that provides ballast against its inevitable pain?

DEVELOPING COURAGE, INTEGRITY, AND A CLINICAL IDENTITY

It takes a great deal of courage to train and practice as a clinician. We have to develop the capacity to be the most intimate strangers imaginable. We deeply care about our patients yet are paid by the hour, sometimes uncomfortably linking our field to that of the "oldest profession." We understand our subjectivity and that we can never, as Steve Mitchell used to say, see outside the perspective shaped by our particular countertransference. Yet when a patient tells us a story, we realize that what we question, what we forget he said, what we hear and respond to, what we nod to, and what we remember next session may have some impact on that patient's life. Becoming a clinician means, to me, embracing the paradox of being aware of my limitations and yet having the courage to go ahead with doing clinical work. From the first session we conduct, when the patient questions what the purpose of the work is or how long it will take, we have to bear how little we often know, respond truthfully, and still believe in the ultimate value of the work. The goals of many treatments can be understood only over time. What courage it takes to believe in the treatment, and sometimes fight for it, when we honestly can't know where it is headed! When facing something is painful, we have to believe it will be worth it in the long run. Most of all, I think, we have to believe in our own integrity and that we are not fraudulent but are genuinely trying to help. Despite a lack of proof, we have to believe (and, at times, persuade the patient to believe) that the treatment will enrich the patient's life in ways we can't yet formulate. It takes courage and a strong sense of integrity to express this belief with passionate, contagious conviction. How is this conviction nurtured in training?

I believe that most people who have just had graduate school training have not yet developed what I would call their signature style of doing treatment. They may have many styles or techniques they have learned. But often they do not have a clinical identity, a core of strongly held beliefs about what is important to them in the work they do. Postgraduate training is a place to develop those beliefs. To me, most of the work in any identity-building task is accomplished through contrasts. By seeing what goes on in his friend's home, the 10-year-old child understands that his parents' way of functioning is not the only possibility. Similarly, in training, by hearing how differently various teachers and supervisors think about treatment, we can examine, validate, and modify our core beliefs about the work and eventually forge that signature style. This style does not tell us what to say in any session. Nothing can, fortunately, I would say. Treatment always has to remain a live response to real moments with another person. It can never be reduced to formulas, recipes, manuals, or preprogrammed sound bites.

But training can tell us about the experiences of other clinicians who have faced and thought through a variety of clinical dilemmas. Theory gives us a map, which, as we all know, is not the territory. But, I would say, it can be a help. That is, theory may tell us something about where we need to go, although it does not get us there. But in every clinical hour, we still need to be brave in order to approach our daunting task.

THE MEDIUM IS THE MESSAGE

I think how we treat candidates often has the greatest impact on the development of their clinical courage, integrity, and love for the truth. In 2009, I published a "letter" to my first analytic supervisor, Ralph Crowley, MD. Although Ralph had been dead for many years, I was still trying to clarify just how he helped me become an analyst. Here are a few quotes from that letter.

Was I so needful of someone to believe in me, that you were simply the right person at the right time? Just a nice guy who communicated a positive attitude about my potential? Is that what beginning candidates most need? I don't think it is that simple. ... You had a consistency of word and deed. Your way of being with me was consonant with the values you were teaching. I learned something about how to be with my patient, from how you were with me. Somehow you balanced curiosity with patience. For me, then, curiosity was a drive that obliterated patience. It sometimes still works that way. Patience is not one of my virtues. But you taught me about it in how you contrasted with me. With you, for the first time, I was conscious of how powerfully contrast teaches.

What didn't happen with Ralph sometimes had as much impact as what did occur. Ralph didn't make me choose between him and my own instincts about what was right clinically. When his views and my own pointed in different directions, Ralph just let the difference hang in the air. He trusted me in a way that helped me trust myself.

Ralph will always be part of what I call my "internal chorus." During training I think it is essential that the candidate "audition" supervisors, teachers, and training analysts for parts in this set of internalized mentors. The voices of these elders can help us feel less lonely as we work with patients. I understand the quality of moments of being alone clinically as dependent on whom I am with when I am alone; that is, it depends on the attitudes of my internalized mentors. My aloneness is less absolute when I can imagine what Ralph might say as I face a difficult moment in a clinical encounter. Even if the patient has rejected me or abandoned me, I still have Ralph to talk to. My aloneness is not permanent and does not define me as unworthy. In other words, clinicians need a relative absence of persecutory inner objects, and a presence of benign inner objects, to bear the strains of the work we do. We need dependable sources of clinical wisdom and strength. In training, many individuals have a chance to become one of those inner objects for each of us.

In summary, I am suggesting that one of the greatest overall challenges of clinical work is maintaining a primarily non-narcissistic investment in life and growth, and many factors can contribute to developing the capacity to make these investments. I believe that if training instills confidence and conviction about the work, those candidates who are characterologically capable of non-narcissistic investments will develop this capacity. That is, we hope, the candidate has come to training equipped with the potential for relating to patients relatively non-narcissistically. But training can cultivate this strength, if it doesn't do severe damage to the candidate's self-esteem, if it helps the candidate learn the "basics" of analytic practice, if it strengthens the candidate's belief in the effectiveness of analysis and his or her competence as a practitioner, and if it gives the candidate sufficient opportunities to develop the supportive inner supervisory objects I have referred to as the clinician's "internal chorus." One way to think about the internal chorus' job is that it keeps the clinician's inevitable moments of aloneness from becoming painful loneliness. Another way to express the chorus' function is that it can help the clinician experience doing treatment as hard work rather than as an impossible, hellish nightmare. We as human beings can suffer intense anxiety when we feel compelled to accomplish something we believe is beyond our capacities. Without the guidance and faith of a genuinely helpful internal chorus, a clinician can easily feel overwhelmed, unable to choose what to focus on, unable to make necessary judgment calls, unfit for the emotional rigors of practice, and, perhaps, too vulnerable to make non-narcissistic investments in patients. That is, without internalized mentors, the clinician may be dependent on positive feedback from patients and, therefore, *narcissistically* (rather than non-narcissistically) invested in the outcome of the work. Without the chorus' reliable guidance and support, the clinician's sense of competence is always at stake, and her feelings of professional worth can be crushed with every abrupt termination, every patient's verbal attack, and every insurance company's dismissive review.

Training analytically is an opportunity to audition analysts, supervisors, teachers, and other colleagues who might become members of the candidate's internal chorus. Training can enhance the candidate's curiosity, courage, professional confidence and identity, sense of integrity, awareness of his or her "signature" style, and capacity to invest in patients non-narcissistically. But, as we will see in the next chapter, when we create a threatening atmosphere, gratuitously shame candidates, infantilize them, facilitate their feeling like cowards, and fail to equip them sufficiently, they may leave training with lasting scars. They may never attain sufficient conviction about themselves as practitioners to work effectively. If they can't believe in the work they do, they are unlikely to persuade patients to invest in long-term treatment. This can further erode their confidence, as their patients prematurely terminate. As subsequent chapters will discuss, training that fails to instill confidence can have a lasting, damaging effect on the whole of a clinician's career.

Chapter 2

Emotional Hazards of Clinical Training

In his witty and highly influential paper "Thirty Methods to Destroy the Creativity of Psychoanalytic Candidates," Otto Kernberg (1996) issued a "plea for the fostering of psychoanalytic creativity" (p. 1031). From my point of view, he rightly asserts that a significant challenge in training is to try not to inhibit trainees' natural curiosity and responsiveness. In other words, if we don't get in the way, trainees will be able to develop their individual voices and creative contributions to the field. But Kernberg went on to suggest that all too often we *do* get in the way. By naming 30 ways we obstruct candidates' development, Kernberg makes it clear that this negative impact occurs quite frequently and is not just a function of the personality issues of particular trainees and faculty. Rather our training institutes as organizations tend to spawn these inhibiting attitudes, policies, and procedures. What is more, we have been very reluctant to examine this unfortunate situation with the self-observational tools that are our stock in trade.

Some of the unfavorable tendencies Kernberg cited seem to me to be likely to inculcate four overall attitudes:

1. a general lack of confidence in candidates' opinions, clinical judgment, and treatment style;
2. a rigid, dutiful compliance with the training organization's points of view;
3. the use of defenses such as splitting to maintain an idealization of the organization; and
4. paranoid fear about what is "really" being said about them, what is "really" going on behind their backs, and what is "really" required to succeed in the program and, more generally, in the profession.

I want to highlight the likely immediate effect and long-term consequences of this process on candidates' professional identity. More specifically, my focus is on how this training affects candidates' curiosity, courage, confidence, integrity, and clinical identity.

TRAINING'S POTENTIAL NEGATIVE
EFFECT ON CURIOSITY

One of the ways Kernberg (1996) suggested we inhibit creativity is by making the candidate feel that he can prevent making mistakes by "following his supervisor's advice without questioning and demonstrating to the supervisor that he has made the kind of interpretation that he understood the supervisor would have done" (p. 1036). Surely this would delimit the candidate's alive, curious play with treatment alternatives. But I think we, as supervisors, are often tempted to try to control the treatment. We may tell ourselves we are just trying to get the treatment "on the right track." Although the supervisor does, I feel, have some responsibility toward the candidate's patient, it is unhelpful to try to use the candidate as a kind of conduit through which the supervisor treats the patient. In a felicitous phrase, Fiscalini (1985) referred to this as ventriloquism.

Another way to think about how training can inhibit curiosity is to look at how it can evoke paranoid anxiety. Because I believe that paranoia is inversely related to curiosity (Buechler, 2004; see also Chapter 1), it is clear that I would think that any training that increases paranoia will discourage curiosity. My understanding of this is that when human beings are profoundly afraid we will be harmed, we tend to crave a degree of certainty that is incompatible with creative curiosity. An example might be the case presentation that most institutes require for candidates to graduate. The more the atmosphere fosters paranoid fear, the less likely candidates will use the presentation as an opportunity to play with new ideas, test out relatively unformulated hunches, and try to find language for intuitions at the edge of awareness.

It is interesting that despite differences in language, culture, and theoretical orientation, a paper by Horst Brodbeck (2008) about training conditions in his society, the DPV (German Psychoanalytic Association), vividly described how case presentations can evoke candidates' paranoid fears in programs that otherwise vary greatly. Brodbeck reported the results of a survey of the experiences of graduates of his program. Although one fourth expressed positive feelings about the "Kolloquium" (case presentation), a third described it as a "nightmare." Some of the phrases used by graduates to describe the Kolloquium could hardly be more expressive of paranoid anxiety. The Kolloquium was characterized as "horrible. It felt like a massacre, an unpleasant experience. Everything I had done was wrong. I suffered a great deal and came out of it with nothing to go on" (p. 336). Brodbeck came to the following conclusion: "For most of them, the Kolloquium thus becomes a 'matter of fate,' a process that one simply has to go through and endure" (p. 336). Brodbeck suggested that the Kolloquium has elements in common with some cultures' initiation rites in which hopefuls learn "at the mercy of anonymous masked figures" and they "are not granted acceptance into the clan (are not taken into the fold)" until they pass through a terrifying ritual. It seems clear to me that those surveyed about the Kolloquium spoke the language of paranoid fears. If many members of the DPV felt they had to simply endure the presentation, how could they have been at their most emotionally open and creative? Wouldn't these fears foster a longing for the safe harbor of an identification with a powerful authority figure or the certainty of an allegiance to established and approved theories? It is hard for me to imagine most candidates in this situation being able to wonder out loud, try out a barely formulated idea, or openly disagree with a supervisor or other powerful figure. In other words, creative individual experimentation is inhibited, and conformity with established doctrine is fostered.

Emanuel Berman's passionate book *Impossible Training* (2004) vividly portrayed some of the problems inherent in each of several types of training. His sophisticated analysis explores the dangers inherent in more traditional, classical training, as well as the pitfalls of the more interpersonal, relational programs. I think no one could be clearer about the paranoia-inducing possibilities of the more opaque, mystical evaluation processes in traditional programs. Here are Berman's own words:

> I discussed some of the pathogenic influences of the hierarchical traditional institute, idealization of the training analyst, infantilization of the candidate, encouragement of regressive and paranoid fantasies, and the potential contradiction between the creative individualistic nature of psychoanalysis and the typical training process. I suggested that these contradictions can be resolved only by changing the structure and climate of training. (p. 130)

More informally, Berman remarked that the training analyst appointment process creates "a persecutory atmosphere paralleling that of candidates in training" (p. 135). He went on to quote a colleague who lamented that in the appointment process, "the demon of intrusive and ruthless judgments, which we unleashed at the candidates, now gnaws at our own feet."

My own thought is that secrecy and judgments of analytic "quality" that are unavoidably subjective, but treated as objective, are bound to evoke anxious paranoid needs for certainty in those being judged. These needs will foster absolute adherence to orthodoxy of some kind. Curiosity and creativity will be sacrificed for a false sense of clarity. The thrill of discovery that can accompany a genuinely free analytic process will be lost or, at least, attenuated. Rich, playful riffs won't be attempted or won't be reported. We will lose innovative approaches that ask, in effect, "What happens analytically if we prioritize b instead of a?"

My supervisory experience tells me that during training, curiosity and play are inhibited if candidates feel they will be subject to an unclear but tremendously consequential evaluation. But perhaps more subtly, I think play is attenuated when candidates are infantilized. I believe that it can be harder for adults to freely play when they are actually being treated as children. *Infantilization of candidates can evoke their need to be seen as competent adults who know what they are doing before they do it.* But in our moments of greatest therapeutic creativity, we can't know where we are going before we get there. We have to risk a childlike (not childish) wonder. Some candidates can maintain wonder no matter how they are being treated. In my experience, a candidate has to be supremely self-assured to remain curious under these conditions. I have often advised candidates to prioritize becoming the best clinical instruments they can forge out of themselves. In the long run this will allow them to become imaginative analysts. I tell them that in my own experience in training, keeping this goal in mind helped me stay centered (to some degree). But I know that this can be very challenging.

It seems to me the assumptions that are most toxic to creative wonder are as follows:

1. Proper analytic technique can be described and assessed. We can make *objective* assessments of whether a treatment is "analytic," whether a candidate is "suitable" material to become an analyst, and whether a graduate analyst is of sufficient quality to be a training analyst.
2. A treatment's goals can be known in advance rather than discovered during the process.
3. Candidates, like small children, are not "ready" to know what is going on behind the scenes. Their evaluation has to happen behind closed doors. Only its resulting judgments should be shared with them.

These assumptions can inhibit playing with irreverent, unconventional possibilities because play can feel too dangerous. The candidate's potential for being seen as a competent professional feels at stake. It becomes too important to look like a "real analyst." Some candidates decide to adopt the part of the obedient supervisee, either omitting mention of their more creative moments with their patients or "cleaning them up" before presenting them in supervision and case conferences. This poses challenges for the candidate's sense of having courage and integrity.

There are many emotional challenges embedded in training analytically. On the one hand, candidates are reminded of the subjective nature of all analytic understanding. Psychoanalytic "truth" is cocreated and colored by interpretive biases. But, at the same time, candidates are expected to look and feel relatively confident and competent. Brodbeck (2008) suggested, "Candidates experience their uncertainty, their incompetence, their not-knowing, their lack of knowledge, and their helplessness and dependency in their work as personal deficiencies with the danger of denunciation and devaluation, and not as the irrevocable consequences of 'connotative theories' " (p. 339). Often, candidates are expected, and expect themselves, to have a clarity that everyone knows is elusive or, perhaps, impossible. In a particularly telling comment, Ben Davidman (2007) said,

> The question I wish to address is not simply what ought to be included in a psychoanalytic curriculum but what is the effect on the candidate of the indeterminate nature of psychoanalysis? In other words, when we choose to pursue an education in a thing called psychoanalysis, what are we studying? (p. 77)

From my point of view, Davidman raised many highly significant questions, but here I address just one: the effect on the candidate of the indeterminate nature of psychoanalysis. I suggest that if you put any human being in a situation rife with uncertainties and assess his or her competence, you will see that any paranoid tendencies are likely to surface. Paranoia often includes feelings of being set up to fail. Whatever insecurities candidates have are bound to be exacerbated *when they know they are being judged on their performance of a task that can't be clearly and reliably defined.* Over 50 years ago, Sullivan (1956) connected feelings of insecurity with paranoid trends. Because I see paranoia as precluding curiosity, what this means to me is that the training situation is not likely to facilitate playful, creative, curious imagining.

COWARDICE IN CANDIDATES

Whether or not a candidate actually lacks courage, I think training convinces many that they are cowards. Briefly, here are a few ways this comes about.

1. In my experience candidates are rather routinely told they are not "confronting" or "direct" enough with their patients. I am sure that my experience is colored by my participation in interpersonal psychoanalytic programs rather than those guided by other theories. But I think the issue probably exists, to varying degrees, in other programs.
2. Candidates (and graduates) who feel afraid of speaking up at meetings often experience themselves as cowards. I think this is exacerbated by their difficulty explaining (to themselves and others) just what they are afraid of.
3. Many candidates are being analyzed, supervised, and taught by members of an older generation that was closer to the field's early battles of mythic proportions. Each institute hands down its own stories of psychoanalytic "gladiators" who fought for what they believed in. It is not hard to read in an implicit comparison between then and now that highlights the commitment, conviction, and courage of our analytic ancestors.

4. In classes and case presentations, candidates often feel cowardly if they fall silent when a colleague is being humiliated or otherwise unfairly treated (from the candidate's perspective).
5. Confusing and elusive taboos about boundaries make candidates feel generally anxious during public meetings and social occasions. Many feel they have to "play the game" without knowing the rules. What is the "protocol" when candidates and their training analysts both attend a function? The lack of clarity leaves some with a lingering sense they were too cowardly to deal with the situation in a forthright manner.

Horst Brodbeck's (2008) survey of candidates' feelings about their training includes some poignant expressions of the anxieties training evokes and their impact on how candidates see themselves. Here are two quotations from this significant and moving report:

> The anxiety in psychoanalytic training proves to be a constant companion. (p. 333)

> Yes, I always felt inhibited when my training analyst was there. At our Institute, it was not at all unusual for me to be sitting in the case seminar with him there. And I was always analyzing myself at the same time, whether I was saying something about the case that referred to my training analyst, or whether he was interpreting something I was saying about the case in relation to my person. (p. 334)

I would say that candidates often feel some equivalent of the experiences of the central character in Kafka's masterpiece *The Trial*. Judgments that will have severe consequences are occurring but are often ambiguous and impenetrable.

SOME SOURCES OF SHAME IN ANALYTIC TRAINING

So far I have addressed some of the ways training can delimit candidates' curiosity and evoke the feelings of being a coward. An obviously related issue is the sense of shameful inadequacy that haunts some of us for the rest of our careers. How we shame candidates is a topic I have explored at length elsewhere (Buechler, 2006). Here I extend this discussion by citing some of the factors that can combine to damage the candidate's sense of self-esteem. Central to my thinking is the notion that the resulting narcissistic vulnerability can have severe long-term effects on our whole careers. First, I will suggest what shame entails and then briefly outline some of its sources in the training process.

Shame occurs typically, if not always, in the context of an emotional relationship. The sharp increase in self-attention (and sometimes the increased sensitivity of the face produced by blushing) causes the person to feel as though he were naked and exposed to the world. Shame motivates the desire to hide, to disappear. Shame can also produce a feeling of ineptness, incapacity, and a feeling of not belonging. (Izard, 1977, p. 92)

It is difficult to imagine an educative process more acutely conducive of shame than analytic training. Every aspect of Izard's definition fits the analytic training process. As candidates our relationships with our analyst, supervisors, teachers, patients, colleagues, and even the institute itself are all emotional relationships. These people matter to us, and we care what they think and feel about us. Self-attention is intense in training, because heightened self-awareness plays such a crucial role in every part of the learning process. The candidate must be extremely self-observant. Without self-observation, every aspect of analytic training, from personal analysis to supervision and even theoretical coursework, would be a disembodied, sterile exercise.

Clearly, then, in training all the ingredients needed to induce shame are present. The candidate intensely examines himself as he is being evaluated by people whose opinion of him deeply matters. But yet another pressure is often added. The candidate is frequently aware of an expectation that not only should he be able to reveal himself while being evaluated but also he should be able to do so relatively *comfortably*. To put it briefly, the candidate is expected to open himself to an unusual degree of personal scrutiny and still maintain enough equanimity to function in his new professional roles. Because he often incorporates these expectations, he also expects himself to be comfortably self-revealing. At the same time, he is involved in a personal treatment process that facilitates less reliance on accustomed defenses, and therefore he is confronting anxiety his defenses previously kept at bay. He is learning a new, highly ambiguous task; absorbing complicated theoretical material; making new friendships; and attempting to integrate this new life with his previous responsibilities and relationships. And, often, any discomfort with this process is seen as problematic by the candidate himself, as well as by others. Here is one graduate's self-reflections, 50 years after his training was completed:

At first, I responded to my analyst's expectations of me to think about myself and others, and reveal to him what I was thinking with no pleasure in the procedure. People used to remark how interesting it must be to have an opportunity to study oneself with the help of a guide and mentor. I don't recall disagreeing very actively, probably out of some apprehension that if I did so, they would think I must have had a terrible past. I resisted the process of self-revelation, often quite pain-fully. (English, 1976, p. 192)

Thus English suffered from shame about his shame. His discomfort at revealing himself felt like it was, itself, something to hide and be ashamed of. As will be further elaborated, it is the shame about feeling shame that, I think, is unequivocally harmful, unnecessary, and potentially avoidable in training.

Even with supervisors who have the best of intentions, shaming occurs in analytic training. For example, which of us has not felt inadequate when we compared ourselves to a renowned supervisor? The following statement shows how a supervisor can inadvertently exacerbate these feelings:

> I think it's a good idea not to overwhelm a supervisee with all the clever ideas that you as a supervisor think you have. This is one of the ways in which I tend to err in supervision. I get very stimulated, and sometimes I talk too much, and it can have a deleterious effect on the work of the supervisee. Occasionally, supervisees who are working through the problems of speaking up against authority in their own analyses begin to indicate to me that I sort of make them feel stupid—things like that. (Schafer, 1984, p. 225)

Personally, I often ask myself what aspects of my reactions to a vignette presented in supervision would be helpful to share. For example, a candidate in analytic training presents his work with an obsessive patient whose language is at a 45-degree angle away from direct communication. That is, for instance, the patient says he is upset (rather than angry) to avoid the part of the message that might make him anxious. As the supervisor, I hear in the material a kind of contagion. The patient's indirectness seems to elicit something similar in the language of the candidate. If I point this out, I believe I am very likely to elicit the supervisee's shame. Although seeing *any* countertransferential defensiveness may evoke some shame, it is my impression that, at least in my supervisees, becoming aware of their own obsessive language is particularly shame inducing. I wonder whether this is, partially, a product of my own attitude. Perhaps not unlike Schafer, I can feel tremendous zeal at these moments. I am excited to impart something I think of as potentially highly mutative. My excitement may lend intensity to my voice. My supervisee may then feel his obsessive defenses have been all too eagerly exposed.

I will merely mention another supervisory situation that I think is likely to elicit shame in my supervisees. When I see the content of the candidate's treatment of his patient being *enacted* in the supervisory session with me, and I point this out, I think it can evoke the kind of shame in the candidate that we all feel when we don't know our slip is showing and someone comments on it. In this situation, as with contagious obsessive language, I believe some shame in the supervisee may be inevitable, but my own emotions will affect the manner and timing of my comments, which may affect the intensity of the supervisee's shame. Do I interpret with glee, with unnecessary emphasis, or with compassion for the courage it takes to train as an analyst?

JOAN'S SHAME: A FICTIONAL CANDIDATE FACES FAILURE

Let's describe, in greater detail, the experience of Joan, the mythical candidate I introduced in the preceding chapter. Joan is in her 30s when she decides to train analytically. Therapeutic passion was instilled long ago. It would be impossible for her to differentiate her wish to help from her need to help. She comes to training with a conscious desire to become a better clinician.

The institute's acceptance letter comes as a bit of a surprise, which, in retrospect, could serve as a clue to her self-esteem issues. As is true in most interviews, Joan tried to portray her strengths but, inwardly, wondered if she would make the grade.

She is excited, and a little anxious, about meeting the other candidates. When she does, she is struck by her own strong tendency to make comparisons. Who is the smartest? Who is the most skilled and experienced clinician? Who will be the faculty's favorite? Who will be most liked by other trainees? Where will she fit in the hierarchy?

She is immediately ashamed of these thoughts and, most especially, her need to be the best or, at least, not the worst. But it is all so confusing. How can she know how she stacks up compared to the others?

Classes start. Now, at least, there will be a way to shine. Hard work and intense, thorough preparation will pay off. She tries to read everything listed in the syllabus for the first week. Some of it doesn't make sense, but she reads it anyway. Or, at least, she reads the words.

In class she forgets what she read. She desperately tries to remember. The instructor, who seems pretty anxious too, asks a general question about what people felt about the readings. There is a painful silence. Everyone squirms and looks around the room. Finally someone thinks of a question. Joan listens, both humbled by the questioner's ability to think of something and also contemptuous, because it is clear that it wasn't curiosity that motivated the questioner but only the wish to be the one who broke the silence. This does not seem to be apparent to the instructor, however, who is clearly relieved that someone asked a question. Joan doesn't exactly understand the relationship between what the instructor says and the question that was asked. She wonders if she just isn't bright enough for this program.

Or maybe she is tired from all that studying. That was foolish. She worked so hard preparing that she is too tired to participate.

With the help of her newly assigned psychotherapy supervisor, Joan figures out her problem. She is too eager to please. She wants to succeed too much. And this is not just a problem in class. It colors her clinical work as well. In supervision she learns that she has trouble with anger. Anyone's anger. The patient's anger, her supervisor's anger, her own anger, her classmates' anger. Anger is her Achilles' heel. At last, she feels, she is getting somewhere. The problem is clear.

Relief mixes with lingering anxiety as she brings this issue to the first potential training analyst she sees for a consultation to assess whether to work with him in analysis. She doesn't really know how she should choose her training analyst. She is thinking about this during the consultation. Of course, she can't ask about it. How can she ask this distinguished analyst about how to decide whether to choose him as her analyst? She tries to avoid the issue. The idea that *she* is evaluating *him* is absurd. She had better not look like she is evaluating him. Maybe it would be best to decide right away just to work with him. How bad could it be? And maybe it is good if it is bad. That is, maybe an easy analysis wouldn't really be worth much. The harder, the more painful, the more shaming, the better. After all, she won't confront her defenses of her own accord. Someone will have to be strong enough to *make* her do it.

During the interview the training analyst says very little. He asks her to tell him a little about herself. Her anxiety level rises. What does he want? Maybe it is a test to see how open she can be. She should tell him something embarrassing to show she has courage. But maybe she shouldn't tell him anything *too* embarrassing. That might suggest to him that she has poor judgment or poor impulse control. What is open enough but not too damning? Her mind becomes a complete blank. She can't think of anything. He asks her what theories she likes. She can't think of any names of theorists. This is going very badly. She feels sure he won't work with her. Why would he want to waste his time?

He asks her if she has any questions. Does that mean she should have a question? Quick, think of a question. She asks about the fee, thinking, "What a lame question! What will he think of me now? I'll bet he will want to work with one of the other trainees and not me."

Then it strikes her. Of course! She is enacting her problem! She wants the training analyst to think well of her. She is living out her central issue, already, in the first session! So this is analysis! It is working! Because she feels quite uncomfortable, she will stay with him. He must be the right analyst for her.

Emboldened by making this choice, she decides to select someone to be her analytic supervisor. This won't be as hard. It will be easier to talk about a patient than about herself. But, here too, how do you choose? She looks at the list of supervisors. Maybe she should ask candidates in the higher year levels. But what should she say she is seeking? Someone who doesn't expect much? Maybe it is best to save the really great supervisors for later, when she knows something.

She gets a few names, makes some appointments, and brings her case notes to a consultation. The supervisor smiles and asks how she chose him. She has the beginning of a panic attack. Oh, God, not now! But she can't tell this man that she chose to meet him because a few older candidates said he didn't expect much and wasn't that bright himself! Maybe she could tell him she likes his theory and wants to learn from him. But what *is* his theory? She can't ask, because, supposedly, she chose to see him because she knows what it is and likes it. Oh, God, she thinks, "If I throw up, I'm finished." She questions the whole idea of training. Maybe she should face her limitations and leave the program.

Time marches on, somehow. She starts work with an analytic supervisor. She has a patient who is ambivalent about moving from twice a week therapy to three or four times a week analysis. She wants to present this patient to the supervisor, but she is ashamed she has not been able to motivate the patient more. Maybe she shouldn't tell her new supervisor about this situation right away. Maybe she can get away with asking some general, innocuous questions. Or can the supervisor tell she is stalling?

Meanwhile, with guilt, shame, and anxiety that she will be caught, she offers to see the patient for three times a week for a very low fee. It is actually less per week than the patient was paying for only two sessions. She feels terrible about this. She resents that she is actually losing money on the deal. But most of all, that is just what it feels like: a deal. Maybe a bribe. She is afraid this will affect the whole treatment. It is tainted. But how else can she persuade the patient to come three times a week? Of course, all the other trainees can easily get their patients to commit to analysis. Obviously, she is inferior. The faculty is wise. They will catch on for sure.

The patient accepts the arrangement. For the moment, Joan is very happy. She likes this patient a great deal. She wants to help him very much. He is a nice guy but not functioning well in his work or love life. He seems like an ideal patient. Maybe training will work out after all.

She comes to supervision, armed with extensive notes. She gets through two sentences. The supervisor tells her to put the notes away, asking why she thinks she needs them. Joan smiles, awkwardly. She doesn't answer the question about why she thought she needed the notes. Instead she begins to talk about the patient's history.

The supervisor stops her again and asks what she feels about this patient. "Thank God," Joan thinks. Here is a question she can answer. She tells the supervisor how much she likes this patient and wants to help him.

The supervisor looks surprised. In an impatient tone he says, "But this man is so aggressive and contemptuous toward you! Can't you see how he is treating you?"

Silence. Joan sinks into her chair. Here it is again. Her problem with aggression. She can't even see it, let alone deal with it.

Fast forward. It is time for Joan to write a case study and present this patient at a meeting of the whole community. Joan experiences the conflicts she has felt before but with greater intensity. Should she be open? About what? Her difficulties in the treatment? Her difficulties in the supervision? Her flaws as a human being? Their history? Her pathetic attempts to overcome them? Her failures, past and present?

Or how about doing something less personal and more theoretical? But to this audience that might sound even more defensive. Well, it *would be* defensive, so, of course, it *would sound* defensive. But, maybe, it would also be wise. But, then, if she wanted to hide, why did she come for training? Why is she spending all this time, money, and effort?

Joan sits down to write the case report. She asks herself what she knows about her patient. What defenses does he use? What is his diagnosis? What are the main themes of their work together so far? What theory is she using in treating him? *Why doesn't she know the answers to these fundamental questions?*

Joan feels she just doesn't have the right stuff to be an analyst. It must be obvious to everyone, her analyst, her supervisors, her classmates, and her patients. Everyone sees her inadequacy. Her patients are probably going to quit treatment any moment now. This will expose her weakness as a clinician. And her failure as a clinician is really about her shortcomings as a person. She isn't just doing a poor job. She *is* an inadequate human being. Everyone at the presentation will see that. Even if she is not thrown out of the program, everyone will feel sorry for her and superior to her. Her classmates will be kind about it, at least to her face. She can only guess what they will say to each other behind her back.

Of course, she isn't really helping her patient. Just yesterday he came to a session asking what good this treatment was supposed to be doing. Lately he has been feeling kind of unsettled. He thought treatment would help him feel better. He wasn't really getting any answers about how he should handle things on the job or with his girlfriend. What gives? Maybe he should go back down to twice a week. Maybe he just doesn't have enough to say for three times a week. What does Joan think about that? What Joan really thinks is that she will die of shame if her only analytic patient drops out of analysis but, of course, she can't say this to the patient. She tries to remain calm or, at least, to look calm and sound calm. Desperately, she searches her mind for something to say that might reassure this man that the analysis is working, but he must give it more time. Just a little more time.

Let's assume Joan gets her wish, and her patient stays in analytic treatment. This means she has the task of presenting material from his analysis to her supervisor. The central goal of this process is to further Joan's development as an analytic clinician. Thus, on a weekly basis, Joan chooses which material to focus on and bring to her supervisor. A potential conflict is built into this system, in that the supervisor is responsible for teaching Joan and also evaluating Joan's progress and reporting it to the training committee. For the supervisor (depending on his or her character issues, level of supervisory experience, transference to the institute, and, probably, many other factors) this can create some conflict. Is it best to encourage the candidate to be completely candid about her difficulties as an analyst (and as a human being)? If so, then, the more skilled the supervisor and the more open the candidate, the more likely it is that significant issues will be revealed. But, then, what is the supervisor's responsibility to report these to the training committee? If reported, these issues might be taken as problematic enough to slow Joan's progress through the program. Of course, the positive spin on this is that Joan is there to learn, and assuming whatever the supervisor and committee suggest is in Joan's interest, her slower progress will be of benefit to her in the long run. But this makes some major assumptions. What if the supervisor is wrong or, at least, biased in some way? What if, for example, the supervisor, because of his or her own proclivities, greatly privileges stark confrontation of defenses early in treatment, or the slow, gradual unfolding of an analytic process, or the exploration of genetic material early in the work, or minimizing patients' experiences of anxiety, or some other stylistic practice? What if, in other words, the supervisor's "vision" of treatment isn't "super" in the sense of unquestionably superior or "super" in the sense of above, over, or outside? What if it is merely another vision of how to do the work, a vision shaped as much by the supervisor's particular character issues as is Joan's?

I am not suggesting that supervisors have nothing to teach or that their input is necessarily unhelpful. But the situation is, in my opinion, potentially conflict laden, for both supervisor and trainee. How hard to try to get the candidate to be self-revealing can be one of the supervisor's dilemmas, whereas how open to be about real difficulties is among the candidate's potential issues. Here is where the character patterns of each play a major role. For example, we know Joan wants to be liked and do well in her training program. I would suggest that to the degree that Joan has schizoid features, she will cope with training by putting a premium on "getting through" it. Elsewhere, I have described the schizoid tendency to try to manage interpersonal interactions and how that characteristic can affect the analyst's behavior in sessions (Buechler, 2002a). Here I suggest how it could impact the supervisee's behavior, as well, of course, as the supervisor's. Both Joan and her supervisor might, if they are schizoid enough, avoid getting into potentially problematic, emotionally intense areas. Or if both have obsessive features, they might get involved in a prolonged power struggle of some kind or a wordy, vague, unclear, faintly unpleasant way of relating to each other. Many other permutations are possible, of course, and they may be further complicated by the training committee's input.

Although any emotion might be elicited in supervision, I believe it is especially important to be aware of the candidate's feelings of shame. I have written elsewhere about the role of shame in analytic training (Buechler, 2006, 2008). Here I am emphasizing potential long-term effects of damage to the self-esteem of candidates. Aside from being painful at the time, shaming trainees can leave a legacy of vulnerability to doubting one's clinical judgment and worth.

Let's return to the interpersonal situation in supervision. The candidate, perhaps feeling her professional life is at stake, comes to supervision, where her countertransference is often a central focus. This seems to me to be especially conducive to evoking shame in the candidate. The analysis of countertransference in supervision has much in common with the analysis of defense in treatment, with one major difference. In treatment, we explore the patient's defensive style in the genetic context, as well as in its current manifestations. We look at *why* the analysand needed to develop her defenses. But in supervision, although the candidate's defenses are also an important focus, the *genetic situations that necessitated their development* are generally not mentioned. Thus my analysand and I understand, together, why she had to become the person she is. But my supervisee and I examine only the defensive *outcome* of her life experience but not the life experience itself. We don't have the shared understanding of the historical context that explains the need for just these defensive patterns. In supervision, as opposed to treatment, the candidate does not have the opportunity to identify with my empathic attempt to contextualize her defenses, to help make sense of them. In treatment we can understand the struggling person whose only way to survive may have been to develop these defensive maneuvers. In supervision, we focus on their professional impact but, generally, not on their genetic sources. The candidate often feels ashamed that she needs these defenses, afraid they make her unfit to be an analyst, unforgiving toward herself for these "inadequacies." This may elicit her self-contempt, scorn, and shame, unmodulated by the compassion she might feel more easily if she were my patient.

I do not mean to suggest that we should explore the candidate's genetic history in supervision. Generally I do not inquire into the candidate's personal life, although if a candidate chooses to disclose I do not discourage it. But I leave the decision entirely up to the candidate. Because most candidates limit how much of their early life they share in supervision, I think they find it easier to feel compassion for themselves in their training analysis than in their supervision. I believe that compassionate love for oneself, as a struggling human being doing the best one can, modulates shame more often in treatment than in supervision.

I think it adds to the potential for shame in the candidate that it is so infrequent that the supervisor's countertransferences (to the candidate, as well as the candidate's patient) get scrutinized. We do not have as firmly established a tradition of looking at supervisory countertransference as we have for examining an analyst's countertransference in treatment. Given the power differentials, this can hardly be accidental. I believe there are also many ways to engage in outright but unacknowledged competition with the candidate, and these, too, can foster the candidate's feelings of inadequacy and shame. The context hardly creates a level playing field. As Edgar Levenson (1982) suggested, supervision derives its clarity from its level of abstraction. The supervisor can address himself to the *class* of patients to which this particular patient belongs. In addition, the supervisor has the advantage of being removed from the patient's pressures. Also, he is already "stamped" with the institute's seal of approval. Competition between supervisor and candidate is, thus, unfair and potentially shaming.

Especially conducive to evoking the candidate's shame is the situation we create when we provide the candidate with a patient who is fundamentally unanalyzable and then judge him on his ability to conduct analysis. An example is assigning the candidate a patient who spends 40 out of every 45 minutes campaigning to break the frame and considers the analytic interpretive process a poor substitute for unlimited contact. In this situation the candidate is extremely likely to feel like a failure with the patient and with the supervisor. In the treatment he feels he is not helping the patient feel better. The patient's troubles are urgent and require relief. What the treatment provides is too slow, abstract, and removed from the patient's crises. With the supervisor the candidate feels equally inadequate but for a contradictory set of reasons. He feels he has been too concerned with the patient's life and not sufficiently focused on the patient's analysis. He is too easily drawn into the patient's mood of urgency. He has let himself be bullied, perhaps even blackmailed, by the patient's implicit threat to leave treatment if he isn't more forthcoming with personally revealing, openly caring, concretely advising behavior. In short, with the patient the supervisee feels inadequate about his ability to help, whereas with the supervisor he feels ashamed he isn't doing enough to analyze.

IS THE CANDIDATE'S SHAME UNIQUE?

How much is shame an inevitable part of being a novice in *any* field? In response to a paper of my own that dealt with the shaming of analytic candidates, Robert Michels (2008) posed this question:

> Buechler discusses candidates' experiences of shame and the power-ful effects that can persist and color their psychoanalytic careers. This

is, of course, true in all forms of apprentice learning and is discussed extensively in the literature on professional education in law and medicine. It would be interesting to explore what, if anything, is unique to the role of shame in psychoanalytic education. (p. 396)

I think this is a crucial question. In what follows, I suggest some ways I think psychoanalytic training poses shaming possibilities way beyond those in any other field.

1. The candidate is being evaluated as a whole, as a human being, and not just with regard to a specific skill or knowledge base. The subjectivity inherent to our work means that, as Brodbeck (2008) suggested, "analytic practice and technique cannot be regarded as distinct from the person who is practicing it, rather, it is only through the person practicing it that it can have an effect" (p. 330). For this reason, Brodbeck continued, "it is always the person, as a whole, that is being trained and evaluated." No clear-cut distinction can be made between competence and character. The "right stuff" to be an analyst is nebulous enough to contribute to *a sense of being sized up, as a human being, rather than merely evaluated in a specific area.*

2. When the candidate submits to pressure to imitate a supervisor's technique (without using his or her own clinical judgment), shame and a sense of *self-betrayal* seem to me to be likely results. Even without any pressure from the supervisor, candidates often feel tempted to merely imitate their approach rather than develop their own unique styles. But we foster rote imitation if we collaborate in the attitude that the way patients will get an optimal treatment is for supervisees to absorb as much as possible in the supervisory hour and hold on to it with all their might until they next see their patient, when they must dispense these precious drops into the patient's ear. What candidates "learn" from this potentially disheartening experience is that the best they can be is a fairly accurate copy of someone else. The pressure to imitate is likely to be stronger if the institute tends to present a united front.

3. If faculty support an idealized vision of their own skills, the candidate is likely to feel unalterably inadequate by comparison. This false impression is reinforced in many ways. Exaggerated needs for power, recognition, and fame ensure that narcissistic injuries will be handed down from one generation to the next. To the extent that a program is hierarchical, it is likely to reinforce perceived differences between candidates and faculty.

4. Brodbeck (2008) wrote of the "sense of mission" that may be necessary to the analyst, suggesting that "this also harbors a risk of self-exultation and social isolation with the proviso of seeking gratification in the

narcissistic sector, instead of earning one's living in an interesting profession" (p. 341).

5. One of the harshest criticisms leveled against candidates (and colleagues, at meetings) is that their work is "not analytic." In a similar spirit, analysis is held as superior to other forms of therapy. This implicitly shames candidates who need to earn most of their living through these "inferior" occupations.

6. At public forums and in classes, the fear of making a fool of oneself can be palpable. Succumbing to this fear and remaining silent can be shaming. Elsewhere, I have expressed my feeling that candidates' shame about having shame can be especially painful (Buechler, 2006). Candidates are entering a field that privileges devotion to finding out about oneself, emotional openness, and selflessness. This makes it hard to bear moments of being so worried about looking bad that one cannot speak.

7. Infantilizing comparisons between candidates and children, who should not know what the "parents" decide behind closed doors, are still all too common. They are shaming in their implicit assumptions. Berman (2004) wrote of the particularly painful impact when supervisors assume that any protest about the system must have its origin in the candidate's oedipal issues. More generally, it seems to me to be clear that pathologizing dissent is an abuse of power, bound to create shame in those who yield to it. It is clear that the genuine respect for individual differences that we believe in offering our patients should be extended to candidates as well.

8. A panel (*Psychoanalytic Dialogues*, 2003) on issues in training brought out some other sources of shame. Margaret Crastnopol commented, "There are many counterintuitive rules that must be learned and followed by the analytic acolyte, who also needs to learn to bear the anxiety and shame arising from lapses from the prescribed role ... with maturity and, one might say, aplomb" (2003, p. 382).

9. Later, Crastnopol (2003) brought up the problem of teaching candidates to "swim" by "throwing them into the deep end (and only later explaining why they drowned)" (p. 385). I think this is a significant source of potential shame in many of the helping professions. Often, we assign the most difficult patients to those with the least training. For example, I think it is more and more common to assign "borderline" patients to candidates as analytic cases. Frequently these patients are openly contemptuous of the candidate's level of expertise and experience. Thus clinicians with the least experience are learning treatment with the most challenging patients, because colleagues with higher status can afford to turn down treating these patients. This situation is bound to create crises of self-confidence in some beginners.

10. Crastnopol (2003) also mentioned that an inadvertent effect of our multitheoretical approach may exacerbate candidates' shame. Presented with many possible ways of working, candidates can feel confused and overwhelmed, and they can despair of ever finding a coherent style that will allow them to feel adequately skilled.

WHEN THE PATIENT TERMINATES ABRUPTLY

As a supervisor, I am often in the presence of clinicians struggling with shame that threatens to overwhelm them. To illustrate this situation, I describe the supervision of Ellen, another fictional candidate. From the moment I saw Ellen in the waiting room, I knew something was wrong. Her smile was too effortful. We took our accustomed places in my office, and she tried to prepare me for her story. A moment of small talk, and she launched in. The patient whose analytic treatment we had been discussing for over a year quit treatment in a telephone message. No warning. Something like, "Look, Ellen, I can't make it in next week. In fact money is getting really tight, and I think maybe I should take a break from treatment. If you need to reach me, you can call me at ..."

Ellen is devastated. She pours a lot into her work. She really cares about Nancy, her patient, and thinks it is hardly a time to stop treatment. Nancy herself is in a mental health profession, but she is still new to clinical experience. Nancy has clearly begun to feel the stress of a life in practice. It seems obvious to me that Nancy is looking for a way to reduce the stress. Her treatment has begun to really confront her defenses. It has gone from an initially supportive once a week treatment to a much more intensive three times per week analysis. Nancy's accustomed ways of functioning are getting questioned. I have promoted Ellen's focus on Nancy's defenses, with my usual supervisory advice that treatment can often progress more quickly if the analysis of defense is prioritized.

Ellen and I really like each other. I know that part of her upset is the feeling she will disappoint me if Nancy drops out of treatment. Also, of course, she will not get credit toward completing her training if the patient leaves prematurely. So we each have a stake in this work going forward.

I can tell that Ellen feels like a failure. She is trying not to cry. What went wrong? She has gone over and over her last session with Nancy. Was she too tough on her? Or was she not tough enough? Was there an empathic failure? An enactment, undetected by both of us? Could Ellen have seen this coming if she had been more alert, smarter, or more talented clinically? Did denial, or some other defensive process, keep Ellen from being in better touch with her patient? She wants me to tell her what to do next. Should she call Nancy (again)? E-mail, cell phone, text, telephone? At work or home?

Send a note, send the outstanding bill? Leave an extensive message or just her name?

I wonder if she wants me to tell her what to do because she is afraid her own choice may turn into another "blunder." Perhaps she is angry with me, feeling that this is all really my fault for influencing her work as I have. But Ellen knows that the training committee won't see it as my fault. They are likely to wonder what aspect of Ellen's character is implicated in her losing her patient.

As Ellen muses out loud about why this happened, she sounds more and more depressed. Maybe she just isn't cut out to be an analyst. She wonders whether I knew this from the start but was trying to give her a chance. No wonder she doesn't have the "right stuff," with her problematic childhood. How could she have thought she could make it as a psychoanalyst? She isn't savvy enough, intelligent enough, strong enough, empathic enough.

I first suggest that Nancy might still continue treatment, but I then ask whether Ellen blames me for what has happened. I reflect on the possibility that Ellen is angry at me and Nancy is angry at Ellen for similar reasons. Ellen is making Nancy's life harder by confronting her defensive maneuvers. And I am making Ellen's life harder by encouraging this approach. Ellen thinks about my interpretation but rejects it. Nice try, Sandra. But, Ellen says, it is clear that she is just no damn good. Maybe she has actually harmed Nancy. With a more skilled clinician, Nancy would have stayed in treatment longer, but with Ellen she has lost hope.

Inwardly, I am asking myself how far I should go in interpreting Ellen's depressive feelings. After all, this is supervision, not treatment. Yet it feels wrong to just let them stand. What should I focus on? Should I insist that Ellen is "really" angry with me but can't let herself be aware of that, so her anger is turning against herself? Should I point out the harshness of Ellen's "superego"? Should I focus on the clinical work with Nancy and strategize about how to get her back in treatment? Should I suggest reasons why she might have left?

From my point of view, any of these approaches can be justified. What seems to me to be most important are the long-term effects of this clinical experience on Ellen. These may include the following:

1. The candidate has shame and a sense of inadequacy not only as a professional *but also as a person*. All the sources of shame, previously mentioned in this chapter, are present for Ellen. I see her shame as operating in a loop, in which a feeling of inadequacy elicits heightened self-attention, which exacerbates the shame, further heightening self-attention, and so on. Ellen's relationships with both Nancy and me are certainly emotional and extremely important to her. With her patient threatening to quit, Ellen feels exposed as a poor clinician.

She certainly suffers from the sense of "ineptness, incapacity, and a feeling of not belonging" that Izard identified as part of the total shame experience. She wonders if she belongs in training and, more generally, in the community of clinicians.

2. The candidate has uncertainty about how to prevent losing future patients and, as a result, a hesitancy about what to focus on in sessions with patients. There is a great deal of second-guessing after sessions and worry about whether patients will return.

3. The candidate perhaps has some reluctance to take on new patients and other professional challenges.

4. The candidate has awareness that the path to hell is paved with good intentions. Ellen knows that she has tried to provide a good treatment experience for Nancy. She is learning the painful lesson that in clinical (and many other) situations, trying hard does not necessarily result in a successful outcome.

What are the surprises in store for Ellen as she pursues training? What is she likely to learn about herself along the way? What aspects of her identity are likely to be challenged? What feelings probably will get stirred up? How will she be altered as a human being, and how will she remain the same, by the time she graduates? I believe that the shifts I refer to are prevalent in the experience of clinicians in general, even without advanced training, although I explicitly describe those that occur during analytic training. The training process enhances and coalesces these personal changes, but many might come about without training, over a lifetime of clinical experience.

Training (regardless of the orientation of the institute) has certain features, which make some personal shifts probable. For example, I think it highly likely that training will offer the candidate an opportunity to be more aware of the role of aggression in psychic life. Of course some candidates enter training quite aware of aggression in themselves and others. And there are candidates who studiously avoid this aspect of humanness. But, at the very least, candidates are likely to encounter some aggression in the (frequently) competitive atmosphere of institute life.

So, Ellen entered training, having had a bit of clinical experience but not a great deal of supervision. Much like growth in a hothouse, training intensifies certain inherently likely processes of change. In her first year, Ellen would never have dreamed she could hate a patient. She saw the world as mostly populated by good guys with benign intentions. It is therefore highly likely she was acutely uncomfortable when she encountered intense anger, aggression, or hatred in herself. How will this affect her as a human being? What will happen to the defenses that have shielded her from this self-awareness? What aspects of her identity will change?

I know candidates and graduates are individuals, like all human beings, and no generalizations are universally true. But, on the whole, I think training magnifies the likelihood a clinician has to face the aggressive potential in us all. With great frequency, I have listened to training committees deliberate about how to help the candidate become more comfortable with aggression. Anxiety also comes up frequently. Although candidate reviews are hardly uniform, I have heard much more about helping trainees deal with aggression and anxiety than I have heard about helping them with their guilt, shame, sorrow, envy, jealousy, or regret. Occasionally the subject is raised of dealing with sexual or tender feelings. Seldom have I heard deliberations about how the candidate might feel more joy, or hope, or kindness.

Why do these disparities exist? I am sure there are many reasons, but one factor must be the type of person who tends to enter the field. I think clinicians cling to what Larry Epstein (1999) might call "good therapist" feelings. We choose our careers partially based on our ability to see ourselves as born caretakers with mostly benign intentions toward others. We are usually more aware of our nurturing and benevolent qualities than our aggressive attributes. In training (and, perhaps more slowly, in the process of gaining clinical experience outside training), we encounter our own and others' aggression and feel its power. Who do we then become? That is, given that, like any other human beings, clinicians have defenses, what happens to the clinician confronted with seeing herself as the aggressive "bad me" or even the "not me" she might most dread becoming?

In other words, what happens to a human being who is confronted with previously warded off aggression? Let's add that chances are the candidate is also undergoing some challenges to her usual defensive style. Who does she see when she looks in the mirror or, rather, when she is mirrored back to herself by her supervisors, analyst, and teachers?

Ellen personifies some of the qualities I am describing. Like many of us, Ellen entered training with certain unformulated but personally significant assumptions about herself. She saw herself as generally well intentioned toward other people. Like a good Winnicottian, she believed she could keep any anger toward patients in "storage" until the patient seemed ready to hear about it (Winnicott, 1949). She thought she could limit herself to expressing only clinically useful, well-modulated, constructive anger. Her anger would obediently wait in the wings until the clinically right time to make itself known.

All through school, from kindergarten through graduate training, Ellen was a model student. She knew that if she studied hard she would do well, and she usually studied hard. She believed in herself as generally intelligent, intuitive, and interpersonally aware. She knew herself to be a "quick study," adept at sizing people up. Her early clinical experience told her that she could form a good therapeutic alliance, even with difficult patients. She was usually able to keep patients in treatment, through the force of her ever-present good will, sensitivity, and clinical talent.

And then she entered analytic training, and Nancy came along as her first patient, and I came along as her first analytic supervisor. Much that Ellen didn't know she assumed about herself was now open to question. For one thing, she found herself furious with Nancy much of the time, and her fury seemed unwilling to wait in the wings. Sometimes it surfaced suddenly, in sessions, moving her to fill Nancy's sessions with "interpretations" that resembled verbal attacks.

Ellen had to see herself as capable of sudden bouts of rage toward a patient. Where was her self-control, sensitivity, compassion? Where was the Ellen she thought she knew?

I am suggesting that if Ellen had not entered training but had accrued years of clinical experience, she probably would have had a more gradual introduction to these ego dystonic aspects of herself. Eventually, in the treatment of some of her patients, she would have come across the angry Ellen who could respond impulsively and vindictively. But I think training often condenses the process of self-discovery. Suddenly candidate Ellen looks in the mirror (and training is like a hall of mirrors) and sees a stranger she neither likes nor admires. Worse yet, this alien Ellen is constantly exposed in evaluations and training meetings.

In Dostoevsky's (1846/1985) brilliant short novel *The Double*, a man wakes up to discover that a duplicate of himself is posing as him and behaving outrageously. To his horror this mischievous replica is replacing him. He pleads for his old life, to no avail.

Such is often the lot of the clinician and, especially, the candidate. Our hardworking, generally successful, well-intentioned, empathic selves mysteriously morph. I am reminded of Kafka's (1948) "Metamorphosis." A grotesque creature seems to have taken the place of our familiar selves.

It is hard to describe the shame that can result. Sullivan (1953) gave us a vivid description of the discomfort we can feel when we encounter the "bad-me" or "not-me." He generally called this feeling "anxiety," but I think it has all the earmarks of profound shame. Although anxiety may well accompany the shame, the central experience is that our insufficiencies are being exposed. In our own eyes, and the eyes of others, we don't measure up.

What do we feel when we have to acknowledge "bad me" or "not me" as part of "me"? What happens to us when our accustomed selves are replaced by a mischievous double or a hardly human creature that claims to be us? Or when (as in Gogol's [1960] memorable short story "The Nose") we find an essential aspect of ourselves suddenly missing (in the story the central character wakes to find his nose has fallen off). I think this relates to what is meant by the expression "dying of shame." The well-known, well-accepted self is lost. In its place is an unfamiliar, alien replica.

In this sense, I would suggest that candidates frequently die of shame. Eventually the self that dies is replaced, often by an expanded, richer self. The phrase that "nothing human is alien to me" takes on greater meaning.

For example, Ellen may find that she could be as aggressive, competitive, self-interested, envious, and vindictive as anyone else. I think it makes emotional sense to guess that toward the middle of her training, Ellen might wake up to find that a strange creature that lacked some of her accustomed features has taken her place. All around her are "mirrors" that call this new being "Ellen," so she has to own it as herself.

From another perspective we could say that Ellen was caught in a bind. To be "good" in her new profession, she has to acknowledge being "bad." That is, to succeed as a candidate, she has to recognize previously disavowed personal qualities. A uniformly kind, capable Ellen has to die so a "more human than otherwise" Ellen could be born.

Briefly, I think the experience frequently includes a few fundamental lessons:

1. Previously "not me" or "bad me" aspects of the self are integrated into the clinician's self-concept.
2. Clinicians have to recognize that hard work does not always bring success in clinical endeavors (unlike many of the academic situations they faced previously). In fact, trying too hard to have a "good" session can be counterproductive and may lead to wordy, overly interpretive behavior.
3. Even the most interpersonally astute, alert clinician can be blind to important aspects of the patient's experience. For example, it seems likely that Nancy had been dissatisfied with the treatment well before Ellen became aware of it. This challenges Ellen's sense of herself as sensitive and empathic. Ellen has built a major part of her sense of self on believing she has these attributes. Who she is to herself, as a person and not just as a clinician, is at issue. Once again, a dentist whose skill is challenged may still see herself, or himself, as a capable parent, offspring, partner, and friend. But for a clinician, bad news about one's equipment as a professional is also bad news about one's equipment as a human being.

Thus, for a clinician, becoming aware of previously unknown negative attributes can elicit exquisite shame. What is being exposed is one's fundamental capacity to function interpersonally. The carpenter can perform poorly on the job and still count on being a good father (or mother). But as clinicians, our professional performance speaks of our essential ability to relate to other human beings. In an unusually broad sense, we *are* our work. When a mathematician fails on the job, he or she doesn't necessarily feel less competent as a friend, neighbor, partner, or parent. The mathematician's failure to solve an equation may evoke shame. But then, that evening, the mathematician will still expect to be the same good parent he or she was yesterday. Not so for the clinician, for whom failure on the job can elicit profound shame about his or her very humanity and capacity for interpersonal relating.

In short, I can envision reasons some shame may be inevitable, and even adaptive, in analytic training. The functions shame serves in training may be similar to shame's role in early life. Shame motivates the child's development of objective self-awareness. The children we all were needed this perspective to become socially attuned. The analysts candidates are becoming need high degrees of attunement, self-awareness, and sensitivity to their interpersonal effect. Candidates are preparing for a professional life uniquely dependent on painstaking self-awareness, honest self-scrutiny, and a willing acceptance of responsibility for negative interpersonal impact. It is human nature to feel shame when a spotlight is thrown on our significant limitations. As Sullivan (1953) suggested, part of how we learn to be social creatures is through experiencing varying degrees of failure, with its attendant discomfort. So perhaps shame in analytic training is inevitable and even has its adaptive functions. In other words, the candidate revealing how her limitations as a human being affect her clinical work inevitably feels some shame, as would any other human being acculturated in our society. But, on the other hand, I think shame about shame is avoidable and destructive and can leave a lasting, demoralizing legacy, as I will elaborate in subsequent chapters.

In sum, in training all the ingredients needed to induce shame are present. The candidate intensely examines himself as he is being evaluated by people whose opinion of him deeply matters. But yet another pressure is often added. The candidate is frequently aware of an expectation that not only should he be able to reveal himself while being evaluated but he should be able to do so relatively *comfortably*. To put it briefly, the candidate is expected to open himself to an unusual degree of personal scrutiny and still maintain enough equanimity to function in his new professional roles. Because he often incorporates these expectations, he also expects himself to be comfortably self-revealing. At the same time, he is involved in a personal treatment process that facilitates less reliance on accustomed defenses, and therefore he is confronting anxiety his defenses previously kept at bay. He is learning a new, highly ambiguous task; absorbing complicated theoretical material; making new friendships; and attempting to integrate this new life with his previous responsibilities and relationships. And, often, any discomfort with this process is seen as problematic by the candidate himself, as well as by others. The legacy of supervision is bound to include some feelings of inadequacy, even when things go relatively well. But what about when they don't?

THE EFFECT OF A NEGATIVE EVALUATION

I now consider the possible long-term impact on the career and personal life of the candidate who is given a predominantly negative supervisory evaluation. Although this situation merits much more attention than I can give it here, I would like to suggest the following:

1. The candidate who receives a highly critical and generally negative evaluation may be profoundly, lastingly affected by this experience.
2. Regardless of the degree of validity, necessity, and educative value of the assessment, I believe that its shame-inducing potential is accentuated by the *secrecy* that often surrounds it. It is my experience that when a negative evaluation is given, candidates frequently feel it is in their interest to hide it from their classmates and other colleagues. It becomes a secret source of shame. The candidate thus denies himself the opportunity to examine the meaning and accuracy of the evaluation, with the help of others who know him. It is as though problems encountered in training are taboo subjects to be shrouded in silence. I think this secrecy itself adds to the potential for evoking lasting shame.
3. Candidates often feel that if any problems occur in their training, they should outwardly comply, uncomplainingly, with what is suggested to them. Complaints about how they are being treated may be seen as further evidence of a character flaw in the candidate.
4. Candidates often assume that others will suspect they lack self-awareness, tend to externalize blame, are unaware of their shortcomings, or are not strong enough to "take it" if they complain about an evaluation. Whether or not the candidate feels the criticism is valid, the analytic culture presses him to act as though he thinks it is valid, if only to show that he can "take it." I think this furthers the potential for lasting shame. It can, at times, add the injury of a feeling of *self*-betrayal to the insult of feeling misjudged.
5. Resulting feelings of failure can remain, unmodulated, sometimes affecting the candidate long after graduation. Perhaps partly because they are hidden they can exert a powerful impact on self-esteem. Because they are not countered, they may feel more accurate, self-defining, permanent, and emotionally significant.

In any other field of study, a student given a negative evaluation might challenge it or might show it to friends, mentors, family members, and colleagues. Its impact might be balanced by other perhaps more favorable reports or, at least, appraisals with a different emphasis. But I would suggest that the analytic candidate can feel that exposing a negative evaluation is, itself, evidence of a character flaw. To complain in any way or even to question the judgment can seem like it proves the candidate is characterologically limited. It is assumed that if the candidate dares to complain, the community's assessment will be something like, "He doesn't even see what is wrong with him" and "He is unable to take criticism." Thus the negative evaluation is hidden in the emotional equivalent of the back of the closet and becomes a secret source of shame, unmigitated by other feedback, unchallenged by other self-experience. I believe negative evaluations during training, rarely discussed in public, can have profound and permanent impact, often reverberating over the span of a long career and perhaps defining the perimeters of ambition. Can those who have been marked by this secret shame dare to aim high? Do they ever go on to realize the fullest expression of their talents?

ABUSES OF POWER IN ANALYTIC INSTITUTES

Recently there has been more attention given to the potential for abuses of power in analytic training (Buechler, 2008, 2009; Levine & Reed, 2004; Raubolt, 2006). This literature has especially focused on the problems that can develop in the training analysis, among other issues. Here are some optimistic and pessimistic visions of the situation:

> There is hope for the reduction of problems within psychoanalytic organizations. Secrecy, insularity, and the isolation of power are decreasing. Consistent with 21st-century science, we understand that the management of organizations is part of a process. Psychoanalytic organizations are in a better position to be more compatible with the humanitarian characteristics of psychoanalysis. (Bornstein, 2004, p. 84)

> I have no doubt that psychoanalytic training often tends to foster in candidates a turn from their original idealism to a kind of quiet fanaticism. I have always been appalled at the religious nature of much of the discourse in the field. The authority to control all aspects of the lives, indeed the souls, of others can all too easily create monsters of senior analysts, teachers, and supervisors. (Raubolt, 2006, p. 5)

> With this authoritarian exercise of power by the training committee, psychoanalytic education became institute-centered as opposed to student-centered. ... The interweave of ideology, power, and knowledge in psychoanalytic education appears to have molded the historical discipline of psychoanalysis into an unreflective and uncritical discipline that has failed to question its most cherished assumptions, theoretical beliefs, and ways of thinking. (Kavanaugh, 2006, pp. 126, 141)

In 2009, I edited a volume of *Contemporary Psychoanalysis* devoted to the question of how various analysts would define the "ideal" psychoanalytic institute training. Of course, in defining ideal training some authors described imperfections in the system as it now exists. Personally, I found it fascinating to look at how 17 analysts approached the question of ideal training. Each had a particular emphasis. For example, Karen Maroda (2009) pointed to some problems stemming from the training analysis, which can foster a kind of inauthenticity. The candidate, fearing being seen as inadequate and unfit for an analytic career, may limit self-exploration. Overall, the system can promote infantile dependence and self-censorship, because candidates and graduates can fear being blackballed if they are seen as suffering from significant pathology.

In the same volume, Marylou Lionells (2009) described the deadening effects of bureaucratization and standardization in institutes as they now operate. When supervisors prescribe and proscribe ways of working clinically, we are going beyond our current state of knowledge. In Lionells's own words, "It should not be the business of psychoanalysis to prescribe that only certain techniques or procedures are acceptable. Despite years of controversy, we are still unclear about what works and what does not, what is effective, what is transformative" (p. 313).

This is an important statement, with which I agree. Yet I think it can be as damaging to be vague about technique as it is to be prescriptive. When candidates emerge from training, many have a sense they still don't know how to work analytically. They often feel shame about this and may try to hide the feeling that they must have missed something. They feel it is a measure of their own inadequacy that they failed to learn more. I have observed that it is not uncommon for recent graduates to feel depressed, partially as an expression of having somehow missed out on developing their understanding of analytic theory and technique, despite years of effort and financial and other personal sacrifices.

Thus, the negative impacts of training can include depression, stifled curiosity, loss of a sense of personal and professional adequacy, and loss of a sense of being good, courageous, and intelligent. In the worst-case scenario (partly depending on the candidate's underlying character issues), the failures of omission outlined in the previous chapter and the failures of commission described in the present chapter can *combine* to severely hamper self-esteem. Subsequent chapters further trace the potential legacy of these experiences during training.

Part 2

Early Career Vicissitudes

Chapter 3

Traumatically Overwhelming Professional Settings

I remember some of my first professional settings in snapshots. While still in graduate school, I worked at two Veterans hospitals and one New York State hospital. What is the personal and professional legacy of these early career experiences? Did they prepare me to bear the incessant losses that are inherent in a clinical career? On the whole, did this powerful introduction to professional life inoculate me, strengthening my ability to witness suffering? Or did it somehow weaken my capacity to withstand the "ordinary" losses and the other stresses of a life doing clinical work?

As background, I would like to mention a required course given early in my graduate school program. I don't remember its title, but the gist of it was that our class made weekly visits to various settings that employed clinical psychologists. Thus, as a group, we toured residential settings that housed developmentally delayed children and adults, severely organically damaged children and adults, and psychotic children and adults. These brief visits usually permitted only a glance at the facilities, a nod to the patients, and a talk by the psychologist.

I think, for me, the effect of these visits was amplified by my other inpatient work with the Veterans and state hospital inpatients. Taken together, I have no doubt that these experiences provided unforgettable lessons about life and, perhaps more important, about my own strengths and weaknesses as a human being and as a clinical instrument.

I am aware that what I am describing is a personal odyssey, but I suggest it may have some relevance for others. I think many of us enter our careers through jobs that place us in the trenches. We occupy the front lines, so to speak, before we have the standing to choose less exposed perches (if that is what we would select, given a choice). Perhaps it is ironic, but I am certain that it is significant that our earliest professional experiences are often with the very most disturbed, difficult patients we will ever see. What impact is this likely to have on our feelings of competence and, more generally, on our professional identities? How does it mold us, and what does it teach us? Perhaps a better way to express this is, which of our potential professional selves is it likely to cultivate in us?

INPATIENT EXPERIENCES

I have often wondered who I might have become if inpatient experiences had not been my introduction to being a psychologist and, more generally, to being an adult. Would I have had more resilience or less, more hopefulness or less, a greater or lesser capacity to mourn?

It is striking to me that my most vivid memories of inpatient life are olfactory. The smell of steamed food often evoked a disgust reaction in me. My years of inpatient work were accompanied by a low but constant level of nausea. It was enough to ensure that I could eat little until I got home. I remember years of being able to get coffee and toast down, but during my hospital shifts, that was all I could manage.

It is not hard for me to see this as a kind of conversion reaction to what revolted me, in many senses. On a concrete, literal level, ward life acquainted us with every imaginable human waste product. Of course the word *waste* can be understood in several senses in this context. I don't think I can express how profoundly I was affected by seeing the incalculable waste of life I encountered every day.

A much later experience, consulting to the nurses in a very large hospital for severely impaired children, also blends into my memories of these inpatient settings. Looking back, I would say that every hour put me close to the edge of trauma, in Freud's sense of the word. My understanding is that Freud saw as traumatic any situation that threatens to overwhelm the ego. *What* was overwhelming was less important in this definition than the sense of almost being overcome. Moments that stand out for me include the first time I entered a ward of hydrocephalic babies, their heads taking up much of the surface of their cribs. I don't remember this, but I imagine I had to stifle shock, prioritizing looking as though I could "handle" my feelings. Of course I am aware that this speaks to who I already was by the time I had these encounters. My own personal life experience, and my character issues, shaped my responses to these settings. But I believe the professional situations privileged certain potentials in me over others. I think my tendencies toward schizoid functioning were especially nurtured and, in a sense, rewarded. I learned to "get through" the day. I gave myself what I remember calling my "marching orders."

For example, consulting in a very large hospital for severely handicapped children, I told myself that I *would* try to make eye contact with each patient. When I entered a ward of children strapped to their chairs (ostensibly because of their self-mutilating behavior) who struggled to find a way to greet me despite being tied down, I was determined to recognize in some way the particular human being in each child. I tried to give each a brief nod or some kind of verbal response. Consciously, I wanted to give each a sense of still being respected as individuals, with personhood. Retrospectively I see myself as willing Sandra forward, giving her a nearly impossible (but wholly absorbing) task. Looking at each child kept *me* going. I was fighting my own pull to drown in misery. I was willing myself to differentiate them, bullheadedly refusing to blur them. Some of them, perhaps just as fierce as I, found a way to rock their chairs forward to get closer to me. I was determined to meet their stubborn will with my own. They were bound to chairs. I was bound to a self-imposed resolution.

What was the short- and long-term impact of these experiences? What did I take away about life, about myself as a person and clinician? At the time, I think what impressed me most was how close I felt to being unable to cope. My own insufficiencies were more palpable to me than my strengths. My ability to bear each hour felt tenuous. The nurses and aides seemed a lot less fragile than I felt myself to be. Most frequently, I think I felt insufficient or, at best, barely sufficient. On good days, I could get through without crying, without retreating to the bathroom, without giving up on my goal to recognize each person. But I felt this was a "minimalist" goal, and even that was a stretch for me, most of the time. I compared myself with someone stronger, who could aim for more than I could. I don't think this more competent "other" was any particular person but just a mythical better version of me.

Long term I think, first of all, my schizoid tendencies to push forward, no matter what, were further etched into my character. Also fostered were some obsessive defenses. I remember dividing up the day, in my mind, and figuring ways to get through each portion. I think continuously living this close to the edge of what I could bear reinforced tendencies already well established in me. One way to see this is that although I entered the profession already equipped with a personal schizoid/obsessive coping style, these early experiences fostered a variation on the theme. Now I had a template for "getting through" 8-hour shifts, as well as "getting through" more personal experiences.

My impression is that my sense of inadequacy in these work situations was more vivid to me than any feeling of strength. Even though I "made it" through all these assignments, getting promotions and doing "well" by external standards, I never felt increased capacity or greater confidence. Making it through yesterday didn't convince me I would make it through today. I think that what I "learned" was mostly about how bad things can be and how close to unbearable they can feel to me.

Other memories take me to the New York State hospital, where I was a nonmedical team leader in charge of one ward of chronic inpatients. Elsewhere, I wrote about the impact of the suicide of one of my patients (Buechler, 2008, chap. 4). He hung himself in the bathroom, shortly after I interviewed him and while I was conducting the team meeting to plan his treatment. Once again, I think what got reinforced in me was the sense of being "in over my head." Somehow I had failed a crucial test. I should have known how dangerously depressed this patient was and put him on 24-hour watch immediately. Why didn't I do that? What was missing in me, or present in me, that resulted in this lapse/mistake? At the time, I concluded that I was in too much of a hurry, in several senses. I had hurried through the interview, perhaps missing signs of the degree of this patient's despair. More generally, I had hurried through my career, quickly getting to a point of responsibility beyond my current, real capacities.

The state and Veterans hospitals showed me how profoundly lost in despair it is possible for human beings to be. Yet I was also struck, and moved, by the survival of hope. I remember a middle-aged woman, hospitalized most of her adult life, so excited at the possibility of being released.

Looking back, what stands out for me in my responses to these environments, in addition to sadness, is my effort to deal with shock. It is impossible for me to remember how much of the time I was girding myself to absorb shock waves. I think I was always trying not to be shocked, or show shock, at the bizarre shapes human bodies and minds could take. Bodies with no limbs were not uncommon during the war in Vietnam in the Veterans hospitals. Damage could be startlingly obvious or more subtle. A patient would suddenly emit a piercing cry. I must have steeled myself not to respond. Another came hurtling at me, threatening me. Another would have animated conversations with hallucinatory friends. I think I tried not to startle, not to look rattled, but to exert a calming force. Because I was younger than a number of nurses and aides, yet in a senior position, some seemed to me to be anxious to find my weaknesses. I felt I had to prove myself by being "strong." For example, one woman went into a frantic, manic episode and started hurling herself onto the concrete walls. Instinctively I positioned myself between her and the wall, counting on her liking for me, to stop her from smashing us both. At least, that was what was conscious to me then. Now, looking back, I think I was taking this as an opportunity to prove myself to be as brave as any of the other staff.

Every morning by 8:00 a.m., I had to enter the ward. What I think was probably most frightening to me was that *anything* could happen, at any time. There were, basically, no holds barred. Many patients knew they were not going anywhere. This was the end of the line. There was no one they cared to impress or were afraid to irritate. Some would say anything, bare anything, hurl anything, do anything. Every moment was entirely unpredictable. Unlike much of the rest of my life, on the ward there was no way to prepare by doing homework conscientiously. I now imagine I spent a good deal of energy stifling my reactions. I was trying to look imperturbable but, all the while, knew this was not the whole truth. So, I must have felt that my real reactions were unacceptable.

How much are my experiences relevant to anyone besides me? To explore this question, I first attempt a quick summary of the main features of these early professional experiences:

1. In many of these situations, I was just on the edge and, sometimes, over the edge of feeling traumatized.
2. Nevertheless, I tried to "get through" the day by dividing it into manageable time periods and exerting my will. I feel that this reinforced my already established schizoid and obsessive tendencies.
3. Being young, and relatively unseasoned, I felt a need to prove myself strong enough to "take" in stride the many assaults to my senses.
4. All of this was accompanied by feelings of being unequal to the tasks. I felt I was "in over my head" in many senses. These feelings were ongoing, not necessarily conscious, but would erupt into consciousness during crises, like the suicide of a patient.
5. Another ongoing effort was the attempt to hide being shocked by all that was bizarre and unsightly. I subdued startle reactions to sudden jolts, trying to seem calm and in charge. But, inwardly, knowing I was doing this made me feel my real reactions were unacceptable.

In retrospect, it seems to me that my early career experiences challenged my identity as a "going concern" or functional, effective person. They were just at the edge of what I could cope with. I used character traits and defenses that were first developed much earlier, but they had to be adapted to these new contexts. For example, I had already learned to "get through" difficult circumstances, and I had already relied on my own will power. Faced with a room full of children tied to their chairs, I concentrated on just one goal: to look at each child separately. I gave myself an order I could carry out. This was not a well-thought-out strategy but rather an instinctive use of myself. I coped with many extreme difficulties well enough to bear their sorrow and learn from them, but I think I emerged with heightened vulnerability to shame. The feelings of insufficiency and inadequacy, the constant effort to stay afloat and prove myself, and the sense that I was hiding my shock underneath a false exterior all predisposed me toward shame.

Elsewhere I discussed three forms of shame (Buechler, 2008, chap. 4). I called the most dramatic form "shame/anxiety." I now wonder how much my own experiences shaped my vision of this phenomenon. Here is how I described this form of shame:

> Each of us has known inadequacy, but which human predicaments have most vividly elicited this feeling differs according to our personal histories. Shame/anxiety is, I suggest, the earliest form of shame, and expresses the helplessness inherent in the human condition. In these moments we feel we *must* be able to do something that we cannot do. (p. 57, emphasis in original)

I am not questioning the existence of shame/anxiety. I still think it exists. But at the time I wrote this, I wasn't (consciously) thinking about my own early career experiences and how they may have heightened my own tendency to feel this combination of emotions. Although I am sure this tendency first dates from much further back in my life, I feel that the many facilities I worked in as a very young psychologist brought me in constant contact with what I felt I "must" but also "couldn't" do. I wonder how many of us have similar backgrounds, with early jobs that face us with impossible odds. We see the worst that life can be and may expect ourselves to "handle" what we can hardly bear. "Handle professionally" may mean different things to each of us, but, I suggest, for many it means trying to look better put together than we feel at the time.

What have been the long-term personal and professional effects of these experiences? I wonder how much they have interfered in my own capacity to mourn professional losses well and resist burnout, much as they may have also strengthened my belief in my own resolve. I learned that I could "carry on" when necessary. But I think the children tied to the chairs are still with me. Their hell-bent determination and my hell-bent determination are joined. Just as they *will* be recognized, even if it costs them physical pain, I *will* recognize them, no matter what psychological pain it costs me. I met them before I had really developed a clinical identity. Being totally overwhelmed by them became the first and, perhaps, a permanent part of my personal and professional identity. I may be "enough" to help many people now, but the children in the chairs, the man who hung himself, and countless other lost souls still tell me otherwise.

To further explore what can be generalized from my career, I look at some accounts of the long-term impact of others' early professional experiences. Susan Bodnar (1997a), in her moving essay on her work with HIV-positive substance abusers and, in the same volume (edited by Mark J. Blechner), in her essay (1997b) on the impact on her of losses in her practice, vividly portrayed her struggle toward life-enhancing mourning. Writing of her work on an inpatient AIDS unit, she remarked, "Death hovered in the air so palpably that it lingered on my clothes" (1997b, p. 221).

One reason Susan gave for taking this inpatient job was to work on the legacy of having lost her husband to cancer the year before. She felt out of step with others in their 30s. As she put it, "The knowledge that life is finite had transported me to the poet's interior palace" (1997b, p. 222).

Entering this hospital unit's world, as a relatively young woman and a stranger to it, Susan expressed something I think is similar to my own feelings of having to prove myself. She described that at first "an odd silence fell upon the nurses' station when I entered it. No one read my chart notes either" (1997b, p. 223).

To me it sounds like Susan earned respect by showing her humanness, willingness to learn from others, humility, and excellent judgment (she made the right call about a dying patient and helped save him). But yet, after this dramatic victory, Susan reported that she "lay awake, terrified by the grim responsibilities of my job" (1997b, p. 225). Once again I see an analogy to my own experience of feeling close to becoming traumatized on an ongoing basis. However, a difference seems to me to be Susan's staff's interdependence and closeness, which sounds much more supportive than the units I experienced. From her descriptions, it sounds as though this atmosphere helped her let go of the constrictions of a strictly "professional" stance, and this enabled her to reach her patients on a more profound level. At the end of her second essay, she concluded that her "way of coping with so much loss of life was to listen carefully to what each person was discovering on his or her deathbed, and to tuck the wisdom away for safekeeping" (1997b, p. 234). It is clear that Susan was trying to learn from these encounters. But I wonder if, in addition, she was finding a way to honor the unique individual in each sufferer, just as I did with the children tied to chairs.

EMOTIONS THAT CAN COMPLICATE GRIEF

It seems to me that it helped Susan that she did not feel defined by how she was initially treated on the ward. Though overwhelmed by the tragedies unfolding all around her, she was emotionally supported by the camaraderie of the staff and her own essentially solid sense of personal and professional competence. When her chart notes were not being read, she looked for what she was *doing* wrong but didn't assume she was fundamentally incapable. In other words, shame/anxiety did not overly encumber her efforts to bear the sadness inherent in the situation.

Another crucial aspect of Susan's evolution seems to me to be the anger wedded to her sorrow. As she told it, when she first came to work on the AIDS unit, after suffering through her own husband's death, "Defiant and proud, I expressed my fury at life by working hard and burning away the edges of my joy. They were the reactions of a confused young widow who hadn't yet found her way in a world that didn't yet understand the impact of loss on young people" (1997b, p. 233).

My thought is that the combination of sorrow and rage, without significant shame, allowed her to forge an effective therapeutic instrument from her strengths. It seems to me that emotions that were missing were at least as important as the feelings that were present. Susan sounds pained, enraged, and sometimes afraid, but she doesn't sound ashamed, guilty, and regretful. She was not plagued by self-doubt. When she didn't know what to say, or what to do, in the presence of a dying patient, she openly struggled with the question. She was able to be transparent in her search because feeling ill equipped became not a defining self-experience but rather more like a temporary (reversible) state.

What seems to me to count most is the predominant combination of emotions, that is, what accompanies sorrow, rather than the sorrow itself.

As I have suggested elsewhere, it is not, so much, the inevitable pain of loss that determines whether we can constructively mourn (Buechler, 2004, 2008). *It is what accompanies the pain.* I believe that, to the extent that shame, regret, and guilt complicate sorrow, they can eradicate the tools an individual needs in order to cope. What I mean by "constructive" mourning or "mourning with strength" is finding a way to live with the suffering that does not add avoidable shame to our inevitable sorrow. Sadness, itself, actually has some survival value. In the words of the emotion theorist Carroll Izard (1977),

> Since separation causes distress, the avoidance or anticipation of distress is a strong force acting to keep one close to one's loved ones and friends. If we did not miss (feel distress over separation from) loved ones and friends, one of the great forces binding us to other people would be lacking. (p. 293)

So, at least potentially, sadness about loss can serve a human function when it is not severely complicated by other emotions.

But what happens when the clinician is unable to avail herself of sorrow's potential to promote connection? My own experience tells me that my pre-existing character trends, the "pull" to look professionally competent and able to "take it," my heightened awareness of the dangers of traumatic shock and disgust, and my shameful feelings of insufficiency compromised my ability to connect with other staff members. Each morning, along with the "marching orders" I gave myself, I think I put on a pair of blinders. I kept myself facing forward and concentrated on getting through each portion of the day. I was surviving, in the only ways I knew how.

FIGHTING DEPENDENCE AT THE EDGES OF SURVIVAL

A short story by Jack London (1965) titled "To Build a Fire" poignantly captures how schizoid and obsessive coping devices can eventually fail in the face of mounting terror. Briefly, this is the story of an adventurer who thinks he can "go it alone" on an unknown path in freezing weather. At first he doesn't understand why old-timers say they wouldn't travel this road without a companion: "Those old timers were rather womanish, some of them, he thought. All a man had to do was to keep his head; and he was alright. Any man who was a man could travel alone" (p. 275). At the beginning of the story, the loner meets every obstacle with well-thought-out strategies, superb observational skills, knowledge of the terrain, and resourcefulness. He divides every task into sections, manages to find a way around every difficulty, and makes light of every discomfort. He controls the environment, and, with the same painstaking care, he controls his mind, keeping fear at bay with fierce concentration on each task. He uses keen observations to master outer dangers and fearful thoughts. When terrifying possibilities "demanded to be heard," he "thrust them back and strove to think of other things" (p. 281). Of course it isn't long before he has to admit that the old-timers were right, and he has to see that his efforts to master inner and outer dangers are doomed to fail. Eventually he succumbs to death. His dog, however, survives, and their fates are beautifully contrasted. The man's inability to keep a fire going parallels and symbolizes his loss of faith in himself as his hardships mount. Gradually, almost imperceptibly, the reader, like the protagonist, gives up hope that the man will live. London vividly portrayed how the loner loses the battle with his own thoughts at the same time as he loses the battle with the cold:

> He tried to keep his thoughts down, to forget it, to think of something else; he was aware of the panicky feeling that it caused, and he was afraid of the panic. But the thought asserted itself, and persisted, until it produced a vision of his body totally frozen. ... He was losing in his battle with the frost. It was creeping into his body from all sides. The thought of it drove him on, but he ran no more than a hundred feet, when he staggered and pitched headlong. It was his last panic. (pp. 282–283)

In contrast his dog survives, unencumbered by romantic notions of going it alone. I think this story appeals to me so much because it so movingly portrays the allures and the dangers of a stubborn, uncompromising determination to keep going, alone, despite the threat of being overwhelmed. At first, fighting dependence may steel us against adversity. We barrel through, as I did in my inpatient work, cutting my days into bearable bits and ordering myself onward. Like Jack London's fire builder, I survived on the augmented pride I got from feeling fiercely independent. But this brittle confidence is easily shattered. As the frost gathered, London's loner could no longer make his mind believe in his ability to withstand it. Similarly, I think, too much of my own pride was staked on being able to keep marching, single file, no matter what life brought.

Working in an equally harrowing setting, I think Susan Bodnar was better able to avail herself of support. She thrived, partially because she embraced her need for help. I conjecture that she was not hobbled by shame when she found herself (temporarily) unequal to her clinical task. At the outset, when the staff doesn't read her chart notes, she understands their reasons. They see that she is young and inexperienced. She doesn't yet command the full respect or attention of her colleagues and patients. But, undaunted, Susan continues to hone her unique identity as a clinician. Her fierce determination is joined by a full appreciation of her dependence on others. In other words, Susan is not so defined by the staff's first responses that she has to brave the "cold" alone in order to prove herself. She can even laugh at herself, as the innocent "Gidget" who welcomes the advice of the old-timers about the harsh world of "Sing Sing." Susan doesn't ignore their advice, like Jack London's loner ignored the wiser elders. Nor does she define herself as insufficient when she feels overwhelmed, as I did early in my own career. She has faith that by initially taking all the help she can get, eventually she will develop a unique and valued voice. And she did.

What can give us enough confidence, patience, humility, and faith to weather extremely difficult professional situations, too early in our careers to have a reliable track record? What allows us to look past the present moment, which may confront us with unremitting demands and a level of human suffering that we, ourselves, feel unable to witness? For now, I am emphasizing one potentially crippling handicap for the inexperienced clinician: an unrealistic pride and determination to "make it" exclusively on one's own resources. London's protagonist loses heart, as he realizes he will not survive the cold alone. Perhaps because his sense of self is too tightly wrapped around being extremely competent and self-sufficient, his self-confidence collapses when his (obsessive and schizoid) strategies fail. Like him, I counted on the force of my own determination and resourcefulness. For London's loner and for me, our strengths stood us in good stead in most of life's circumstances. But in the face of extreme situations, it wasn't enough to sustain us.

BRUSHES WITH FAILURE

Ann-Louise Silver (2002) in her work with severely disturbed patients reported many daunting, and sometimes defeating, inpatient treatment situations. But she also described another kind of "failure": the closing of Chestnut Lodge. In response to this poignant paper, I wonder whether every generation of analysts feels that things will "never be the same." Do we all come to feel obsolete, like cowboys at the close of the Wild West? Does the analytic world, as we have known it, have to (seem to) die as we, ourselves, grow dim? Does every generation feel we have failed to pass on a thriving field to the young professionals we taught? Is this simply an eternally recurring part of growing old professionally, or a format for professional insecurities that had their origins in our training, or something *unique* that is really happening at *this* time in *this* generation?

Regardless of how we answer that question, many of us sense defeat now. Silver (2002) wrote that many mental health professionals feel that "somehow we have failed in our mission" (p. 38). We may blame ourselves, feeling we don't have personal strengths and professional talents the work requires. Or we may blame our analytic community, or managed care, or the wider culture. In any case many of us feel like a dying, doomed breed that deserves our fate. It seems likely to me that we each feel some shame about this, among many other possible emotions.

Silver also wrote poignantly about specific cases she saw in her years at the lodge. After a patient, Jody, terminated because she was "fed up," Silver was left feeling "a bit like a bag lady, carrying around my tattered possessions—clipboard, pen, my dog-eared copy of *Principles of Intensive Psychotherapy*, mumbling, 'I can't do it. I just can't do it' " (pp. 55–56).

Silver mourns the sexual abuse she failed to discover in one patient until after the woman had a debilitating relapse. She mourns another woman who fired her and subsequently committed suicide. She also mourns the family feeling at the lodge, which is forever lost.

I quote from Silver's work because I find it particularly moving, but numerous analysts have written about their sense of personal failure and the profession's defeat (see Reppen & Schulman, 2002, for some especially evocative expressions of these feelings). Analysts have used a wide variety of terms for our failures, calling them "vicious circles" (Berman, 2002, p. 270), "negative therapeutic reactions" (Eidelberg, 1968, p. 253), and "impasses" (Vida, 2002, p. 27), among other descriptions. Whatever word we use, it seems to me that we are trying to bear our sense of our own failure by linking it to the experiences of other analysts. Failure is lonely. If we give our failure a name that connects it with the troubles other analysts report, it may soften our self-reproaches. Perhaps labeling failure sometimes serves to induce the feeling we are still part of the analytic fold. Maybe it changes failure from a personal event, with meanings about our own character issues and professional competence, to a more global event. But whatever we call it, I think we cannot avoid some of the shame that comes with the territory of failure.

Rita Wiley McCleary (1992) in her book *Conversing With Uncertainty: Practicing Psychotherapy in a Hospital Setting* reported a particularly poignant account of the struggles of a young clinician in an inpatient setting. McCleary told the story of her treatment of Kay, a highly disturbed adolescent, as part of a psychotherapy practicum at a state hospital. In writing a foreword to this book, Stephen A. Mitchell recalled some of his own experiences as a young clinician in an inpatient setting:

> My first experiences doing psychotherapy took place at a large, prominent teaching hospital in New York City at the beginning of my psychology internship. As in most training institutions, we arrived on July 1 and were assigned our patients, in my case, two community service inpatients and several outpatients. Although there were supervisors and administrative staff to help us, we suddenly had primary responsibility for the lives of those assigned to our care. With an allowance of some time to get to know them (a few days!) we were expected

to make decisions having major implications for their lives: privileges and restrictions within the hospital, privileges to leave the hospital, discharge, disposition, and so on. (p. xi)

In his characteristically candid voice, Mitchell went on to describe the dread he felt as he approached the Monday "morning rounds," because he feared finding out that his patients got into trouble over the weekend, and, somehow, he would be held responsible. Mitchell succinctly expressed a feeling I mentioned in the first section of this chapter. He used strong language to describe an aspect of inpatient care in our country:

> Perhaps the greatest irony, absurdity, and cruelty of the mental health care system in the United States is that the most difficult patients are treated by the most inexperienced therapists. People with the most complex psychological problems, compounded by social and economic hardship and chronically traumatic backgrounds and living conditions, are the patients first encountered by beginning therapists. (p. xiii)

From my point of view, Mitchell captured an essential issue and beautifully framed McCleary's discussion of a clinician's struggles in an inpatient setting. I find her account of her work with her patient, Kay, extremely touching, stunningly honest, and resonant with my own experiences. I think that initially McCleary, a relatively inexperienced therapist at the time, made efforts to master her feelings in order to look and feel competent, just as I did. In her own words, "I tried to minimize my nervousness as I listened to staff members grumble that this kid had an awful lot of baggage to sort through and that her nose ring was disgusting. I did not know what to say or think" (p. 1).

McCleary struggled to find her footing with Kay, an utterly unpredictable, disturbing, traumatized, and traumatizing teenager. As a relatively inexperienced clinician, she hoped theory would ground her, and she tried to apply various theoretical frameworks to guide the treatment of Kay. McCleary forthrightly described the benefits and drawbacks of relying on three theoretical guideposts: Masterson's ideas about the treatment of borderline conditions, conceptions of projective identification, and notions drawn from the literature on milieu therapy. I deeply admire her honest portrayal of the confusion, anger, and sheer pain that accompanied her conflicts with other staff members as she struggled to find a way to reach Kay. No one could more clearly express how personally and professionally challenging this position can be. I think it is often especially hard for those who have yet to prove their therapeutic talents to others and to themselves. In the book's foreword, as already mentioned, Mitchell poignantly recalled the anxiety he felt early in his inpatient experience. Similarly, McCleary remembered, "The confusion, shame, and eventual anger that characterized this initial encounter with my colleagues formed what I have called the 'noisy' backdrop to my early months at State" (p. 79). At the same time as McCleary went through these troubling encounters with staff members, she also had to bear how she was seen by the patient. "If anything, I had imagined my role as a beneficent godmother whose mission was to empathize and bequeath insight and understanding. Kay seemed to cast me in the role of evil witch instead. The more she perceived me as oppressive, the nicer I tried to become" (p. 28). As I imagine it, McCleary's situation is fundamentally different from the position of a math student when an equation is hard to solve. *McCleary's sense of her potential as a human being was at stake, along with her belief in her capacity to become an effective clinician.*

When I read McCleary's account, I was immediately reminded of a challenge to my own identity that I encountered several times in my early experiences on wards at Veterans and state hospitals. As I saw it I was frequently confronted with the choice of whether to speak out about a staff member's hurtful behavior toward a patient or remain silent. For me, either choice often had serious drawbacks. For example, I can still see Tommy, an obese, whiny, towering man with very limited intelligence. Many mornings he greeted me with tearful stories about being beaten up in the stairwell by the night nurse, a man I knew to be sadistic toward some patients. Tommy could probably get on most peoples' nerves, and I felt sure he had provoked the nurse in some way, and, at least some of the time, the nurse had actually abused him. Tommy certainly had enough bruises to corroborate his complaints. But I said nothing and did nothing about it. I really can't tell you why. I am sure that doing nothing had a very bad impact on me. It challenged my sense of being who I want to be, comparably, I think, to McCleary's struggle cited above. I don't remember what I told myself about Tommy, but I imagine it was something like, "I can't prove who hurt him. No one will believe me. I can't fight everything."

I wasn't always silent, but I soon discovered that speaking out could be a complicated business. For example, in my first outpatient session with a young woman recently discharged from inpatient care, she told me that the unit psychiatrist had been sexually inappropriate during their medication consult that day. I knew this woman well, having worked with her when she was an inpatient, and I believed her story. In the hospital the patient had had serious bouts with depression but had never been hallucinatory or delusional. Her husband, who had accompanied her to the clinic but had stayed in the waiting room during the medication review, was furious. The woman felt terribly guilty, convinced that she had somehow provoked the doctor's sexual advances. At the same time she was very worried about how these events would affect her husband. I sensed her fragility, and I feared that she would not be able to remain outside the hospital if her guilt overtook her. I felt that telling her it was not her fault would not be enough. I also suspected that the psychiatrist might be behaving inappropriately with other patients.

This time I decided to make an issue of it and went to a hospital administrator. At first, I got little response. So, with full awareness that I was risking my job, I told the administrator that if nothing was done about this, I would advise the husband to go to the local newspaper. This seemed to get the administrator's attention. My patient's psychiatrist soon left the hospital. Either he was fired or he resigned. I never found out which it was. But, later on, I found out something that was terribly disconcerting. The state system had reassigned him to head an adolescent ward at another hospital!

This incident recalls to me the many times I felt I was taking a huge risk, endangering a job I sorely needed. But, just as often, I kept silent about terrible things that were going on. The residues of these experiences included profound disappointment in myself and in others; sorrow over lost illusions; sorrow and anger about how unfair life can be, most especially to those most vulnerable; and ongoing questions about my own integrity. I had initially idealized mental health professionals. I expected that we would put patients' welfare ahead of all other motives. When I saw that in countless situations that simply wasn't true, I felt confused and, most of all, ashamed that I didn't fight harder and more often. In fact, I gradually became a "key swinger." That was a phrase many of us used for hospital workers who could last in the system. In a literal sense, we were "key swingers" because we held the huge keys to the locked wards. I was proud to be tough enough to become a "key swinger." But I was also deeply ashamed and confused about what it said about me. In retrospect, I think the 8 years I spent working in these hospitals taught me many valuable lessons but also left a legacy of shame about failing a vague, but crucial, test.

In an afterword to McCleary's book, Glen Gabbard (1992) described the plight of the novice therapist in an inpatient setting. I think his comments relate to the kind of shame I felt. Gabbard stated, "The new therapist's need to master sadism and aggression is only one of a myriad of needs that are activated in the hospital setting. Professional self-esteem is on the line when one enters a new inpatient unit" (p. 146). Gabbard went on to describe some of the pulls the neophyte regularly encounters from the rest of the staff, from patients, from her training requirements, and from her own psychological tendencies. Sometimes these pressures profoundly conflict and can even challenge our belief in our own capacity to cope.

My very earliest inpatient experiences were in two Veterans hospitals, while I was still a graduate student. These brief placements occurred before the longer state hospital stint I just mentioned. Whenever I try to describe my experiences working in the Veterans hospitals, I feel no one will believe how bizarre they were. Perhaps some snippets will give the reader the flavor of these settings. In one hospital (in the late 1960s) I was placed on one of the chronic care wards. The patients' average stay on my ward was about 20 years. Most patients were entirely docile, having long ago adapted to ward life in one way or another. Some worked in the laundry, some sat in front of the television in the day room, some yelled at hallucinated enemies, some wandered the halls in a dazed state. Some spent most of their lives looking for cigarette butts that had not been completely smoked down. I remember the yellow/brown color of the tips of their fingers. Many of the patients had found ways of avoiding taking their medications. It was rumored that many fed their liquid medications to the cats that prowled around the hospital's facade. I don't know whether this was true, but I did see some patients develop special fondness for particular cats.

The bizarreness of the sights, smells, and sounds of ward life profoundly challenged my coping skills. But even more difficult, at least for me, was the extreme peculiarity of the behavior of some members of the staff. My first supervisor, a psychologist who had been on the unit for many years, was unabashed in his delight in having a young, female trainee. He seemed to me to derive great entertainment value from my states of confusion. For example, once he told me to schedule an appointment with a man who was marching around the unit, seemingly lost in thought. My supervisor told me this would be my first "patient." It turned out the man was a psychiatrist on an adjoining ward. Eventually, thankfully, I was transferred to another supervisor. Perhaps it goes without saying that I didn't feel I could look to my first supervisor for help with my earliest attempts to treat patients.

I don't know how common my experiences of ward life were, either within that time period or now. But my sense is that although many circumstances may differ, the feeling of being "over one's head" is not uncommon for young trainees in inpatient settings. Some complain of the sheer volume of paperwork and other duties. For some, this is the first time in their lives they have seen such hopelessness, poverty, strangeness, and desperation. Each patient feels like a bottomless pit of needs that the trainee will never be able to fill. To care, to remain empathic to the patients as fellow human beings, can elicit overwhelming sorrow. But (for some trainees) to become impervious to the patients' suffering (so as to survive in this atmosphere) can feel like a bartering away of a part of the trainee's selfhood. As is often true, I get comfort from the humane words of Harold Searles. Writing about the young clinician in training in a hospital setting, Searles (1965) said, "We need to see how vulnerable he is to feeling caught between the patient's intense criticism on the one hand and the supervisor's disapproval on the other, so that his beleaguered areas of healthy self-esteem very much need our support and encouragement" (p. 587). Possible legacies of these early threats to self-esteem are discussed further in subsequent chapters.

REACTIONS TO THE SUICIDE OF A PATIENT: NEOPHYTE CLINICIANS AS SURVIVORS

It seems obvious that a patient's suicide can have a serious impact on any clinician's confidence. My experience suggests that clinicians are quite likely to be severely affected, perhaps for the rest of our careers. I include myself in this category. As mentioned earlier in this chapter, I have written about the aftermath of my own experience of a patient who committed suicide shortly after I had interviewed him, when I was a team leader in the state hospital (Buechler, 2008). I don't know whether the impact of this event was greater because I was still so young and had so little experience as a clinician. But I suspect that not having a track record of good treatment outcomes played a role in my experience of this event.

The American Association of Suicidology created a task force to address the concerns of what it calls "clinician-survivors" (DeAngelis, 2001). Describing what it was like when one of his practicum patients attempted suicide, James L. Werth Jr. emphasized his strong need for reassurance from his supervisors that he had been appropriately empathic and helpful. Writing about the needs of clinicians whose patients have killed themselves, Campbell said, "We've got to get to the point where we can face ourselves in the mirror and look at the faces of others without the fear they will judge us" (in DeAngelis, 2001, p. 70). I am fascinated by Campbell's emphasis on faces and mirrors. I would suggest that he is making reference to the shame that can complicate the clinician's grief.

In a paper on suicide's toll, Levin (2005) reported that clinicians "may feel overwhelmed by shame and humiliation at 'failing' a patient. Some psychiatrists may even endure a crisis of faith about their training and therapeutic work" (p. 10).

I strongly believe that patients who suicide can have a lasting, destabilizing impact on clinicians. I think shame, or a sense of insufficiency, can be an especially potent legacy for the "clinician-survivor." Personal character patterns, events in training, and experiences early in the clinician's career can predispose us toward mingled shame and grief. Constructive use of the sorrow is inhibited by shame. When we are in hiding, we isolate from the very contact that might help us heal. The "clinician-survivor" in hiding can suffer from grief that knows no bounds and a sense of unalterable insufficiency.

As is often the case, I gather some consolation from the words of Nina Coltart. Among many other valuable points, Coltart (1993) discussed the difference between being surprised and being shocked by her own patient's suicide:

> This extreme situation—which I hope none of you has to endure, and yet which comes to many therapists at least once—has its own logic. I knew this woman would be a severe suicidal risk. ... While I was not

surprised when she finally did kill herself, I felt profoundly shocked. It was as if the event was a complete bolt from the blue ... we have to be prepared for anything, and yet have faith that the extraordinary process is worth involving ourselves in. (p. 54)

Earlier in the same chapter, Coltart wrote of how we need to support our own sense of self when a patient suicides. In her blunt, matter-of-fact style, Coltart stated, "From whatever angle one studies it, one cannot escape the stark knowledge that suicide stands for failure" (p. 45). Coltart remarks that it is often as beginning therapists that we encounter patients who kill themselves. At that early point in our careers, we might not yet understand that

we are not infinitely resourceful, though it may have been conveyed to the public that we are. There is a pretty strict limit to the help which can be offered, and, moreover, there may be an even narrower limit to how much of our sort of help such people can assimilate. (p. 46)

When we first enter the field, many of us (myself included) don't really understand or accept the limits of our power to heal. The more we believe we should be capable of curing the patient, the greater our sense of failure when we don't. This can make a patient's suicide even harder to bear than it otherwise would be. Added to the absence of a "track record" of more positive outcomes with other patients, failing to prevent a suicide can severely try the young clinician's professional (and personal) self-esteem. Subsequent chapters will trace potential legacies of these challenging early career experiences.

Chapter 4

Difficult Patients as First Cases

Because I do a great deal of supervision, I often sit across from young clinicians coping with feelings about their first outpatients. Before the initial sessions they are often anxious and excited, worried about "blowing it," but hopeful. Usually they are aware that this patient means too much to them. There is too much pressure on the clinician and, in an indirect sense, on the patient. When things go wrong it is easy for *me* to have something similar to a parent's long-term perspective (don't worry, sweetheart, you will have other patients), but for the beginner it feels defining.

Increasingly, in my experience, the cases referred to newcomers are patients who present tremendous challenges. Generally, they are not people who have heard about the advantages of the analytic approach and want to know themselves better. They are more likely to be people whose lives are falling apart. They have already been through several therapists, and maybe a few medications, and nothing has really worked. They may have figured out that if they work with a newly minted clinician, they are likely to get relatively low-cost treatment and, perhaps, the added benefit of the insight of a supervisor. Or they have read on a Web site that this young clinician takes their insurance.

I am going to draw a composite sketch of what can happen next. The clinician and patient meet for the first time. Let's say the patient is a recently divorced man, in his mid-40s. We will call him Mike. Mike came for treatment because he is depressed and anxious. He has been sober for 2 years, but he used to drink and use cocaine. His career has taken a nosedive, along with everything else in his life. Because he was unhappy working for others, he is trying to make it as an independent consultant and is barely making ends meet. His early history was a horrendous tale of abuse and abandonment.

Let's call the clinician Laura. Laura is in her mid-30s, has a Ph.D. in clinical psychology, and has decided to be in supervision to advance her therapeutic skills. Mike is her first private patient. Laura came to me for supervision before even meeting the patient. Laura is sophisticated enough not to ask me her real question (What should I say when I first meet Mike, and what should I avoid saying?). Laura knows how to couch her real question in more acceptable terms: What might be the best approach to this patient?

Now I enter the picture. I like Laura and am glad to be supervising her. It might be partly because I see my younger self in her. Was I that eager, sincere, serious? Was I that scared? Was I that naturally talented?

I tell Laura to try to relax, but I know she can't. It seems to her as though her whole life, and Mike's, depends on her saying the right thing, only she doesn't know what it is. Or, what is even more terrifying, it all depends on her not saying the wrong thing, but she doesn't know what *that* is either.

I tell Laura to keep in touch with her own feelings. No matter what happens. She can't make herself know what to say, but she can try to notice her impact on Mike and his impact on her.

Laura makes a mantra out of my words. Although that is a bit too mechanical for my taste, it does help her bravely face the first session. They meet. Miraculously, Mike seems to want to be in treatment with Laura. Mike looks older than Laura imagined he would, but he is otherwise unremarkable in appearance. Still attractive, relatively fit, casually dressed. Mike has the body of a former athlete who hasn't played ball in a while but hasn't altogether given up on staying trim.

Mike wants help getting his life back on track. He admits that it was mainly his fault that his marriage fell apart. He had an affair. Both relationships are over now. He looks back with guilt, sadness, and some agitation. Will he have another chance with someone new? Will he be able to do better?

Work presents an even scarier, bleaker prospect. The economy is in bad shape. Nobody wants to hire people with Mike's background. He admits that he feels his "skills" are nebulous. He is a good salesman. He used to be a good sales manager, when he was sober. He never quite finished college. He is not sure why, except he remembers that he was more focused on the beer parties than the courses.

By the third session Mike is getting restless. He has told Laura a lot of information. He has felt worse after each session. He feels clearer about what he has squandered. How is this supposed to help?

Laura feels increasingly anxious in anticipation of her sessions with Mike. In fact, now she feels anxious the night before her sessions with him. What can she do, or say, to make Mike feel therapy can help him have a better life? What can she do to keep him coming to treatment, at least for a while?

Laura tries hard not to pressure me. She has read about parallel processes in supervision. She doesn't want to do that to me. But she really would appreciate some help.

And then, in the fifth session, the bomb shells. There are a few things Mike hasn't mentioned. He has had sex with men. A lot of one-night stands, starting in high school. He has gone to prostitutes. He has cheated on everyone.

He doesn't know why. He feels terrible. He also didn't mention his financial situation. He is deeply in debt. He doesn't know how it happened. It just happened. One day, he had to face that he owed more money than he could imagine ever being able to pay back. He doesn't like to think about it. The panicky feelings are taking over. How will spilling all this help?

Laura tells him that it is good that he is admitting all this to her and to himself. Telling it all ("verbalizing it") will help. It clarifies it. Putting it into words will help them understand it. Then he will be able to change it. He won't be running away from himself any more.

Mike looks doubtful but doesn't say much. Laura feels uncomfortable. The session ends. Laura feels a sinking sensation. She's not sure what she did wrong, but she feels scared. So when Mike's e-mail comes, saying he has decided not to come back, she isn't totally surprised.

Mike's e-mail is matter-of-fact. He has decided that treatment is not for him right now. He tells Laura not to take it personally. It's just that he realizes that it is not "practical" to pile up more debt. He implies that quitting is the psychologically responsible thing to do. He doesn't spell this out but seems to suggest that Laura should be glad for this. She should be pleased that, at last, he is facing reality. Of course he hopes he can always come back to treatment. This is just a hiatus, for right now. Please send him the bill.

Laura tries not to cry. She is devastated. She is having nightmares about Mike. She doesn't know what to do. What is "appropriate"? Can she call him? E-mail? Write? What can she say? Offer to see him, once, for free, to "terminate" properly? Insist on saying good-bye in person? Let it go? And what should she learn for next time (if there ever is a next time, with this or any other patient!)?

Laura gets my blessing to call Mike and ask him to come in for a last session. It seems to her that when she calls, he picks up the phone, says nothing, and quietly puts it down. She sends him the bill and gets a check for half of what he owes. No note. She never hears from him again.

What did Laura do wrong? Or was this inevitable? I ask Laura if she is angry with me. She says she is not, but I still wonder. Did we all fail each other? Or is Mike someone who just can't benefit from a talking cure? Why would that be?

There are many assumptions built into this situation. First of all, Laura assumes I would know what to do, even though she knows that I have not seen any new patients in a long time, other than people in the field, so all *my* new patients *do* have an interest in self-exploration and in putting experiences into words. I am protected from discouraging experiences like these, even though they would probably be less devastating for me, because I have a backlog of "successes" with patients to draw on. I would be less likely to blame myself. Or, at least, I would know that I *have* been able to help many people. I wouldn't feel as defined by the outcome of my work with this one patient. I might still feel bewildered, sad, regretful. But probably not as ashamed and worried about my skills and my future as a clinician. It is possible that because of my many years of clinical experience, I have refined my judgment and could make a good assessment of what Laura should do with Mike. But I think no one *really* knows what to do in these situations. We each would do something that makes sense and that we feel we can live with. So many questions about our actions in treatment have no right answers yet seem crucial to "get right."

It seems ironic to me that Laura is feeling a sense of guilty insecurity, not unlike Mike's. Whether we see this as some sort of projective identification or repetition or understand it in other terms, there is something interesting about how things started with Mike and Laura and how they ended.

My sense is that (no matter what Laura decides to do) in order to bear this experience, Laura needs the "backup" of a relatively benign "internal chorus." What I mean by this is that if Laura's training experiences prepared her well, she has a better chance to bear Mike's abrupt termination without losing her sense of competence. Laura looks to me, as her supervisor, to help her understand what happened. But she sees me only 45 minutes a week. For all the other hours of the week, she has to rely on what she has already internalized. Laura needs a relatively benign internal voice who tells her that although she still has a lot to learn, she is a fundamentally well-intentioned, well-trained, intuitive, empathic therapist who did the best she could in her work with Mike. Sometimes I help Laura most by admitting that I am not sure what I would have done differently in her shoes. I don't think she made an egregious error, or has a fatal flaw, that caused Mike to leave treatment. I am not denying that there might be ways she could do better. For example, in the third session, when Mike was asking how treatment was supposed to work and telling Laura he felt worse after each session, perhaps there could have been a way for Laura to engage his resistance more directly. Maybe both Laura and I dropped the ball, in a sense. Would Mike have been more likely to stay longer if Laura had asked, in that session, whether he was tempted to quit? Or could she have been more attuned to the extent of his narcissistic vulnerability and the injuries to his pride that he was suffering after each session? Could she have handled the work differently and enabled him to stay? Could I have sensed this and warned her in time? Why didn't she/I/we?

Perhaps feeling my own regret will help me help Laura with hers. Somehow I have to communicate to her that we should face our limitations and learn from them, but we must not become so self-punitive that we "die" of shame. Laura's training has to have fortified her in dealing with the inevitable self-esteem injuries, and the inevitable losses, that come with a clinical practice. What happens with first patients can sorely test the clinician's feelings of competence. There is a big difference between feeling "I am generally clinically able, but I could have been more sensitive to Mike's feelings" and feeling "I don't know what I am doing, and Mike was wise to quit."

In supervision, I have the chance to help Laura compensate for any gaps in her preparation for a clinical career. If she is too self-critical, I can add my own voice to her "internal chorus." I believe that we can never subtract voices, but we can add others that ultimately change the mix. If she (in external reality and, later, internally) hears me saying, "You can use this experience to become a better clinician," but "You are not disqualified because it happened," I think she can learn from it and move on. A kind of emotional resilience is the goal. We have to bounce back, every time we are thrown. No matter what happens in a session, we need to register it but, at least at some point, regain the ability to function. Someone inside us must tell us there is reason to be hopeful about our future as a clinician. Some voice inside must persuade us to pick ourselves up, dust off, and move on. We must believe that this moment, with this patient, is meaningful but not our only source of feedback about our professional worth.

If a therapist doesn't have a strong, fundamentally positive sense of professional identity, early "failures" with patients can be devastating. They usually take on a personal meaning that makes them utterly defining and exquisitely painful. For example, one young therapist asked me to supervise his therapy with his first private patients. A few months into our work together, he seemed unusually agitated. Without preliminaries, he said there was a patient he needed to tell me about. For the next few months, our only subject matter was his work with Sam.

Sam is a gay man in his 40s who presents with a history of dramatic successes and failures in his creative work. He entered treatment complaining of depression, alcohol abuse, and job dissatisfaction. In the initial consultation his dramatic gestures, appeals for help, tears, pleas, and self-recriminations were striking. When asked, he admitted to coming to the session drunk. His recent history included a great career opportunity he lost because he came to work inebriated and had to be fired. In the first session he veered from grandiosity to tremendous shame, from fantasies of being a great hero to feeling "less than human." Sam showed up an hour early, appearing even larger than his six-foot-five-inch frame, because of his dramatic self-presentation. He frequently stared straight at his new therapist with a desperate expression. At other moments he would raise his hand over his head, pleading for help, making a big show of misery that also seemed quite genuine.

Sam entered his second session, again drunk and visibly bruised from being beaten by his partner. Apparently utter frustration with Sam's drinking had driven the partner to violence. Sam had not stopped drinking after the first session. Daring his new therapist to get rid of him, Sam insisted that it was useless to order him to get a medication evaluation or recommend that he attend an AA program, because he had tried medication and it had done nothing for him, and he would be insulted by the mention of AA. Sam also informed his therapist that he would violate the rules if he were told not to drink the day of a session.

Presenting problems centered on his difficulties getting work in his creative profession, because of his reputation for taking jobs and then showing up drunk. Employers have had to walk him to emergency rooms and have him hospitalized. Word travels pretty fast in his world, and it has become controversial to hire Sam for any project. Yet he is obviously enormously talented and engaging, so some are still willing to give him that "one more chance" that he so pitifully begs for.

Sam immediately revealed that he was on an antidepressant that, he felt, was doing him no good. When asked what he wanted from treatment, he replied that he "wanted to be normal." He understood that he was "screwing up his own life" and attributed this to his anger. He admitted to unbelievable excesses of alcohol abuse, as well as abuse of cocaine, but reported that he had stopped using drugs. His history of alcohol abuse began at age 16. By 17 he was aware he had a problem with beer and bourbon. He would go through a gallon of bourbon every few days. Thus, he had been abusing alcohol for decades. His history included many failed attempts at rehabilitation. Staying dry, for Sam, was a very fleeting experience. He seemed only momentarily capable of giving up drinking vast quantities on a daily basis, starting in the morning and going through the late hours of the night. When asked for his understanding of why he drank, he said, "To face the day."

Sam's life was a remarkable story of glorious successes creatively and horrific benders, sometimes with near fatal results. His behavior seemed poised to dare everyone to reject him—friends, employers, his partner, and, now, his therapist. He came to sessions drunk, or late, or not at all. He could be alternately pleading or abusive. In his behavior, he seemed to be asking how much his therapist would tolerate, but by being so extreme, he seemed to be guaranteeing that he would eventually get the rejection he feared and expected.

Sam's history seemed, at least as he first told it, to reveal nothing that would begin to explain his self-destructiveness. The oldest of three siblings and the only boy, Sam was born to a lower-middle-class intact family. He was generally popular and, fairly early, showed promise creatively. He was particularly close with a grandmother, with whom he lived for periods of his adolescence. This grandmother was very important to him, because she was especially encouraging of his talents.

Sam could not pinpoint when he became aware of being gay, but he felt he always knew that other boys turned him on. His early life seemed unremarkable, although there were several moves and consequent disruptions of his social and academic life. But, on the whole, things seemed relatively calm (which left his early alcohol abuse unexplained). One great disruption occurred shortly after he entered college, when his parents visited and announced their separation. In his own words, the patient "lost it." He was enraged that his father was leaving his mother after so many years to marry another woman. Although Sam already had a history of alcoholism, it did seem to escalate after this event, and he had convictions for DWI, was in jail for one night, and wrecked a truck.

It was not long before this history became more complex and troubling. Incestuous experiences with family members began in his childhood years. Very shortly the history would become even darker, as Sam's sisters volunteered to tell their stories of being sexually abused by other family members. As the three siblings talked about their past, more began to make sense but also to horrify them. Sam seemed genuinely flooded with grief that his sisters' lives were marked by repeated abuse. Their early family life was, apparently, highly erotically charged, with inappropriate behavior on the part of both their parents and all the siblings, with multiple pairings between them and other teenagers in their family. By a few months into the treatment, it seemed as though none of the immediate family was left out of this history of incest.

Sam wondered how he could have remained oblivious of his family's dramatic story until now, and his therapist wondered what to take as veridical. Certainly the patient was responding with full acceptance of the details as factually accurate. But his therapist felt disconnected as he listened. What to believe, what to question, became a preoccupation for the therapist but not for the patient. The therapist asked himself, "Why aren't I more horrified? Why am I so skeptical?" After all, this is not just Sam telling a story, this is a tale being pieced together by several members of his immediate family.

At this point Sam brought in some violent dreams of animals murdered. It would have been easy for the therapist to piece together that the abuse of the sisters was dissociated by all the family members, that Sam drank to forget, until he entered this treatment. It seemed real and not real, too neat, but also not wholly fabricated.

What is very clear is that greater consciousness of his history did not lead to a decrease in the alcohol abuse. If anything, it seemed to operate in the reverse direction. As Sam and his family talked about the past, Sam's drinking escalated. He showed up to sessions drunk, seeming to dare his therapist to throw him out, or take him to an emergency room, or have him committed to a hospital.

Although the therapist, eventually exasperated, did try all these approaches, as well as a variety of treatment strategies, Sam's attempts to stay dry worked only for a limited time. He would make and break promises to his therapist, to his partner, and to his employers. All three increasingly lost patience with him. He always seemed to be pleading for another chance, asking, in his behavior, to be treated as so special that nothing he did would make others give up on him for good. At the same time, he acted in such a way that it was inevitable that people would run out of goodwill toward him.

Eventually, Sam was found on the street, having had seizures, and was taken to an emergency room. This led to a longer hospitalization, but the usual pattern recurred. His therapist found his evolving history of family incest less and less moving and credible. Sam said he was drinking again "out of boredom." Sam drank publicly, even though he had sworn to his partner and others that he would quit. When caught he said he "did it to get caught." Sam seemed to be toying with everyone, including his therapist. Could any approach really "get through" to him? What did he really want, from his partner, from his work, from his treatment, from his life? Could we ever really know?

Sam came in ready to quit treatment. He said he felt he had "exceeded" what his therapist had to give to him. He was not getting enough out of the work to make it worthwhile. He seemed to feel the therapist's well had run dry, at least for him. He said he didn't know if he was really angry at himself or the therapist, but he felt it wasn't working.

Was this yet another test of the therapist's love? Was there a way to pass? To continue seeing him felt to the therapist like collusion with his alcohol abuse, but to stop felt like giving up.

It seemed as though the best answer to the question "What is this *really* about?" was "all of the above." Sam was testing his therapist's love for him, testing everyone's patience, wearing everyone out, angry at everyone, angry at himself, wanting to die, wanting to live, wanting to succeed, wanting to fail, wanting to quit, wanting to stay. It would be "real" to terminate, to continue the treatment, to insist on AA or another round of hospitalization, or to refer him to another clinician. Was Sam, more than anything else, insisting on being traumatic to others? Was he wanting most to "stir the pot"? Was it most important to him to be unusual, memorable, difficult? Sometimes he cried for most of a session, begging for a hug. Sometimes he growled or yelled, saying his therapist didn't care enough. The only emotion that seemed foreign to him was calm.

The usual patterns (Sam coming to work and sessions drunk and returning home in a stupor) escalated until he was fired again. He threw himself on the therapist's floor and wailed that he had destroyed his own life. He accused the therapist of cold indifference because he wouldn't give him a hug. Maybe it was really the therapist's homophobia. His family had told him they gave up on him. He abruptly left one session, went into the therapist's bathroom, and threw up. The therapist got angry enough to tell Sam that he felt Sam just wouldn't give the treatment a chance to work.

The treatment ended in mutual exasperation. Both felt worn out. Ostensibly, Sam left treatment unable to afford it any more, but both Sam and the therapist were clear that this was not the main reason. The therapist asked me whether he had failed and why. Could there have been a better approach? Could it have gone differently if the therapist had been tougher or more insistent on AA or longer-term inpatient treatment for the alcoholism or a psychiatric hospitalization? Would any way of working have had a different outcome?

In both of the cases so far, the patients are male and tend to act out impulsively. Perhaps it is important to note that in each case, the shared sensibility of the clinician and supervisor markedly differ from the patient's style. Each of the clinicians and I have many qualities in common that we don't share with the patients. The clinicians and I tend to be introspective, reflective people. It is our nature to think (sometimes obsessively) before we act. Mike and Sam, the two patients, are quite different from their therapists and from me. Is that part of the problem? Could it be that the clinicians and I simply can't understand, or fully enough respect, people so different from ourselves?

Hearing about Anne's treatment presented other challenges. In a bizarre twist of fate, I had already heard about her when Ellen, her therapist, presented the treatment during her internship. Now in private practice, Ellen began talking about her work with Anne again.

During Ellen's internship, Anne presented problems that, although interesting, were not very unusual for someone in her late 20s. They had a rather schizoid cast. Anne's relationships with men, friends, and family weren't fully satisfying, and her career was still unformulated. She longed for her father, who died when Anne was a young child. I felt Ellen worked well with Anne. Ellen understood Anne's confusion about what she wanted from her life, and they made some significant progress. Anne moved into her own apartment, was planning an extensive trip on her own, and seemed to be starting to really live her life rather than letting it pass by.

And then, in a moment, Anne's life changed forever. She slipped on a balcony and fell several stories. She couldn't feel her legs. She soon found out that she would be paralyzed, confined to a wheelchair, for the rest of her life.

What was it like for Ellen to hear about these events? What was it like for me? What did Ellen and I have to summon for Ellen to help Anne through the ordeal of operations, faint hopes, and resignation to a lifetime forever altered by the accident? As I like to put it, who did Ellen have to be to help Anne? Who did I have to be to help Ellen?

For purposes of confidentiality, I won't go into the specific details of the accident, but I will ask you to understand that it was possible to wonder how much it was preventable. Thinking about it, second by second, Anne, Ellen, and I could ask, if we had made more progress, might Anne have made different split-second decisions? Might she still be able to walk, to feel her legs, to sit in a chair only when she wants to sit?

I can't find adequate words for the pain that accompanies these reflections. I had many fantasies of being able to roll back the clock so Anne could make different decisions and avoid the fall. Two of the saddest words I know are "if only." Hearing about the details of Anne's physical condition made me feel nauseated. Her injuries made her unable to urinate or move her bowels normally, and in the first months she suffered from bedsores. Imagining myself into Anne's mind, I attempted to understand what it would be like to be her. I tried to leap the gap between this young woman I would never meet and myself. Inevitably, I could be only Sandra-thinking-about-Anne's-life rather than Ellen-thinking-about-Anne's-life or Anne-thinking-about-Anne's-life.

There is a bizarre quality to the situation that makes it hard for me to take in. Can there really be such a monumental consequence of a momentary choice? Can we know that things can alter in an instant and still go on with our lives? The brakes in the car behind us fail. Riding our bicycles, feeling free, we don't notice the pothole. For a blinding moment we are Icarus, daring the sun. Will we really have to pay for that moment of unbridled joy for the rest of our lives? For me, there is a surreal quality to hearing about these events. It feels too horrible to be real. My own defenses limit what I can take in. At some point my mind refuses to see the pictures of Anne it nevertheless continues to create.

What can adequately prepare Ellen to be Anne's therapist, and how will the experience of treating Anne affect the rest of Ellen's career? In a strange version of parallel process, although Anne and I are strangers, I had heard about her before the accident. How can I use that to benefit Ellen? Can I find a way to harness the dread in my stomach? Can something of use come from my own feelings of revulsion and regret?

As the weeks went by, in the aftermath of the accident, Ellen and I wondered what role the treatment could play in Anne's recovery. Might it do more harm than good? More generally, does the truth always set us free? Maybe, sometimes, it makes the bearable into the unbearable. Anne said that seeing her therapist, Ellen, reminded her of her preaccident self. She felt sad and also wondered whether Ellen was trying to act like a "professional" but was really "freaked out." From my point of view, the patient was wondering about *her therapist's* potential for emotionally cutoff, schizoid functioning.

I wondered when denial should be left alone and when it should be explored. If Ellen and I help Anne think about the accident, might we stir up feelings that are beyond Anne's capacity for guilt, shame, and grief? Ellen thought about this dilemma and about Anne's increased envy of her. What could save each of us from sinking into despair? Can we/should we still aim to work with the issues that predate the accident? New dependencies were forcing Anne to face her feelings about dependence on her friends, family, and therapist. Her nearly unbearable regret about the accident brought out Anne's perennial need to find someone else at fault. Who can be blamed without causing Anne even more loss? If she blames herself, will she sink into a depression that saps the strength she needs, now more than ever, in order to fight for her life? If she blames Ellen, or members of her family, will she destroy relationships crucial to her survival?

I felt Ellen and I had to think about our own guilt, trusting that this would eventually lead somewhere. In supervision, as well as in treatment, we are so frequently lost in the woods, without any sense of direction. And yet, as I have often reflected, the worst thing to do would be to stand still. We have to move (ironically, in this case, given Anne's paralysis) in order to go on living. That means, to me, that we sometimes have to choose a direction without knowing whether it will lead us astray. Ellen and I were rather like Hansel and Gretel, in the fairy tale, but we hadn't known to plant "bread crumbs" that could direct us toward home. That is, in the preaccident treatment period, we hadn't formulated insights that we believed could act as signposts for our work now.

I tried to use theory in place of bread crumbs. How could my own studies help me help Ellen help Anne? Aware that I could be using "intellectual" (obsessive) defenses to ward off unbearable anxiety, I nevertheless turned to the emotion theories (Buechler, 2004; Izard, 1972) that have always been such a major source of strength for me, clinically and personally. I thought about how some terrible feelings were inevitable for Anne, but what did I believe might modify them to make them bearable? Sadness simply couldn't be avoided, but what of her fears? What of her intense envy? What of the longing for the conspicuously absent father?

My sense was that loneliness formed an important part of Anne's feelings. Ellen *could* make a difference in how unalterably alone Anne felt. Theory told me that because the emotions form a system, with an alteration in any feeling having an impact on all the others, if Anne's loneliness decreased, that change would affect her experience of sadness. In an important sense, Anne blamed her mother, as well as Ellen, the doctors, and others, for not being the father she missed even more profoundly since the accident. He would have saved her, somehow. Everyone else was a very poor substitute for him. How dare they try to fill his shoes!

I believed that Anne's sadness was inevitable, because she was suffering such significant losses. But I thought Ellen could help her with her envy, rage, fear, and loneliness.

This supervision confronted me with some of life's (and treatment's) most significant questions. How do we all bear the limits of our power and influence? How much do we really believe that the truth sets people free? What can give us the strength we need to bear life's gravest assaults? What beliefs can we each turn toward to provide the "bread crumbs" that give us a sense of direction in our moments of most intense confusion?

Personally, I always turn toward my feelings. Anne's story deeply disturbed me. It was so awful that I could find no "redeeming" feature of it. But I did feel enough commitment to my work with Ellen, and enough warmth toward her, to profoundly want to help her through this. I felt it wasn't only Anne who would never be the same. Anne, helpless in some senses, was having a powerful impact on two women, only one of which she would ever meet.

What did it take for Ellen to be able to bear this experience relatively early in her posttraining career? This question leads me to think about an experience early in my own career. Though different from Ellen's in countless ways, it might shed light on one aspect of the legacy Ellen carries from her work with Anne.

Very early in my own career, shortly after I began seeing outpatients in a clinic attached to a hospital, I treated a man I will call Joe. I found Joe to be a pleasant, highly intelligent man with profound interests in music and art. Though fairly young, his talents had already received public recognition. It looked as though he was headed for a promising career. I had also had occasion to meet his wife and young daughter. Both struck me as good natured and clearly loving toward Joe.

In the midst of this promising picture, there seemed to be only one major problem. Joe had a history of exposing himself to children in public places. Numerous convictions had already led to incarcerations. Each time Joe came before the court, the judge was more exasperated and gave him a harsher sentence. It seemed pretty clear that if it happened again, Joe's career and marriage would end.

Joe's descriptions of his experiences in jail were truly horrifying. By his account, other inmates were especially physically abusive to men who had committed his crime. In inmate society, Joe was considered the lowest of the low, not only because of the nature of his crime but also because he was a sensitive, artistic man, unaccustomed to physical labor or roughness of any kind.

Although I was still a very inexperienced clinician, I was assigned to treat Joe. I thought about trying to refer him elsewhere, looking for treatments with a variety of other approaches, but he wanted to be seen in our clinic (where he already knew some of us and would receive medication and therapy). I felt extremely unprepared to work with him. I was baffled by him. Early on, he told me he was equally baffled by himself. Why did he risk his whole life to have the moments of excitement he got from dropping his pants in front of children he didn't know? When I met with him together with his wife, they both assured me nothing inappropriate had ever occurred between Joe and his daughter. I found a bit of relief from this but still felt deeply troubled and lost as to how to help him.

This was one of many times I remember feeling unqualified for my job. The economic and other practical reasons I had taken the job didn't justify it at those times. I felt it was wrong for me to "treat" a man whose behavior puzzled me as much as it did everyone else, including his wife, the various judges, and the patient himself. What did I have to offer him? Had my training provided anything potentially useful in my work with this man?

I am now about 40 years older than I was when I saw Joe in treatment. I look back with a mixture of many feelings. In some ways I recognize myself and feel I have not changed all that much. Although my own "internal chorus" has certainly multiplied, I can still feel overwhelmed and unprepared and, at times, self-critical. But these feelings are not as intense or frequent. I am not sure I would work "better" with Joe today, but I do think I would be somewhat more confident that I had something to offer, despite my bewilderment.

Joe, his wife, and I felt desperate. Along with his lawyer, we all felt that if Joe committed another offense, the result would be a long jail term. I remember thinking about this treatment after hours and feeling there must be some way I could help prevent another episode. Were there any words I could say, logical points I could make, that had not already occurred to me, his wife, or Joe himself? My feeling was that this was a situation where theory (as I understood it) failed to provide what I needed. No matter how many hypotheses I conjured up to explain Joe's behavior, they didn't lead to any greater understanding of a "therapeutic action" that would be likely to help.

I fell back on an intuitive guess. Pouring over Joe's history, I wondered if the two things that seemed to stand out most, his accomplishments and his exhibitionism, were somehow related. Each was risky in its own way. In each he "showed" himself (in a sense). Each was very exciting for him.

On this extremely slim basis, I recommended to Joe that he stop all musical and artistic activities. He was devastated. When he questioned me about how that would help, I admitted my uncertainty but, nevertheless, strongly urged him to do it. I tried to explain that perhaps the excitement of creativity somehow spawned the urges that got him into trouble. I felt terrible telling him this. I felt I was taking away something that had greatly helped to sustain him, based on a flimsy guess on my part. I tried to tell myself that Joe was an adult and that he didn't have to listen to me. The situation was dire, and I reasoned that I had to do something. Many other approaches had been tried. All this was true but, as I recall it, didn't offer me much comfort.

Many years of training and clinical experience later, different hypotheses occur to me about Joe's behavior and its meaning. I wonder now whether he might have been bipolar. If so, other treatment approaches might have had some effect.

In any event, I continued to treat Joe for a few months, in which he found a rather mundane office job. During those months, and in the several years I remained in this job, I never heard that he had any repeat episodes of exposing himself. Does that make what I suggested right?

I raise this question not, so much, to explore treatment options in working with Joe but more for the purpose of thinking about the effect of this experience on my own professional (and personal) development. Of course I may well still be blind to some of its meaning and impact on me because of the operation of my own defenses. But some of the legacy of this experience is conscious to me.

First, let me say that I believe it was a highly significant, meaningful early experience in my career as a clinician and in my development as a human being. Although by no means the first or the only time I felt baffled, yet responsible for doing something, it was a time I felt this dilemma acutely. It came to represent a quandary, in work and the rest of life, where a decision is necessary but the path is very unclear. The stakes are high, and time is limited. Whatever I can think of doing will have unpredictable consequences, as would refraining from any action.

I am very well aware that my experience of this quandary is mainly a product of my own character structure and personal life experience. All clinicians would bring a childhood history, character traits, and a set of defensive proclivities and professional resources to their work with Joe. Some might be less or more troubled, baffled, active, problem solving, and significantly affected by this work. But I think most clinicians would share a few aspects of my experience:

1. I believe that this experience had more impact on me because I was young and inexperienced clinically and therefore hadn't yet had the chance to see that there were many people I *could* help.
2. I think that some of my psychic proclivities (looking for my own part in what happens between me and others, feeling acutely responsible for my impact, expecting to be able to help, being prone toward guilt) are not unusual in people who choose a clinical career. I feel they played a role in how I experienced, behaved in, encoded, and "stored" my work with Joe in my memory and, most especially, how it affected my confidence as a therapist.
3. Therapists are frequently confronted with a particular set of challenges. Although inherent to the human condition and, therefore, common to everyone, they regularly occur in therapists' *work*, as well as their personal life. In the treatment context, the therapist is called on to provide something valuable to the patient. Of course we clinicians differ in what we each feel required to provide (advice, attention, our knowledge of theory, concrete help, guidance, influence, modeling, empathy, attunement, mirroring, interpretation, access to our own emotional responses, among other possibilities). Regardless of these important differences, I think most of us feel obliged to provide *something* to our troubled patients, if only because we are paid for our services but, usually, also because we are listening to a suffering human being who is asking for our help. We try to have impact, without overstepping our appropriate role. Walking that thin line is not unfamiliar to the parents of teenagers, the adult offspring of aging parents, and many other human situations. But as clinicians we are called on to be prepared to intervene professionally. The similarities between the tightropes we walk in our personal lives and those we meet in our work may help us in both arenas. But I think there are times when the challenge can be nearly or truly traumatic. Elsewhere,

I have written of the shame and anxiety a person can feel when the "impossible/necessary" requires us to deal with a human situation for which we feel ill equipped (Buechler, 2008).

Even though it has been 40 years, and I have no way of contacting Joe, I still think about him. He comes to mind frequently when I teach, especially when I am trying to express something about treatment's uncertainties and the array of moment-by-moment decisions we invariably have to make. Many would advocate "following the patient's lead" and, therefore, feel less subject to guilt about influencing the patient's decisions than I did, at least, in my work with Joe. In principle I can agree with this, but in practice I often feel it is not enough merely to follow the patient's lead and reflect what he or she says.

AUTOPSIES WITHOUT THE BODIES

Frequently these very difficult early cases end without any real sense of closure for the clinician. I know, for myself, that I would very much like to know what happened to Joe. Did he stay out of prison? Did he ever go back to his artistic pursuits? Over the years, how has he felt about the treatment and about me?

Most likely, these will remain unanswered questions. My curiosity comes partially from concern for Joe but also from an interest in learning whatever can help me in my work as a clinician and writer. I believe that part of the challenge of life as a clinician is living with many permanent question marks.

I am convinced that a truly daunting clinical situation, faced early, can affect the rest of the clinician's career. Of course much of its impact is shaped by the character and personal experience of the clinician. But throughout this book I am suggesting that a clinical identity is first formed in training, partially shaped by the "clinical values" communicated in supervision, classes, personal treatment, and peer interactions. The basic shape of this clinical identity follows the outlines of the trainee's character structure and patterns of defense. But, I think, one's identity as a clinician also has a life of its own, in a sense. That is, my identity as a clinician may not exactly coincide with my identity as a private person. I may, for example, feel more loving, or less competitive, or more impatient as a therapist than I feel in general as a human being. I think it is not uncommon for clinicians to feel we are "better" people when "in role" than we are outside it.

THE FORMATION OF A CLINICAL IDENTITY

Our training experiences can leave lasting imprints on our identities as clinicians (as I suggested in previous chapters). But difficult cases posttraining can also leave their mark, particularly if they occur before the young professional has a track record as a therapist. Perhaps this is similar to how an adolescent's sense of self can be profoundly affected by first romantic relationships. When an identity is still relatively unformulated, powerful interpersonal experiences can have a lasting impact.

Freud (1926/1959) understood trauma as potentially stemming from any situation that threatens to overwhelm the ego. Thus, we can't list what should, or should not, be traumatic, because what profoundly threatens one person's ego may not have the same effect on another. I would argue that some early clinical experiences operate like traumas. Their impact on the individual's clinical identity resembles the effect of any trauma. The ego overwhelmed never forgets that it *can* be overwhelmed. I believe that this is similar to Winnicott's (1965) understanding that a fear of breakdown is really a memory of a very early, unhinged state. This is also akin to Andrew Solomon's (2008) idea that once people have suffered from a severe depression, they carry "breakdown knowledge" for the rest of their life. Similarly, I would say, the clinician who has been truly overwhelmed is never the same.

Do all clinicians have such experiences at some time in their careers? I don't know, but I would argue that a very early brush with what I call the "impossible/necessary" (Buechler, 2008) often has the most profound impact on one's clinical identity. Feeling called on to do something that is entirely impossible yet also absolutely necessary is a recipe for a potent mix of anxiety and shame. I think that both within and outside the clinical setting, the impossible/necessary can engender lasting feelings of inadequacy, of not being "enough," or of being deeply flawed.

For me it felt necessary, yet impossible, to have conviction about my treatment of Joe. I did find a way to work with him, and it may have been "successful," in one sense. He may have been able to stay out of prison. Even if this is so, I will never be sure what part the treatment played in this outcome. In any case, what a price he paid! Looking back I would say that he and I took a leap of faith. Without firm conviction (at least, on my part) we forfeited a profoundly meaningful aspect of his life. To me, it felt like the decision to cut off someone's gangrenous leg in order to have some chance of saving his life. But was there another, less costly way to save his life?

As a very young clinician, I keenly felt that I was ill prepared for my role with Joe. Although ultimately it was his decision, I knew that it was inevitable that I would play a part in it, through whatever I chose to say or not say. I acted on the basis of a hunch that his exhibitionistic impulse could not be contained unless he forfeited his artistic activities. Together, we bet on this hunch. We gambled with his life. In that encounter with risk I flinched, in a sense. I couldn't bear just waiting it out and seeing what would happen. Like a scared poker player with a bad hand, I couldn't just take a chance, hold pat, and bluff. I folded, in effect, and Joe paid for it, with something that meant almost as much to him as life itself. Would a clinician with more experience and/or more guts have been able to wait longer, risking that Joe might "act out" before the treatment had helped him develop the strength to contain his impulses?

SIMILARITIES AND DIFFERENCES

In the first example in this chapter, Laura took a chance that her patient Mike could bear facing his regrets and feelings of failure. Ironically and, perhaps, not coincidentally, Laura was left with regrets and feelings of failure of her own.

Sam and his therapist couldn't curb Sam's excessive drinking. Eventually they wore each other out, and Sam left treatment. As in the first case, this therapist wondered whether he should have more aggressively confronted the patient's resistance to treatment. Would that have resulted in a better outcome?

In the third case, Ellen had to help Anne face the tragic consequences of an accident that, perhaps, might have been avoided. Ellen certainly felt that it was necessary, but sometimes impossible, to bear her role in Anne's life. Was something vital missing in their earlier treatment? Did this contribute to what happened to Anne? Could Ellen now find the strength to help Anne forge a reasonably fulfilling life?

My own experience with Joe brought me to moments of feeling inadequate to face what I felt was impossible and yet necessary. Any action, and inaction, could have grave consequences, yet I couldn't feel a reasonable degree of conviction about how to help.

Although differences abound, I would like to focus on some similarities:

1. All four clinicians are young and relatively inexperienced in doing outpatient treatment.
2. All four therapists keep trying to treat their patients, despite feeling profoundly unprepared and uncertain.
3. All the clinicians are left with a feeling of having failed their patients in some crucial but vague sense.

I remember, as a child, asking for a "do over" when I didn't do something well. All four of us might have wanted a "do over," but I think we all would have felt unsure what to do differently, even if that wish could be granted. If Laura had confronted Mike's resistances in that third session, he might have left even sooner. If Sam's therapist had insisted on AA, Sam, too, might have quit therapy in a huff. If Ellen had more fully addressed Anne's impulse issues in the period before the accident, perhaps their strong attachment would not have developed so fully. Anne came into treatment asking for help with conflicts about important relationships in her life. It may be true that the profound positive bond they developed together by exploring these issues helped Anne depend on Ellen after the accident. And I am not sure what I would do differently in working with Joe if I could have a "do over." Levenson made the argument that sometimes we are effective in treatment despite having the wrong theory about what we are doing. I thought, somewhat concretely, that Joe's artistic excitement pushed him toward uncontainable exhibitionistic impulses. Even if Joe did stay out of prison after our "intervention," there could be many explanations for this result. Maybe my radical prescription (or, rather, proscription) effectively signaled to him that his whole life had to change. Or perhaps he inwardly experienced his own acceptance of my suggestion as a pledge to fight harder for a life outside prison. In short, without the patient, it is hard to conduct a decisive "autopsy." Each of us can't learn as much from these experiences as we might with the collaboration of the patient.

To the extent that we, the four clinicians in these examples, second-guess ourselves, I think the memory is more painful if we feel like our "errors" seem to stem from our most profound personal limitations. That is, in my case, if I feel that my own urgency about Joe's situation stemmed mainly from my own serious, unresolved difficulties taking risks, I am likely to feel the results negatively define me as a clinician. When our clinical failures seem to match our most significant character problems, we can feel permanently flawed as therapists. So, if Laura sees herself as terribly lacking in backbone, her "failure" to confront Mike more quickly may register differently than it otherwise would. Instead of being merely one case among many, it could become *the* case that defines her as a clinician. Instead of being an incident to try to learn from, it could become a painful source of profound shame and anxiety. Instead of recognizing that the "lesson" to be learned from this case is far from clear, if, indeed, there is *any* lesson to be learned, Laura could feel as though she is different from other, more competent clinicians who would have gotten it right. More generally, I am suggesting that a sense of oneself as having significant liabilities as a clinician that is reinforced by unsettling early clinical experiences can exert a powerful effect on one's career.

In cases where the patient suddenly terminates, the clinician can never have any real closure about what happened. This can leave us feeling very vulnerable and likely to interpret the situation as having been caused by shortcomings we believe ourselves to have. If our earliest patients leave prematurely, it is easy for many of us to feel we "failed" because of who we are, in some fundamental sense. It may seem to us as though there is nothing we can learn in order to do better. We just have to go on trying, without knowing what to do differently. In the absence of greater clarity about what happened, it is easy for some of us to feel that we lack a crucial form of courage, or integrity, or intelligence, or sensitivity, or some other vital (but somewhat nebulous and certainly hard-to-develop) characteristic.

I think the legacy of these experiences, early in the clinician's career, may include an enduring insecurity about whether we can ever have the "right stuff" to help patients. Reading Kohut (or anyone else), getting more supervision, or even going back into analysis may not feel like it will really "cure" what ails us. What ails us is who we are as human beings. Partially because the clinical experience is so nebulous, it feels like its cause is too bred in the bones, too pervasive, too encompassing to change. There is nothing to memorize or practice. We are left feeling that we can't clearly say what we did wrong. It isn't really what we did that is wrong. It is who we are that is wrong.

I am suggesting that early in our clinical experience, it is more likely that "failures" with patients can leave a lasting mark on us, particularly if they seem to have the ring of truth about who we are as human beings. If our training has not imbued us with a fundament of confidence, if it has left us open to our own (and some of our patients') critical assaults, shame and anxiety may be lasting legacies. If we have not developed an adequate "internal chorus" or colleagues who serve as resources for us when we are troubled by our work, we can feel besieged and alone. In short, if our resilience has not been adequately nurtured, we may never fully really recover from some of these troubling early clinical experiences.

The final section of this book is devoted to the question of how emotional ballasts can be cultivated. Here I can only mention my belief that in our training we need to build a firm sense of clinical worthiness, as well as a clear outline of the areas we could profitably develop further.

Some events early in one's career, together with negative self-evaluations and discouraging training experiences, can operate like traumas, severely compromising our personal and professional confidence. Like anyone who has been traumatized, there is something we have lost our ability to depend on, which is vitally important for our basic security. In my language we are unable to take it for granted that as professionals, we are generally adequate "going concerns." We feel that our character flaws will forever limit our positive impact and may even result in harm to our patients. Like the overwhelming settings discussed in the previous chapter, early "failures" with challenging patients can call our career choices into question. Before we have built up a track record, it is easier for us to wonder whether our character issues, defensive proclivities, experiential limitations, and other liabilities will preclude us from ever becoming effective clinicians. Any professional needs to feel he or she has the basic equipment to do an adequate job. As clinicians our instruments are ourselves, and our equipment includes our empathic and relational capacity. We may well know that we will have to work hard throughout our careers to keep our instruments in good working order. But I don't think it is possible to have enough vitality for the challenges of a long clinical career without first setting down a fundamentally solid, confident clinical identity. I am suggesting that, both during and after training, when we encounter an overwhelming professional setting or a profoundly challenging patient, crucially important personal and professional self-confidence can be severely, and perhaps permanently, compromised.

Part 3

Evolving Requirements

Chapter 5

Ongoing Challenges to the Clinician's Sense of Self

"Good-me" is the beginning personification which organizes experience in which satisfactions have been enhanced by rewarding increments of tenderness, which come to the infant because the mothering one is pleased with the way things are going; therefore, and to that extent, she is free, and moves toward expressing tender appreciation of the infant. Good-me, as it ultimately develops, is the ordinary topic of discussion about "I."

—Harry Stack Sullivan (1953, pp. 161–162)

Sullivan went on to describe how moments of escalating anxiety form the basis of the infant's sense of "bad-me" and how our most poorly grasped, dreadful moments create "not-me." He called good-me, bad-me, and not-me three personifications and stated, "The essential desirability of being good-me is just another way of commenting on the essential undesirability of being anxious" (p. 165). Thus, the consciously knowable sense of self ("I") stems from experiences that have been interpersonally successful in avoiding anxiety.

This chapter applies Sullivan's conceptions of good-me, bad-me, and not-me to the analyst's ongoing professional experience. As analysts, what happens to us when we encounter "bad-me" and "not-me"?

First, a note about how these "bad-me" and "not-me" experiences are described. Sullivan used the label *anxiety* to refer to the unpleasant feelings that accompany bad-me and not-me moments. Elsewhere I have suggested that current usage would sometimes substitute the word *shame* when Sullivan used the word *anxiety* (Buechler, 1995). More specifically, I would argue that the word *shame* and the word *anxiety* often fit "bad-me" moments. That is, when I perform badly I feel ashamed of myself. I have not been at my best. My inadequacy has exposed me to criticism. As I described at greater length in Chapters 1 and 2, shame experiences frequently occur in clinical training, in supervision, in evaluations, and elsewhere. Candidates are confronted with limitations in themselves that may be relatively unfamiliar and painful to see. This may well evoke anxiety and is, I suggest, quite likely to evoke shame.

But our shame and anxiety in response to "bad-me" and "not-me" reflections don't end with our graduations from training. I think they can recur often in the professional life of a clinician. I believe that shame is so integral to our daily clinical experience that we often fail to formulate its impact on us. To anticipate, I will isolate some of the sources of shame inherent in our work and some of the ways we express its cumulative effects on us. I suggest that partially because we are frequently challenged to prove our worth by our patients, colleagues, and insurance companies, we often take out our frustration and humiliation on each other. We engage in "shaming games," implying our colleagues are not well trained or otherwise deficient. I think this is having a devastating effect on the field in general and on us as human beings.

The second chapter of this book dealt at length with training experiences that can exacerbate the clinician's shame about personal shortcomings. The third and fourth chapters looked at professional settings and first outpatients that can elicit painful feelings of professional and personal inadequacy. Here I recall the definition of shame that I have found most useful in order to comment on the "bad-me" moments that are likely to recur and shame the clinician *throughout* her career:

> Shame occurs typically, if not always, in the context of an emotional relationship. The sharp increase in self-attention (and sometimes the increased sensitivity of the face produced by blushing) causes the person to feel as though he were naked and exposed to the world. Shame motivates the desire to hide, to disappear. Shame can also produce a feeling of ineptness, incapacity, and a feeling of not belonging. (Izard, 1977, p. 92)

Like all human beings, analysts developed good-me, bad-me, and not-me "personifications" in our infancies. So every encounter with "bad-me" and "not-me," in training and beyond, brings shame and anxiety along with it. That is, every clinical encounter that tells us about our interpersonally problematic qualities can threaten our overall sense of self. This seems to me to be a central factor in why clinical work is often personally disturbing. Encounters with patients bring to the fore aspects of us that have been outside our conscious awareness. Although training heightens the likelihood of these expansions of our self-knowledge, all clinical work potentially informs us about "bad-me" and "not-me" aspects of who we are. This heightened self-awareness can create shameful feelings of inadequacy as a professional *and also as a person.* Briefly I see shame as operating in a loop, in which a feeling of inadequacy elicits heightened self-attention, which exacerbates the shame, further heightening self-attention, and so on.

For example, when a patient precipitously threatens to quit, the therapist may feel exposed as a poor clinician. She may suffer from the sense of "ineptness, incapacity, and a feeling of not belonging" that Izard identified as part of the total shame experience. She may wonder if she belongs in the community of clinicians. Each of us brings our early history to these moments, so just what they recruit will differ. But when we feel we have significantly failed, we are likely to come into contact with some form of the "bad-me" or "not-me" personifications that formed part of our earliest interpersonal experiences. It certainly would not be surprising if shame and anxiety lingered after a clinician's encounter with "bad-me" or "not-me."

In the second chapter I described moments when the candidate looks in a mirror and sees a stranger she neither likes nor admires. Comparisons with characters in fiction occur to me. Like the beleaguered hero of Dostoevsky's (1846/1985) short novel *The Double*, the candidate may feel stalked. Somehow the candidate is being seen as though she were a terrible replica of the person she knows herself to be. But this kind of experience is not limited to training. We often look into the "mirror" of a patient's eyes and see someone we don't (consciously) know ourselves to be. Patients can construe us in horrible but somehow convincing shapes that severely challenge our sense of self-esteem and self-awareness.

As previously disowned or unknown aspects of the self are revealed to us, we may struggle to integrate them into our sense of ourselves. Like all human beings, we need to retain some version of "good-me." Thus, for example, experiences with our patients may confront us with insensitive and nonempathic qualities in us. These experiences may severely challenge a "good-me" personification we have long held dear (see Epstein, 1979, for a similar concept). In fact, it seems very likely that those who would enter the field have developed such personifications in important relationships earlier in their lives. In short, we are people who have probably always needed to feel empathic in order to retain a sense of being good. Challenges to this self-perception would affect not only our professional sense of adequacy but also our personal self-esteem. For a clinician, a bad performance on the job exposes our shortcomings as human beings and not just as professionals. Our essential ability to relate to other people can seem to be at stake. Failure with a patient can elicit profound shame and anxiety. Something we rely on as human beings, and not just as professionals, feels called into question. At least for the moment we may lose touch with the "good-me" that we have depended on all our lives.

ASSAULTS ON THE CLINICIAN'S SELF-ESTEEM

One of life's mysteries, from my point of view, is why analysts tend to shame one another so frequently. There are endless ways to tell someone they are inadequate and not a "real" analyst. We all know the history of how major thinkers, such as Bowlby and Sullivan, have been treated as second-class citizens. The targeting of individual analysts, and institutes, is legendary. Given that, in the present era, analysts can consider themselves an endangered species, it is especially amazing that we still indulge in these hurtful political intrigues with each other rather than band together to try to survive. Why do we do it?

Recent work (Raubolt, 2006) has suggested that clinicians who are not analysts are at least as likely to humiliate colleagues. It could seem as though clinical work attracts people whose narcissistic character patterns incline them toward this behavior, and personal treatment does not deter this tendency. This may be closer to the truth than I would like to believe, but, even so, I don't think it is the whole story.

Let's add to the picture the way we cherish status and vie for recognition, sometimes at a colleague's expense. For example, at conferences we often use the position of discussant as an opportunity to publicly humiliate a peer. Are we an unusually narcissistic group, edging each other out of the limelight, fiercely competing for crumbs of recognition?

Although this may be part of the truth, I think the frequent assaults on the clinician's self-esteem play an important role in our status-seeking and competitive behavior. I suggest that ethical considerations and the boundaries of the role limit the ways we can boost our sense of self with patients, although we still indulge in this in many ways. With our colleagues we take out our frustrations and soothe our sore egos by "getting a little of our own back," as the humiliated character Eliza Doolittle, in the play *My Fair Lady* (Lerner & Loewe, 1956), might say.

To expand my idea, I create a mythical analyst, Dr. X, and follow him for one workday. Conveniently, Dr. X is attending a conference in the evening, after a full day of clinical hours. Literary license will enable me to ask him what he is feeling at various junctures of the day and evening. This will allow me to illustrate my suggestion about the *connection between how we are treated clinically and how we treat each other professionally.*

Drinking his second cup of coffee, Dr. X thinks about his schedule for the day.

DR. X: Why did I schedule a new patient, as well as Dorothy, Lucy, the Smiths, and Elliot back-to-back? Am I a masochist? I've got to change this, somehow. Mondays are a nightmare. Better get ready for the first hour. Jeffrey, a new patient. The phone call didn't tell me much, but given his insurance he probably won't be interested in long-term work.

JEFFREY: I don't really know why I am here. I think I have some kind of attention disorder. Do you know how to treat those? Is there a medication for it? Can you prescribe it? I get distracted at work. I'm in finance, and you know what that is like nowadays. I'm lucky to have a job at all.

I should be trying hard, but my mind wanders away from the reports I am writing.

DR. X: Tell me a little about yourself.

JEFFREY: Look, Dr. X, I know the game you shrinks play. You can't really do anything to help me with my attention disorder, so you muck around in my childhood for a few years and bilk the insurance company until I finally call a halt to it. I don't want to waste my time and money. Can you really help me?

Dr. X gathers his thoughts together as he considers Jeffrey's question. Does he know enough about attention deficit disorders? But wait, that may not even really be the problem. Jeffrey comes on pretty strong. Only the first session, and he is already making demands. But maybe he's right. How do I know I won't waste his time and money? But I have to find out about him first, and that will take time. Should I try to "engage" him in treatment somehow? Is this just stalling, because I don't really have anything to offer him? Am I a fraud? Oh, God, how will I get through this day? It is only 9 a.m.!

Jeffrey leaves after 40 more minutes of voicing his skepticism, and Dr. X buzzes in Dorothy, his next patient, a 52-year-old schoolteacher. Dorothy is a little overweight but dresses so as to hide it. She is wearing just a touch too much makeup. She gives Dr. X a forced, strained smile as she heads toward the couch.

DOROTHY: Well it was another empty weekend. I couldn't stop thinking about killing myself. What is the point? I'm never going to find someone to be with. Too old, too fat. I can't go to bars anymore. Most of the men are married. Or they want 25-year-olds. Too late to have kids. Saturday I didn't get out of bed at all. Just couldn't. Kept thinking, what if I just never get up again? Not as if the world would stop spinning. No one would give a shit. Including you. By the way, how long have I been coming here?

DR. X: You are feeling hopeless about your life and our work.

DOROTHY: What life, what work? We have no work, and I have no life. You can't help me. What could you do, besides marrying me yourself? And you won't do that. Not that you are such a great catch. But you are probably married already. It is easy for men. You can get married any time, but my shelf life was over long ago.

Dr. X feels defensive but doesn't want to sound defensive. He thinks about whether he and Dorothy have been coasting. Maybe it *is* too late for her to find someone. But should that even be one of the treatment's goals? He wonders if he took the easy road with her, confronting her as little as possible, keeping things smooth. Maybe she is right to be angry and disappointed. He sinks into his thoughts: "Another failure. Am I just no damn good? How did I imagine doing treatment was the right profession for me, when I can't even think of something to say?"

After a prolonged silence, Dorothy mentions suicidal impulses again but says she won't act on them until her mother dies. She cries for a while, occasionally choking back the tears enough to get out a few words about it all being pointless. Mercifully, the session finally ends, with Dr. X feeling terrible. He buzzes in Lucy, his next patient. Lucy is wearing a skin-tight leotard and short, knit, clingy skirt. Her perfume, carefully arranged hairstyle, and adroitly applied makeup suggest that this is an important date rather than a therapy session.

LUCY: You don't look happy to see me.

DR. X: What does that mean to you?

LUCY: Oh God! There you go with the therapeutic mumbo jumbo! Can't you just be a human being for one day? I bet you would prefer to see any of your other patients rather than me. Is that right?

DR. X: It seems like you want to focus on my feelings rather than your own.

LUCY: I don't know why I keep coming here. I think I should stop. I feel worse when I leave than I did before the session. You are a rigid, programmed robot. You don't have any sympathy or even basic humanity. I have had it! Why should I pay you for this? I am out of here, and I am not going to come back, so please don't bother to call me. I will send you a check for what I owe. And I don't want to pay for this session. I did you a favor by telling you the truth about yourself. You should pay me!

Although it is only 10 minutes into the session, Lucy gets up from the couch and leaves, dramatically taking three tissues, with a flourish, on her way out. Dr. X stares after her for a few minutes before he can collect himself and go to the kitchen to get a glass of cold water.

Dr. X drinks the water slowly, staring out the window. He thinks to himself, "What *do* I offer these people? Why should they want to see me, let alone pay me? What do I know more than they do? All the theories contradict each other, and, lately, everyone in the field is saying it is wrong to enter sessions thinking we know what's what. The fallacy of logical positivism. So if I really don't know anything, what am I selling? I thought I knew myself well. I thought I was a responsible, kind, empathic, capable human being. Am I really an insensitive failure and a fraud?"

Dr. X hears the buzzer and realizes that the Smiths have arrived. He has just begun to see couples. Although he has no special training in marital therapy, he finds it interesting and hopes branching out will help him get referrals. A colleague referred the Smiths, and Dr. X wants them to be satisfied with the treatment, so they might tell the colleague how good Dr. X is. This could lead to more referrals and an increased practice with couples. He could charge a little more for this work, and people didn't tend to try to use their insurance as much. So it would be good to do more marital therapy.

The Smiths enter, a good-looking couple in their late 30s. She is a very successful, up-and-coming lawyer at a prominent law firm. He is a struggling writer, earning occasional, small chunks of money doing freelance magazine articles.

MRS. SMITH: The week was pretty good, at least until last night.

MR. SMITH: That wasn't my fault.

MRS. SMITH: You always deny you are responsible for anything. You never change.

DR. X: What happened?

MRS. SMITH: We finally got a sitter and went out for the evening with the Joneses. I thought we would have a nice time, a good dinner, some drinks. And it *was* nice, until he brought my parents up. He said I was *some* big cheese lawyer, not able to stand up to my own father. It was humiliating. I had to concentrate on not crying and making it worse. Finally I just escaped into the ladies' room. Mildred came in, to see if I was okay. She had a very sympathetic tone. I felt like she pitied me.

MR. SMITH: Well, the prosecution has had her turn. Now, I suppose, it is time for the defense. Or don't I even get a chance to speak?

DR. X: Of course you can speak.

MR. SMITH: Look, I thought we were having a nice time. She is so sensitive! Everything I do is wrong. I can't open my mouth anymore. First of all I thought we would never get out of the house, with all the directions she was giving the sitter. "If the baby wakes up, don't go in for at least 5 minutes. But if he really starts to cry ..."

MRS. SMITH: Get to the point. What does that have to do with ...

MR. SMITH: Oh, so the only point you want him to hear about is what you think *I* did wrong. Nothing else counts! Well I am sick of this. How is this helping us? I don't want to go through this mockery. Every week, the same bullshit. Poor, long-suffering wife at the mercy of a son of a bitch bastard husband. Why don't you just divorce me and get it over with? Why do we have to play this therapy game? Why should we pay this bozo to listen to us fight, when we can fight at home for free?

Dr. X tries to surreptitiously look at the clock to see how many minutes are left in the session, but Mr. Smith catches him.

MR. SMITH: That does it! I am out of here. I'm not paying for this! This idiot is just counting the minutes and counting the fees on the way to the bank! I have had it with this crap. What the hell is he going to say that will change anything anyway? [*Mr. Smith gets up to leave, saying a few more words to Mrs. Smith.*] As far as I am concerned, this therapy is over. You can get home on your own. I'll be home later. I'm going out for a drink. Or two or three.

Mrs. Smith is crying, as Mr. Smith puts his coat on and leaves. Through tears she says, "He will come home drunk and wake me and the baby. I won't sleep and won't be able to concentrate at work tomorrow. Just when I have a huge case, with the toughest partner. I can't take it."

DR. X: [*to himself*] I can't think of anything to say. [*to Mrs. Smith*] Our time is up for today. I hope you both come back next week.

MRS. SMITH: I'll call, to let you know. But I don't see how this is helping us. We have had our worst fights after these sessions. What is supposed to be happening? Whatever it is, I don't think this is working.

Mrs. Smith leaves just as Elliot rings the bell and sits down in the waiting area. Dr. X thinks to himself, "Thank God only one more patient. I will just get through the 45 minutes, somehow, and then take a cab to the meeting. I hope I prepared enough. Who is discussing my paper? Oh, that woman from the Freudian track. She will probably attack what I did with the case. I hope I can speak up for myself."

Elliot, a tall, rugged-looking, middle-aged man, has obviously been crying. He tries, and fails, to contain himself: "We lost her. Mom died last night."

Dr. X. says, "I'm sorry" and struggles to recall the situation. Should he know more than he remembers about it? Has Elliot's mother been ill for a while, or is this sudden? What illness did she have? Should he ask or wait a bit? Maybe Elliot will say something that jogs his memory. Better wait and hope for that.

ELLIOT: Did you think she would die?

Dr. X panics. He can't think of what to say. Everything he can think of reveals that he had not been on top of the material and, what is worse, he didn't admit it right away. Should he "come clean" now? Maybe that is best. But poor Elliot! Grieving for his mother and now also finding out his therapist doesn't pay enough attention to keep track of what is going on and isn't honest enough to admit it right away. Dr. X rethinks what to do: "Maybe that's bad timing. Maybe the less I say the better. Maybe I should just try to be empathic. Oh, God, and there are still 30 minutes left to the session."

When Elliot's session finally ends, Dr. X has little time to think about the profound grief he has just witnessed or his own guilt about covering up his blank memory. With regret he reflects that had he decided to reveal his thoughts, it might have led to something productive. Maybe there is valuable information in it, for both of them. Doesn't he believe in the value of exploring countertransference? Was this an enactment? What did it mean about who Dr. X really is? Dr. X thinks of a few possibilities: that it has to do with his own fear of death, or with feelings about his own mother, or something he feels or does not feel toward Elliot, or something he intuits Elliot feels.

Dr. X then realizes he has to leave for the conference and almost forgets to take a copy of his paper. In the cab, he thinks, "The Freudians will make mincemeat of me with this paper. They'll say I was too active. They'll question whether I am a real analyst. Oh, they'll be polite on the surface. But everyone will know what they are really saying. But two can play at that game. I will expose how stodgy they are, how they don't listen to their countertransference enough. I'll show that their methods are outdated. Nobody really believes that stuff anymore. They think they will show me up. Well, I'll show them up. Let's see, who will be there ..."

Anyone who has attended case conferences can imagine what happens next. Dr. X presents his paper, with case material illustrating a theoretical point. In the discussant's first remarks, she thanks Dr. X for his fine presentation. But then, in order to have a point to make, she must find where she disagrees with his technique. Without consciously formulating it, she feels as though doing a good job as a discussant requires her to find something to differ with. She also feels compelled to raise the flag of her analytic alma mater. There may be some members of her classical school of thought in the audience, and they would be disappointed in her if she didn't say a few words to advertise their theoretical stance. So, at first gently and then more sharply, she takes Dr. X to task for what he left out of his paper. Perhaps, she suggests, Dr. X didn't feel he had sufficient time to discuss the transference thoroughly or mention the patient's defenses. Or maybe he doesn't believe in focusing on them so early in the treatment. Of course, this is a very difficult patient, so proper technique may have been impossible to apply in this case. But maybe countertransferential issues have pulled Dr. X to try too hard to give this patient advice and concrete help. She hopes the patient is engaged enough to stay in the treatment long enough for a real analysis to begin. But if Dr. X continues to work on such a surface level, the treatment will never deepen, and the patient will leave, having changed very little. Of course, we all fail with some patients. It takes courage to resist the temptation to please patients and work superficially. And that courage is in short supply nowadays. So, in conclusion, Dr. X has ably presented a very difficult case. He has focused on surface material, either because he didn't believe the patient was capable of real analytic work or because he doesn't know any better. But we can have confidence that Dr. X and his patient will recover from this false start in the future because, after all, Dr. X is well intentioned. The discussant concludes with some reasons why this case illustrates some of her teachers' favorite points. Nonclassical technique results from gutlessness, pandering to patients, and poor training. The discussant thanks Dr. X and the organizing committee for the opportunity to discuss this rich and evocative clinical material.

Several in the audience praise Dr. X's clinically sensitive and illuminating paper and the discussant's lively response. Both were excellent, and this conference illustrates how tolerant we have all become about theoretical differences.

Gradually, audience members' comments start to cluster. It becomes more and more apparent that something is terribly wrong with the way the case is being conducted, but the participants see the problem differently. Four points of view are articulated:

1. This patient is a nightmare. Who could do good work with such a person? No wonder Dr. X is utterly failing to do anything more than hand-holding. Dr. X is a trooper for staying the course and baby-sitting this patient for so long. And what courage, to share work this inadequate with an audience! Dr. X should be commended.

2. Our discussant has helped us separate the men from the boys. You have to be tough to withstand temptation, face truths, and do real analytic work. Some losers (perhaps like Dr. X) are not up to the task.

3. Theory isn't important. Only having the right feelings counts. It doesn't matter what Dr. X thinks he is doing. What counts is his human response to the patient. And Dr. X is very human, so although Dr. X is wasting time on theoretical bullshit right now, everything will turn out well in the end.

4. Everyone here, including Dr. X, is missing the boat. We have all forgotten the essential truths that Freud (or Sullivan, or Kohut, or Winnicott, or Klein, or Fromm, or whoever) taught. Tragically, no one is getting good training nowadays. This is all too clear in Dr. X's clinical work, the presentation, and the discussion.

The moderator regrets that time is limited, so no more questions can be raised. Before concluding, he asks whether Dr. X would like to say anything. Dr. X has pages of notes in his hand. First he thanks the discussant for her thoughtful response and everyone else for being there. His tone becomes more urgent, as he explains how hard it was to write this paper and how no one really understood what he was saying. If anyone had paid attention, they would have heard how deftly he did deal with the transference and the defenses. Sure, he didn't use the lingo, but nobody really does nowadays. Psychoanalysis is dead, but no one in this room (aside from himself) can face up to that. All the comments show that analysts are out of touch. With such people in the profession, the field deserves to die.

The moderator welcomes everyone to stay for wine and cheese. But first, Dr. X and the discussant must again be warmly thanked for doing a terrific job. We need many more presentations like this so our differences can be bridged and our profession can flourish as, no doubt, it will.

Dr. X moves toward the plastic cups of wine and carefully but quickly downs his first drink. He tells himself to take it easy but reaches for the second right away. People are coming up to him to congratulate him. What a wonderful meeting this was! Halfway through the third drink, he begins to slur his words a bit. He says little but smiles to everyone. The inner debate, however, is quite lively. Should he tell the discussant what a bitch she is? And Dr. Y, that so-and-so! What a bunch of hostile bastards! He wonders why he did this presentation. Well, he reflects, he will never do anything like this again.

THE IMPACT OF ASSAULTS ON THE CLINICIAN'S SENSE OF SELF-WORTH

I am hoping to clarify how assaults on our self-esteem, from patients, colleagues, and, of course, insurance companies and others, cumulatively affect us. This chapter deals with their shaming impact and my speculation about our tendency to respond by shaming each other. The story of Dr. X's day and evening is meant to illustrate several aspects of the shaming that I believe clinicians generally have to endure. I refer, once again, to the general description of shame that introduced this chapter. Shame most often occurs in the context of an emotionally important relationship. It operates in a kind of feedback loop. Feelings of inadequacy heighten self-attention. One notices more flaws in oneself, and the shame escalates. One feels exposed, inept, naked, and like an outsider who does not belong in a competent group. Just how are these feelings elicited in us?

Patients, like Jeffrey, the new patient with an "attention disorder," often challenge our usefulness and our approach. I think therapists undergo more frequent questioning of our worth than, for example, dentists or bus drivers have to endure.

Being questioned this way puts us in a difficult position. It is hard to respond without feeling we are being defensive. We also don't want to lecture the patient on theories about the therapeutic action of treatment. Perhaps partially because we feel we don't have a good enough answer, we may be left with lingering questions about our worth in our own minds. The implication that we are fraudulent, that we are just trying to drum up business to make more money, can be very demoralizing. Not answering can sometimes feel like agreeing that we are guilty as charged. I think chronic feelings of shame may easily result from these encounters.

Dorothy, the lonely and suicidal 52-year-old patient, also asks whether she is being helped, but her attitude is more depressed than angry. I think she might elicit an anxious shame in her therapist. Will she really hurt herself? This would, of course, be a tragedy for her, as well as a possible source of shame for her clinician. It is hard to avoid a profound sense of failure when a patient suicides, no matter what other explanations we might be able to provide. So, in addition to asking hard questions about how we help, patients evoke our anxiety about what they might do to themselves. Elsewhere, I have written about the particularly painful impact of the combination of anxiety and shame (Buechler, 2008). The two emotions can easily exacerbate each other.

An accountant can define the service clients pay for. A baker can count the loaves of bread created that day and provide the number promised. But Dorothy's therapist is not satisfying the needs she loudly proclaims. Can Dr. X feel comfortable that he is providing what she *really* needs, despite her declarations to the contrary? Can he be clear about just what that is?

Lucy, the sexy patient who wants a more "human" and less clinical response, can elicit her therapist's own frustrations with the limitations of the role (this issue is discussed more fully in Chapter 8). Briefly, to whatever extent Dr. X is ambivalent about his therapeutic role, he may inwardly agree with Lucy's complaints. Perhaps he actually feels like the constraints of the therapeutic boundaries are unnatural. Dr. X may feel uncomfortably sandwiched between Lucy's demands and the constraints his professional identification prescribes. To her, he is too analytic, whereas colleagues might see him as not sufficiently analytic. Both judgments might have some of the ring of truth in his own ears. And both could contribute to a sense of insufficiency, inadequacy, and ineptness and a feeling of not belonging. In short, Dr. X is likely to feel shame, no matter where he turns for validation of his stance.

The couple raises the question, extensively discussed by Irwin Hirsch (2008), of what happens when the analyst attempts to coast or just get through a session. I think most therapists will recognize the hollow feeling that can accompany coasting. I believe it easily recruits a sense of fraudulence and shame.

Elliot, the patient whose mother died, can elicit the clinician's guilty shame. There are so many ways to feel you have failed a patient. Focusing on one part of a session, we may neglect other vital aspects. Being worn down, distracted, or burnt out, we may provide too little attention, or empathy, or understanding. We may lack the energy, concentration, stamina, courage, or wisdom that a particular session requires. We have countless opportunities to feel unequal to our task. Perhaps it is especially painful to fail a person in dire need, which is often the situation we face.

More generally, all these fictitious patients confront Dr. X with "bad-me" and "not-me" aspects of himself. Wherever he looks he sees, reflected back to him, an image of the person he never wants to be. Some shame and anxiety seem inevitable for him, as he struggles through hour after hour, with little time to think about the personal meanings of these self-reflections.

So, Dr. X enters the conference acutely aware that he has been tried and found wanting by several of his patients. This is the backdrop for the interplay between Dr. X and his colleagues. I think it makes it more likely that Dr. X will suffer severely from their challenges to his clinical adequacy.

Depending on his defensive style and character issues, Dr. X may respond with a counterattack, with depressive self-loathing, with obsessively indirect intellectualizations, or in some other style. I am suggesting that in professional exchanges, we challenge each other's worth so often partially because we are so frequently narcissistically wounded by our patients (and by representatives of managed care).

FEELING PROFOUNDLY UNEQUAL TO THE CHALLENGE

Early in my career, I felt a kind of awe about clinical work. Sometimes I can still feel it. What a heavy responsibility! Generally people don't come to us with easy or even clear queries. Clinicians face ambiguous and hard challenges about finding the strength to endure tragic losses, questioning the meaningfulness of our lives, bearing our knowledge of death, carrying out our responsibilities toward each other, and countless other complicated aspects of being human. Is it any wonder that clinicians frequently feel insufficient and, consequently, vulnerable to shame? With a task so nebulous, yet vast, how could we feel otherwise?

I think we are more easily shamed about relatively minor lapses because of our knowledge (however unformulated it may be) of our more profound limitations. We forget whether our patient's mother had heart disease or cancer or exactly what happened in the last session. These gaps take on great meaning because, on some level, we know what we are not providing, in a more profound sense. In my imaginary example, Dr. X didn't remember Elliot's mother's condition, and he didn't admit it. Consciously, they may both focus on these "failures." But, somewhere in him, Dr. X knows Elliot is really looking for something beyond his therapist's reach: Elliot wants to know how to live without his beloved mother. They both know this is one of the questions Elliot is asking. How much can any of us really say about bearing life's more profound losses? How much does all our training tell us about living without someone we dearly love and miss more than words can ever express? I think shame can relatively easily be induced in us because, in our deeper recesses, we know that no one is an expert in living life. Our patients often learn which questions to ask us and which to leave unspoken. They may ask for help settling into a career and leave unsaid (though, perhaps, implied) their questions about whether, regardless of which career they choose, their lives will matter. But we know their real questions, because they are not all that different from our own. And we know that although we have studied theories for many years, there are still many more questions than answers.

It is obvious that our work can be compared to the roles of the shaman or religious leader. In addressing the everlasting questions, we also mine territory similar to the terrain of philosophers. Although anyone occupying any of these professions might tremble at the enormity of the task, I would suggest it is today's clinician, more than anyone else, who is likely to suffer shame. In my opinion, we have reached our peak season for being ashamed. This readiness or ripeness for shame results from the confluence of several factors:

1. We have outgrown our field's early reliance on identifiable techniques. Previous generations of analysts could learn how to apply techniques, such as free association and the analysis of defense. Over time, they could gain confidence in their proficiency. They could feel that practice was helping them become better clinicians today than they were yesterday. There were skills that could improve with practice, such as fluency with analytic terms and the capacity to notice transference derivatives. Training and ongoing clinical experience seemed to have a vertical trajectory, in that each of us could see ourselves as always moving closer to an ideal analytic proficiency. But, as we all know, with the proliferation of schools of thought has come the end of an unquestioning belief that there are "techniques" that can be learned, skillfully applied, and improved with practice. Like Adam and Eve, we have eaten from the tree of knowledge and are aware of our nakedness. But, at least, of late, we have no dependable theoretical "fig leaf" to hide our shame.
2. Less confident that there are techniques we have learned how to apply, we are nevertheless still asked for help with life's most complex dilemmas. People come to us with difficulties loving, working, playing, risking, feeling, and bearing their sorrows. We are asked how to help young people mature and older people age gracefully.
3. It has become axiomatic for us to assume we don't really have answers about the "right" way to be a parent, a sexual partner, or anything else. Post-postmodern, we have tried to make a badge of courage out of our uncertainties. But, at the same time, insurance companies and prospective patients pressure us to demonstrate that we have something worth their time and money. The vaguer we are about what we have to offer, the more likely I believe we are to suffer shame when quizzed by those who hold the health care purse strings.
4. All our gods are dead. Unlike the priest or the Freudian, who could claim authority derived from a higher power, we have no gods from whom to receive the Word. We have only our fallible selves.

For many of us, our analytic identities were forged in interactions with our teachers, whose careers peaked in an earlier era. Thus, we grew up (analytically speaking) with the expectation that someday we, too, would have their knowledge and expertise. I think that we can't help experiencing our profound uncertainties as failures to live up to the standards of our forebears. Even though we may have rejected their airtight methods, we nevertheless expected to have their level of confidence.

As time goes by analysis itself sheds the marks of its individuality. It is no longer automatic for it to occur five times per week or on a couch. As we attempt to assimilate, in a sense, can we still retain our identity? As we bow to today's necessities (partially for the sake of business) and give up some of our more stringent requirements, who are we now? What more will we have to give up to appeal to a wide enough audience? As a field, and as individual practitioners, will we be able to retain pride in our profession? Or will we be increasingly subjected to the shame of failing to convince consumers that we "provide" a "service" worth their time, money, and effort?

Subsequent chapters will explore the impact on the practitioner of our own losses of hope and faith in our work. But, here, I am focusing on the issue of shame or the sense of inadequacy or insufficiency. I suggest that the overt challenges coming from insurance companies, patients, and colleagues so wound our pride partly because of the more profound and daunting human challenges we face. Whenever a patient abruptly terminates or an insurance company refuses to pay for our services, I think it reminds us (however consciously or unconsciously) of all the moments we bowed before an immense dilemma. We may protest that, of course, we are not sages and should not be expected (or expect ourselves) to know the answers to life's most essential questions. But the next patients crossing my threshold will still want help living their lives. Although they may know (or learn) that they shouldn't ask me whether or not to try to have a child or whether or not to change careers, the questions still hang in the air. I can explain (at least to myself) that the help I offer will allow them to find their own answers. But there are so many moments when this feels like too little too late. People ask for help facing illness, poverty, trauma, and uncertainty. They feel meaningless, loveless, or awash with grief. Can I meet their eyes without feeling inadequate? Can I bear, without crippling shame, the vast discrepancy between what they want and what I have to give?

Chapter 6

Cocreated Dysfunctional
Patterns of Relating

One way to understand how doing treatment challenges the clinician's sense of self is that working with our patients can highlight problematic aspects of our own character styles. Elsewhere, I have explored how my own schizoid tendencies emerge more clearly than usual in relating to schizoid patients (Buechler, 2002a, 2004, 2008). Confronting this can bring discomfort, anxiety, and shame, particularly if being "schizoid" raises life-long "bad-me" or "not-me" specters. I suggest that the same may be said for the obsessive, paranoid, narcissistic, depressive, and other aspects of the analyst. Each may be brought into the fore in coping with the behavior of a particular patient. Depending on how I most need to see myself, when my paranoid, or obsessive, or narcissistic aspects are highlighted, I may suffer especially painful bouts of shame and anxiety. For example, those of us who *pride ourselves* on being non-narcissistic are likely to suffer acutely when faced with our own narcissistic tendencies. In that situation, I may dread seeing the patient who brings out my narcissism (perhaps without consciously understanding why).

Before continuing, I would like to clarify how I use words like *obsessive* and *paranoid* and other terms borrowed from the language of diagnosis. This is shorthand for me. These words encapsulate styles of coping with the human condition. There are, in my way of thinking, paranoid ways to deal with being human, and they differ from more obsessive ways. Usually diagnosis looks at people in one-person terms. An individual may be seen as obsessive, or paranoid, or borderline. Here I am, in a sense, "diagnosing" analytic pairs, but not so as to label them as pathological. I am using these terms as descriptors of *styles* of living.

An obsessive lifestyle involves, at its fundament, an effort to exert more control than we realistically can. In individuals this often leads to a conflict between what one wants to do and what one is obligated to do. One example would be the child who wants to play baseball but knows that he or she should do homework. Other characteristics of obsessive styles include perfectionism, overattention to small details, procrastination, and reliance on defensive reaction formation, undoing, and compartmentalization.

What is an obsessive style of living, cocreated within the analytic frame? How would it play out in any one session and over the course of treatment?

First, as a couple, an analytic pair coping with the frame obsessively could use the "rules" to try to control their feelings to an unrealistic degree. There are myriad possibilities for how this could be expressed. For example, if analyst and patient are trying to exert control over aggressive feelings, they might engage in endless legalistic debates about details of their arrangements. These "debates" might be expressed in words or enacted in behavior within or outside awareness. The analyst might focus on every minute "infraction" as "meaningful" and interpret it in a subtly blaming tone. The patient might find endless "legitimate" reasons for breaking the frame.

It is possible for the frame, itself, to become a mutual obsession. For example, one patient I have heard about in supervision stages unrelenting protests and work stoppages over aspects of the frame. I believe that this is one way she is expressing some of her lifelong disappointments. But it takes two to tango. Her analyst plays a role in the obsessive style of life they have cocreated. By being unwilling or unable to directly deal with (her own and the patient's) aggression, the analyst is helping to forge their obsessive style. Together, they procrastinate about addressing frame issues and use words to cover over intense angry feelings. Together they cocreate an obsessive atmosphere, with constant competitive power struggles and an unremitting, vague sense of dissatisfaction in the air. Reaction formation and undoing characterize their brief interludes between battles.

My point is that this way of living within the frame could not be entirely the product of just one of them. If both didn't play a role in cocreating an obsessive lifestyle, the ambience would have a different feel.

I have no crystal ball, but I would expect that over the course of the treatment, the thin veil covering their mutual anger will disintegrate. This may, or may not, lead to an abrupt termination. I am hopeful that their sense of the treatment's purpose, primarily to help the patient lead a more satisfying life, and their appreciation of many qualities in each other will be enough to sustain the relationship.

With one of my own patients, adhering to the frame has become a kind of mutually constructed performance art. This is a subtler obsessive lifestyle, in that it is not rife with overt power struggles. The frame is obeyed religiously. I am reminded of Sartre's (1956) concept of "bad faith," illustrated by a waiter pretending to be a waiter. Similarly, my patient and I are an analytic couple pretending to be an analytic couple. We impress each other with exaggerated shows of compliance with the rules. We are exactly on time. Payment of the fee has the regularity of clockwork. I have found it difficult to make good analytic use of my (admittedly partial) understanding of our lifestyle. But I feel certain that our perfectionism avoids strong feelings of some kind. I hope this will become clearer in time. Once again, my point is that my patient could not create an obsessively perfectionistic style of living within the analytic frame on her own. In ways that are not always apparent to me, I play a role in it. Like any two people in a long-term relationship, we have implicit knowledge of each other. We respond to each other according to unwritten rules. As I understand it, part of the treatment's goal is for us to attain greater consciousness of these rules and how and why they have been cocreated. Seeing my role in this construction has the potential to bring me pain that varies in intensity, depending, in part, on how much these qualities represent deeply shameful aspects of the human condition, from my perspective. Is obsessive doubting or an obsessive quest for interpersonal control anathema to me? Does it make me feel particularly unworthy? If so, interchanges that bring out this potential in me may significantly affect my sense of self.

GIVING UP AND HOLDING ON

Elsewhere, I have discussed the nature of hope and its role in treatment (Buechler, 2004, chap. 2). Here I ask how it affects the clinician to try to maintain hopefulness, particularly when an obsessive atmosphere has been cocreated in the treatment. Briefly, here are some of the ways I have previously understood the role of hope in treatment:

1. For both participants hope can be active and not just a passive cognitive expectation that things will improve. It can be a powerful motivating force. As an emotion hope can inspire an effort to change rather than an attitude of waiting for change to happen.
2. In treatment hope can require the willing suspension of disbelief. Continuing to believe the treatment will be beneficial sometimes requires us to look past a current absence of improvement. Maintaining hope can depend on an ability to accept that some human processes work in mysterious ways that require faith.
3. False hope or "hope for the wrong thing" can impede real hopefulness. "Hope for the wrong thing" means hoping for something magical, like continuous narcissistic gratification.
4. Hope can be a gift one person gives another. For example, in treatment maintaining hope can be a kind of tribute the participants pay each other.

Nothing else in treatment is as contradictory and paradoxical as hope. A middle-aged "veteran" of decades of warfare with her irritatingly obsessive husband finally seems ready to give up her (I would say unrealistic) hope that he will change. It seems to both her and me that giving up this "hope for the wrong thing" is a prerequisite for her to create a decent life for herself.

She and I have (cognitively) understood this for quite some time. Yet, mysteriously, she seems unable to grasp it emotionally. Each time she encounters his stubborn rigidity, she is outraged as though she were discovering it for the first time. What would it take for her to genuinely realize whom she married?

What is most relevant to this chapter is my experience of being part of this patient's slow evolution toward realistic hoping. How have I maintained my own hopefulness about the treatment and at what price?

In some senses this husband and wife are not unusual. The wife has the edge when it comes to expressing affect, but the husband is more adept in an argument. They each need to prove they are right, all the time. My patient feels that if her husband could sometimes say he was wrong, she could feel she has gotten through to him. That would be enough for her. Time after time, she polishes her ammunition against him in our sessions. I am expected to wholly agree with her and, perhaps, add a few rounds to her ammunition stockpile.

Here are some of the phases of my own countertransference:

1. For a long while I waited for her to stop complaining about him. It felt as though we were in a kind of pretreatment antechamber. I wanted to get through this phase, and get to the "real" treatment, where my patient would be the main character in her own life story. So in this early phase, I hoped she saw me as enough of an ally to stay with me so we could eventually get to the "real" treatment.
2. At some point I realized that this *was* the real treatment. I had to stop hoping this "phase" would be over.
3. To maintain hopefulness about our work, I had to accept the possibility that we would never move "beyond" discovering her husband's limitations. This treatment is filled with parallels and paradoxes. The patient and I both have to bear whatever severely limited functioning means to each of us. Paradoxically, for the patient in her marriage and for me, in the treatment hope arises from giving up waiting for someone's limitations to disappear. The patient has to stop waiting for her husband to give up his obsessive defenses, and I have to stop waiting for her to focus on herself.
4. Maintaining hope for our work also requires of me that I bear the (internalized) criticism of my analytic forebears. I feel many of my teachers (in my language, my "internal chorus"; Buechler, 2004, 2008) would be highly critical of my treatment of this patient. I can almost hear them telling me that I shouldn't gratify this patient's wish for us to analyze her husband's character flaws. I feel sandwiched between my supervisors' and my patient's requirements.
5. To me this means I have to bear feeling alone and, sometimes, lonely. No one else understands my point of view. Perhaps no one ever will.

PARANOID PARTNERSHIPS AND
THEIR EFFECTS ON THE ANALYST

When a paranoid environment is coconstructed, hope feels dangerous. As I have already suggested, I think analysts and patients create schizoid, paranoid, narcissistic, and other textures. In a coconstructed paranoid frame of mind, hope is an enemy. A patient adamantly insists on maintaining her vigilance against hopefulness about her husband's career. If I cite reasons to be hopeful, she responds as though I were a dangerous temptress. In hope, she might relax her vigil. My optimism shows I am a sucker and a danger to her.

Elsewhere, I have characterized paranoia as on a continuum with the capacity to bear being surprised (Buechler, 2004). Paranoia is a search for more certainty about the future than we mortals can have.

The paranoid atmosphere in this treatment results from a cocreated striving for greater certainty than is possible. My patient wants to be sure she doesn't get disappointed by expecting her husband to succeed where he fails. Not unlike her, I am trying too hard to "confront" the "truth" about his potential.

Another way to say this is that in a paranoid world, hoping seems to require knowing the score in advance. The patient feels if she "knows" her husband won't succeed, she is safe from disappointment. But I am also relying on "knowing the score." I label her "defensive," just as she labels her husband a "loser." Each of us is reaching for certainty about another person by putting him or her in a neat box.

I hope I can see this parallel and give voice to it. I may be able to break through our mutual paranoid, stultifying, pigeonholing tendencies. But I think no matter how well I do this, I will still be the person who holds the hope for us both. I will be the one who is trying to climb outside the box.

Personally, this elicits some anxiety in me. First of all, there are so many ways for me to be wrong. What if her husband really fails in some catastrophic way? She will feel that I have helped dupe her. I coaxed her into submitting to hope. What is worse is that, for a host of reasons, I may not be sufficiently able to disagree. It won't be the first time I am accused of seducing someone to hope. The accusation is uncomfortably familiar. Furthermore, no matter what happens she may envy my hopefulness. I may be told (not for the first time) that my optimism means I (unfairly) have benefited from a better upbringing than most.

Being hopeful and yet cocreating a paranoid climate may seem contradictory. Yet I feel I have inhabited this territory many times. How has it affected me, to be the keeper of the flame in a dangerous world? For one thing, it feels unaccountably anxiety producing. There is likely to be a villain by the end of the story, and I am likely to be "it."

In addition to being the bad guy, I am the "fool," the naive child who hopes, when a sensible adult would be wary. Given that I have this tendency, how dare I occupy the position of a mental health professional?

Uncomfortable with being accused (again!) of leading people astray, I am likely to fall into my own version of paranoia. I will try (too hard) to know what I am doing.

So why don't I just embrace a safer, more neutral stance? How *could I* know whether her husband will succeed or fail? Why shouldn't I register willingness to wait, with my patient, and help her deal with the outcome, no matter what it is? And, on another level, why can't I steer a more neutral course for the treatment itself, accepting that it, too, may succeed or fail? Why must I be so damn hopeful?

These are good questions, in my opinion. In that my own character issues play out in my countertransference, my dilemmas are my own and not necessarily representative of other clinicians' experiences. Yet I think therapists are often the ones who live in hope, before their patients can inhabit it. When one of my patients had to go through yet another serious operation, for yet another life-threatening illness, I think my hopefulness served a purpose. When another had yet another bout of depression, I feel that my ongoing belief in our work meant something to him.

Being the one who has hope makes me feel both grandiose and humble. I think the grandiosity stems from a sense that hoping for someone else is a high calling. But the humility comes from knowing what may happen in the future. I will have to brace, as I am accused of wasting the patient's time, money, and effort, in foolhardy emotional ventures.

I wonder how much my gender affects what it is like for me to be accused of being too hopeful. Sometimes I feel doubly condemned. I know I will be seen as not only a cockeyed optimist but also a superficial, empty-headed, scatterbrained woman. I think that in a paranoid climate, hope is always derided. But my gender may play some role in how my patient and I experience my attitudes. Hope has often been portrayed as a dangerously and foolishly seductive woman. I have explored this at greater length elsewhere (Buechler, 2004), but here I will just mention one example. In an adaptation of the play *Antigone*, Anouilh (1951) had a character proclaim,

> We are of the tribe that asks questions, and we ask them to the bitter end—until no tiniest chance of hope remains to be strangled by our hands. We are the tribe that hates your filthy hope, your docile, female hope; hope, your whore. (p. 43)

In a sense, in a paranoid atmosphere, when I hold out hope I become the seductive whore. Or, as another patient has labeled me, I am the "doctor of adaptation." I am the preacher exhorting my flock to have faith and trust that things will work out in the end. I am a danger, in that I tempt people to relax their vigilance. I would suggest that, paradoxically, a paranoid way of coping with the human condition partially stems from desperately wanting to live in a world where total trust is possible. Suspiciousness seems vital when someone is constantly battling an urge to give way to absolute trust. By asking for my patients' trust, I bring this urge to the fore and tempt them to indulge it.

In a more general sense, I am a danger in that I tempt people toward riskier living. I feel that this stance is implicit in my role, regardless of my analytic orientation. The classical Freudian analyst "asks" the patient to dare to face what has been defended against. Making the unconscious conscious is like conquering new territory. Each of us has a personal "Wild West" to explore and, ultimately, to consider as a potential home. The behaviorist, the cognitive therapist, and the Jungian all invite abandoning defensive strategies. Clinicians hold out hope that what has been renounced for the sake of safety can be reclaimed. I think we cannot do otherwise.

A patient who has immersed herself in professional activities, partly to avoid more frightening social contacts, comes into treatment with me. She expects me to vote in favor of change. Privately, *I* may characterize my effort as an attempt to help her have more choices. I tell myself that I am not advocating that she live a more social life, but I am merely following her lead and helping her feel *able* to socialize. Just how she chooses to live is, after all, her business. But helping her have a greater capacity for coping with life is mine.

To me that sounds fine, but in practice it is extremely difficult to differentiate helping her be *able* to socialize from advocating a *shift* toward being more social. No matter how "neutral" I might try to be, the patient will see me as holding out hope that she can enter social situations with less anticipatory terror, actually enjoy them, and emerge unscathed. But this is not just her projection of her own desires onto me. I am a willing participant in this division of labor. For now, I do hold most of our hope that she can become freer socially. This sometimes leaves me with my heart in my mouth, so to speak. What if her latest experiment in socializing backfires?

What is it like for me to spend so much of my day with my heart in my mouth? When my patient and I have cocreated a paranoid atmosphere, I think I am looking for a hiding place for myself, at the same time as I am encouraging her to hide less. In our session she runs through her budding social calendar. She mentions some of her fears of feeling overwhelmed, unable to meet obligations, ashamed of her limited conversational skills, and exposed to criticism. Am *I* being paranoid when I worry she will blame me for anything that goes wrong? My own need for a safe hiding place takes the form of inwardly searching for "theoretical" backing for my stance. I consult the "internal chorus" of supervisory inner objects I have written about elsewhere (Buechler, 2004, 2008).

My inner Sullivan tells me I have promoted her healthy capacity for learning from new experience. My inner Fromm assures me that I have facilitated her greater freedom. But even with the backing of these wise elders, I remain uneasy. Have I really been a "whore," selling the easy virtue of hope? Hiding behind a theory is harder today than it used to be. As happened at the end of the story of *The Wonderful Wizard of Oz* (Baum, 1900), someone is likely to look behind the curtain and see that the "wizard" is no wizard at all. Ultimately no theory fully protects me from the (self-) accusation and the patient's accusation that I have acted out my own need for hope in how I have responded to her. For example, she tells me she is afraid to go to a holiday party at work. What if the colleague who hates her is there? What if he tries to talk? What if he doesn't?

A theory tells me that my patient is projecting her own dislike of her colleague and then feeling endangered by him (Sullivan, 1956, chap. 7). The word *projection* flashed across my mind as I listened to her. At the same moment I formulated a response. I said something like, "Why are you afraid?" The patient (correctly) hears that my question makes several assumptions:

1. She could be unafraid, in my view. I am implying that this would be preferable.
2. I must have some hope she will become less afraid, because I am choosing to focus on that aspect of the material. I could have said nothing, or reflected back that parties at work are stressful for her, or commented on something else.
3. Her fear is proper subject matter for the treatment.

Even asking this question can position me as the temptress, inviting the patient to hope. In a paranoid atmosphere, there are countless dangers. Experienced clinicians know that eliciting too much of a sense of danger can cost the treatment, because the overly anxious patient may abruptly quit. In paranoid territory the "good" or "good enough" can suddenly turn "bad." In a flash the patient can "realize" his supposed friend is "really" an enemy. Appearances deceive. That damn analyst may seem well intentioned, but she spells trouble!

I am aware that each clinician would have a personal response to being in this situation. I mention some aspects of the feelings it elicits in me to facilitate the reader's self-reflection. What does trying to survive in paranoid territory bring out in you?

For me, probably the greatest challenge is to bear the frustration I feel when someone externalizes responsibility. I can feel impelled to "prove" that an internal locus of control is better than an external locus. I want to "show" that experiencing the quality of one's life as externally imposed truncates hope. How can we have hope if we merely receive, rather than create, our lives? What impact can treatment have, without the assumption that, to a significant degree, each of us authors the meaning we give our life experience? The impulse to fight against an externalizing attitude has often gotten me into conflicts.

Part of what this recruits in me is the feeling I am being set up to fail. How can treatment succeed, if everything is the patient's husband's fault, or mother's fault, or teacher's fault? How can a patient of mine who is single see her own issues if the only problem is that there are no good men out there? I feel set up to fail because even though I am being prevented from having impact, I will be held responsible if things don't change for the better. I am fended off (sometimes by the patient's unrelenting barrage of words) but still held accountable for progress. The treatment is static, and I feel stalemated. This can engender my own version of paranoia. I want to show that I have acted in good faith, to prove my innocence and therapeutic intentions. This can be very problematic. Like the patient, I see my difficulties as originating outside me. Both of us are externalizing responsibility. In effect I am saying to the patient, "You are making it impossible for me to do my job well. Don't blame me!" My paranoia will make it hard for me to provide the contrast I believe the treatment needs. Elsewhere, I have expressed my belief that providing a contrast to the patient's essential ways of operating is crucial, so we can clarify the patient's unformulated operating procedures (Buechler, 2004, 2008). I can't contrast with the patient's paranoid style if I respond with a paranoid attitude of my own.

Of course because I believe paranoia is cocreated, there will always be contributions, by both participants, to a paranoid tenor in treatment. But to the extent we can withstand the pressures I am describing, we still have some chance to provide sufficient contrast.

I have to try to hold my theories about the patient lightly, in the face of the patient's longing for an airtight theory that explains everything. A patient insists on my giving her an "explanation" of her family's ill treatment of her. She must know what I think of their latest outrages. Otherwise she can't go on. I could so easily fall into labeling her, just as she wants me to label her family members. But, once again, that would not allow me to contrast enough to help her recognize her way of operating.

Fundamentally, despite the part I play in creating a paranoid atmosphere, I have to have a separate enough stance to embody hope for the patient and the treatment (and for myself as a clinician and person). This "hope, anyway" maintains basic faith in the work, regardless of how things look at the moment. This hope, although steadfast, must not feel like blind hope. For example, the single patient (who sees the paucity of good men as the problem) needs a clinician who believes that even though presently she creates stalemates, her life can work out well in the future. My hope for her must be based on genuinely positive aspects of her functioning. It has to reflect knowledge of her, and not just blind optimism about life.

If I truly trust that her interpersonal strengths are sufficient to forge a decent relationship, my hope may be contagious.

Elsewhere, I have described the continuum between intense curiosity, on one side, and paranoia, on the other (Buechler, 2004, chap. 1). As I suggested, I see paranoia as an effort to deal with the human condition by insisting on absolute certainty in areas of life where certainty is impossible. So the ultimate (and psychotic) version of paranoia is something like, "Now I understand everything that I have felt, and everything that has happened to me. It is because I am Jesus Christ."

To recap, what would a cocreated paranoid style of coping with the analytic frame look like? First of all, the participants would be aiming for more certainty about something than is possible. Absolute certainty is never available about one's own motives or the motives of another person. Why did I work so hard to understand something about my patient's history last Thursday and not last month? Why did I smile today when I first saw her in the waiting room? Why didn't I remember anything about the dream she told me in our last session? Why did she forget that our sessions on Mondays are scheduled to start 15 minutes earlier than our sessions on Tuesdays?

A paranoid lifestyle looks at what must "really" be going on beneath the surface. Paranoia assumes there is a cover-up. So, living the analytic relationship in a paranoid way would incline both participants to develop a Sherlock Holmes approach to understanding each other's motives and behavior. A patient frequently asks me why I was more involved with her last week than I am today or why I am (or am not) leaning forward in my chair.

In this situation, I would say that my part in cocreating our paranoid world is complicated. Unlike in the previous examples of obsessive living styles, in this paranoid situation my behavior is not parallel to hers, but it facilitates hers. That is, I tend to tell her less than usual about what I am feeling. By being less transparent than I usually am, I make it easier for her to be paranoid. This interaction is mutually constructed in that I feel so minutely observed by her, my every movement so thoroughly examined, that I feel like hiding, even though I know (rationally) that this will not be of help to either of us.

I am calling this a mutually constructed paranoid style of coping with the frame of the relationship and not just a paranoid transference–countertransference, although it could certainly be characterized that way too. But I think paranoia especially describes the issues about the frame, in that the patient appeals to my sense of our obligations to each other. Implicitly she says, "You owe me your fullest attention, honesty, and full disclosure about your motives toward me. It is in our contract." I could question where that is written, but I am sure that she would then get suspicious about my *real* reasons for this question. There would be nothing wrong with having this interaction, in my view. I think it is likely to lead to another iteration of the paranoid interchange.

There are paranoid lifestyles that play out in a more symmetrical way, where each participant is suspicious of the "real" motives of the other. In fact, I think that analytic training often promotes this way of being. I once described some treatments as like "high noon" confrontations, each participant armed with an airtight theory about the other (Buechler, 2004). Like paranoid patients, analysts, too, look under the surface for the "real" motives of the other person. We, too, are well versed in explanations for what is "really" going on. Our theories also reduce uncertainty and its attendant (possible) anxiety. I think it is not uncommon for both participants in treatment to play out paranoid styles of living. Not able to bear some uncertainty about why the other person lived out our contract differently on one day than on another, we attempt a version of nailing down Jell-O. What is particular to this style of living is suspicion about the motives of the other person and an overreliance on a theory to explain it completely. Generally, paranoia poisons the atmosphere. The fundamental trust that is so vital to treatment never develops or is lost. I think it is essential that both people in treatment believe that the other is trying, to the best of their ability. Without that trust, we can become fixated on nothing other than proving our theory of what is going on. No genuine, open-minded curiosity can flourish. Treatment needs curiosity. Wondering what would happen if we connected two previously unattached thoughts is essential to the work. Just as a child throws a ball in the air, merely for the sake of seeing what happens, in treatment we need to feel free to turn ideas on their heads, to scramble sentences, to go wherever our minds and hearts rove. This spirit can't exist in a paranoid world. But, of course, when analyst and patient create a paranoid atmosphere, it is vital to do all we can to explore the meaning of it rather than try to overcome it. But if our own sense of being "good" is predicated on trusting others and being curious and open to news about ourselves, we are likely to suffer when our paranoid potential is brought out, and we may give in to the impulse to try to overcome rather than explore the meaning of this dynamic.

NARCISSISTIC INTERPLAYS

So far I have looked at how the treatment frame can be lived as a set of rules engendering power struggles (by obsessive analytic couples) and the frame as hiding the truth (when the interaction has a paranoid sensibility), and I have explored how these interactions can affect the analyst's sense of self. The next situation I discuss is when the frame is experienced as a set of potential insults. Although it is true that, more often, initially the patient is more likely to see the frame this way, once again, it takes two to tango. Both participants play a role in the meaning of the frame becoming a potential assault on someone's sense of self. Eventually, if not at first, the analyst's pride, as well as the patient's, comes to be at issue.

In a supervisory session I hear about a patient who experiences the very existence of the frame as a direct attack on her worth. If all she can be is a patient, she has been judged as inferior, lacking any value as a human being. Every aspect of the frame, from the fee, to the schedule, to the seating arrangements, to the location in an office, is like a slap in the face.

At first glance this looks like a situation where it is the patient cooking up narcissistic issues all by herself. The only contribution the analyst seems to be making is his introduction of the frame, which it is necessary for him to do. But a closer look reveals how the issues are cocreated.

I am reminded of one of life's ironies. I have found that often when we try to avoid being like our parents, our behavior may take a shape diametrically opposite from theirs *but still on the same dimension.* The daughter of extremely frugal parents may be a spendthrift, but money is still central in her life. The son of messy parents may be obsessively neat, but order is still an issue.

Similarly, in trying very hard to avoid wounding the narcissistically vulnerable patient I hear about in supervision, her analyst's overly wordy, defensive explanations highlight the frame's potential to injure. This is (at least on a conscious level) inadvertent. He is trying to spare her from shame.

How does the analyst's pride get involved? In this case, at least, the patient takes her unwillingness to adhere to the frame to such heights that it challenges the legitimacy of his role. By prioritizing almost any activity ahead of attending sessions, she effectively communicates her analyst's (apparent) lack of worth. His sense of himself as able to function as a professional can become shaky when this behavior persists. I'll bet most of us have seen how a vicious circle can result from such an interaction. Under constant pressure to make exceptions to the frame, the analyst becomes increasingly insistent on adherence to it, where, previously, he was willing to bend over backward to accommodate the patient. As the analyst becomes stricter, the patient objects more strenuously, and as the novelist Kurt Vonnegut used to say, so it goes.

Elsewhere, I have written about becoming what I call a "fool for love" when treating a narcissistically vulnerable patient (Buechler, 2004, 2008). That is, I think it is especially important for analysts to pay attention to shifts in their own self-esteem in these treatments. Becoming a fool for love means, to me, being willing to prioritize the health of the treatment and, more generally, life itself over our pride. I think we have to be willing to choose risking looking foolish for the sake of getting to valuable insights. Admitting we broke aspects of the frame, in a sense, in being inattentive is a frequent example. If my mind wanders in a session, do I try to let the moment pass unnoticed, thereby sparing possible shame for myself but, perhaps, losing an important thread? Becoming a "fool for love" would mean, to me, highlighting my inattention rather than trying to hide it. This openly prioritizes the treatment over pride. It shows a willingness to "go first" in taking interpersonal risks. It says (implicitly) that moments of shame pass and are bearable. Potentially it breaks the cycle whereby both participants are (often subtly and surreptitiously) protecting their own pride at the expense of the other.

When either or both participants treat the frame as a measure of their worth, it becomes an opportunity to work on narcissistic vulnerabilities in each of them. In these situations the frame is truly a microcosm of much of the rest of life, where every limit can be seen as a threat to one's sense of self. I think seeing our own narcissism is especially likely to challenge our feeling of being "good" enough or "good-me." So many of us went into a field that promised we would feel we are helping others and generously giving our time and effort to enrich their lives. Seeing our own narcissism is often quite unwelcome news. I have found it extremely difficult to address when I am supervising candidates, as well as when I am thinking about my own clinical work.

SHAMEFUL SKIRMISHES AT THE BORDER OF SELF AND OTHER

Borderline dynamics are notorious for creating difficulties with the frame, for both participants. In these situations I would say that the frame becomes a constant testing site. Who is subject, who is object, who is aggressor, who is victim, who is sadist, who is masochist? In borderline situations both participants play roles in making it hard to discern who does what to whom. Perhaps more clearly than in any other situation, both contribute. And, even more often than usual, each participant's identity feels like it is up for grabs.

Another way I think of these interactions is that they can resemble the game of musical chairs, where, when the music stops, the winners are ensconced in their places, and the loser is left standing.

Borderline jockeying is frequently played out around concrete aspects of the frame of the treatment. From the analyst's point of view, it becomes impossible to set up a schedule and stick to it. There is always a reason that this week is an exception. Something is always happening in "borderland." Chaos threatens. Things are almost out of control. Babysitters fail to show up, someone misses the train, illnesses appear last minute, or session times are misremembered. Something is always going wrong. The question of whether anyone is at fault and, if so, who it is, is in the air. The patient couldn't make a session, so a makeup was scheduled, which each thought was arranged for a different hour, so someone didn't show. Whose fault is it? Should the patient be charged?

For the clinician, the part he or she plays in these interactions can feel all too defining. The patient "just can't make it today." The analyst often feels threatened by the possibility the patient will get discouraged and quit treatment. So the analyst agrees to an unusual time, or a phone session, or a waiver of the fee, or some other variation. The two participants collaborate in muddying the frame. This continues, until exceptions become the rule. Pretty soon it is hard for both to remember what the frame was originally like.

Treatment is a perfect microcosm for borderline issues. It encapsulates questions about responsibility. I think of the borderline as the place where, in Kleinian terms, paranoid/schizoid and depressive dynamics meet. In other words, there is ongoing uncertainty about who the "bad" guy is. Who did what to whom? Where is the border between your responsibility and mine? The frame gives an analytic couple a perfect place to play out their potential for involvement in borderline issues. Although these enactments can resemble "narcissistic" interactions (see above), borderline interchanges have more of a "splitting," good guy–bad guy flavor.

A middle-aged female patient frequently telephones her analyst in between sessions. She starts with an apology for bothering him. She hopes she isn't being too much trouble. She offers to pay him for the moments it takes to listen to her call. As her analyst describes the situation to me, he confesses that with this patient, he often feels like a "heel." This interaction has just gotten off the ground, and it is already unclear to him who is victimizing and who is victim. These are the earmarks of "borderland," a place where high noon encounters between the good and the bad are cocreated.

And here is where things can quickly get unbearably complicated. Some patients actually *make us into* the people they most fear we will become. This patient, for example, probably most fears her analyst will become resentful of her unwanted presence on his telephone answering machine. As he *actually* becomes more resentful, he feels accused of being resentful by her but also by himself. He feels a greater and greater desire to avoid this patient as much as possible, dreading her sessions and telephone messages. Thus he *becomes* the withholding person she (eventually more openly) accuses him of being. She has succeeded in making her worst nightmare come true. She is dependent on a person who wants to get rid of her. Needless to say, this isn't the first time this has happened in her life.

How were these issues cocreated? The analyst must be capable of becoming withholding. But the analyst is implicated in this interaction in more ways than one. For a borderline flavor to be cocreated, the analyst has to have at least a potential Achilles' heel about the issue of who is to blame.

Another aspect of a borderline atmosphere is its emotional intensity. The air is often electric with tension. Some of us feel charged up, in a positive sense, in such situations, but, for many, it is hard to bear. I think it may be most difficult for us if we expect ourselves not to dread being with our patients. Especially early in a clinician's career, living at the "borders" is challenging because it is relatively new territory. It is literally new, in that we have not yet therapeutically dealt with some of the issues. But, more important, it is also new in that it acquaints us with alien aspects of ourselves. Once again we become more acquainted with our own "bad-me" or even "not-me" in Sullivan's (1953) terms. Borderline frames are cocreated by two people, each of whom feels the other is bringing out his or her worst qualities.

The frame can be the place where analyst and patient severely test each other. How much trouble will each take from the other? When is enough too much? It can often feel to the clinician like dealing with an acting-out teenager. Where is the point where a line *has* to be drawn? The responsibilities inherent in the frame make it an ideal microcosm for borderline dynamics. For analyst and patient, the frame can easily occasion questions about where the fault lies.

It is often possible to use oedipal terms to describe the microcosm of unsatisfied human longings that the treatment frame creates. In fact, we can see *each* of the cocreated atmospheres as styles of coping with this universal dilemma. Obsessive, paranoid, narcissistic, borderline, and other behaviors are attempts to find a relational pattern that helps us bear what we can't have. Whether we use power struggles, exaggerated assertions of certainty, overly entitled claims, or intense blame games, we are compelling each other to play out one (or more) of the ways people try to live within the limits of the human condition. And when patients bring out our borderline tendencies, we are extremely likely to feel "off our game," at our own personal worst, ashamed, and anxious that colleagues will hear of our personal and professional shortcomings.

TREATMENT AS A MICROCOSM OF SCHIZOID RELATING

In some senses the treatment relationship can be extremely intimate. Depending on the style of the work, it can allow two people to explore their own and each other's minds and hearts. But there are also inherent limitations. Some "projects," such as the bearing of children together, are, of course, not viable. Sexual and most other forms of physical contact are not acceptable. The ambiance cocreated by the pair may allow for greater or lesser self-disclosure on the part of the analyst. The time frame, the financial element, the location, and so many less tangible aspects differentiate treatment from other intimate relationships. How does this affect its capacity to function as a microcosm of the rest of life?

I would suggest the limited intimacy in treatment suits it perfectly to serve as a microcosm of schizoid issues. As with the other styles (such as obsessive, paranoid, narcissistic, and borderline) described previously, I am referring to both intrapersonal and interpersonal schizoid qualities of relating. I am using the word *schizoid* in Guntrip's (1969) sense. The treatment relationship *is*, in some senses, fundamentally a schizoid relationship. The characteristics of schizoid functioning that have been emphasized include

1. an "in and out" pattern of interpersonal relating (Bromberg, 1979; Guntrip, 1969) (Schizoid coping can take the form of intermittent relating. People form relationships that are intimate, but because of geographic distance or other reality factors, contact is periodic.),
2. pleasure in self-reliance (Impert, 1999),
3. "need-fear" dilemma (Guntrip, 1969),
4. pervasive underlying fear that one's love is potentially dangerous to others, and
5. muted affect.

Treatment can be seen as the quintessential microcosm of schizoid relating. The time spent together has predetermined end points, limited duration, and periodicity. Thus the schizoid's preference for going "in and out" of relatedness is mandated in treatment! Other aspects of the schizoid style of functioning, such as self-reliance, can also help both patient and analyst adapt well to treatment's regimen.

How does this similarity between the schizoid character style and treatment's mandate affect the participants emotionally? It seems likely, at least to me, that some of the feelings of emotional deprivation that others consciously feel in treatment will not be as intense for schizoid participants (unless their character styles significantly change). So, at least at first, the participants will be spared the most profound feelings of disappointment, rage, and unsatisfied fantasies I have discussed in the preceding sections. I think this makes treatment a comfortable medium for the intimacy style of the person with strong schizoid proclivities. Schizoid analysts and schizoid patients will feel, in more than one sense, right at home.

But, as is frequently the case in life, this positive fit is also a potential drawback. I think it is very easy for schizoid patients and analysts to get stuck in a never-ending, only moderately productive treatment relationship. The interpersonal balance of emotions leads to a kind of stasis. No disruptive feeling reaches enough intensity to upend the relationship. The participants are not angry enough or afraid enough to completely withdraw, and they are not curious, eager, and comfortable enough to fully connect. Treatment can become a kind of "womb-tomb" for *both* people.

In one treatment I have discussed elsewhere (Buechler, 2002a), I found myself in what I would call a schizoid dilemma. Briefly, the patient was a high-functioning eldest son, whose father expected him to provide financial security for his two younger, adult siblings. The patient was going along with this request and, in my judgment, defensively consciously unaware of the resentment, hurt, and anxiety it evoked. As is often true, my patient had always seemed so self-reliant that his parents could conveniently forget he might have needs of his own. Their ability and willingness to take him for granted hurt him deeply, but it was part of his role to ignore, dissociate from, selectively inattend to any evidence of the pain.

But then I entered the situation, with my own schizoid proclivities and balance of emotions. Perhaps mainly because of my identification with my own training analyst's nonschizoid character style, I was aware of the pull ("in" myself) to silently "go along" with the patient, who was "going along" with his father's request. That is, I was aware that the patient (consciously) wanted me to accept his compliance with his father as a *fait accompli*. I wasn't to question this or react as though it had significance.

Looking at the situation now, I would suggest the following:

1. This treatment easily served as a microcosm, in particular, for the patient's overall interpersonal style, though in some ways for mine, too. This brought us both a sense of familiarity and relative ease with each other.
2. But nonschizoid aspects of my own functioning eventually made our smooth glide through sessions unsatisfactory to me. Partially out of identification with my own analyst, I felt a strong need to disrupt our schizoid, complacent, seemingly imperturbable calm.
3. In terms of the balance of our emotions, I think my escalating turbulence was anxiety producing for him. As his anxiety increased, I felt more and more avoided by him, which increased my own loneliness. However, as I described in my 2002a article, "Fortunately, I was also angry. How dare this patient's father be so unconcerned for his son! How dare this patient expect me to quietly go along, like a good little girl!" (pp. 492–493).

So, previously, I had proven myself to be schizoid enough for the patient to get into a familiar style of relating with me. But when he tried to deal with his father's request in his characteristic schizoid way, I had a relatively nonschizoid, emotionally intense, angry reaction. With my feelings tipping toward anger and loneliness, his took a more anxious turn. From that point onward, I think we were involved in a very delicate, mutual, emotional balance with a life of its own. Increases in his anxiety and distancing triggered my escalating loneliness. But I was also angry, at least partially on behalf of this too-stalwart son. He responded to my increasingly vocal anger with more anxiety, and so on. I could say that the two of us were similar enough, in both having some schizoid tendencies, to relate well to each other. But I had enough other qualities to be willing (and able) to disrupt our cocoon. From an emotional standpoint, feelings we triggered in each other pierced the calm, and calming, surface.

One of the most elusive issues in treatment is the question of what makes a good "match" between clinician and patient. (For an extensive discussion of this subject, see Kantrowitz [1996].) I am suggesting looking at the participants' characteristic interpersonal styles of relating and the ways they affect each other's emotional balance.

Was the match between this patient and me a good one? It is years since he left treatment, and I do feel he benefited from it. But I don't know if someone with a different character style and emotional balance would have done him more good. I can only imagine that a less schizoid analyst would have "upset the apple cart" earlier. Or, said another way, a less schizoid analyst probably would have had less emotional stasis in the early phases of the treatment. Whereas it took this incident, about the patient's father's unthinking request, to disturb my equilibrium, I imagine many other analysts would have been angered by something or felt some other disruptively intense feelings earlier in the work. But once my own loneliness and anger were aroused, our emotional détente was over. Perhaps all this made us a very good fit, in that neither of us was made uncomfortable enough by the other to prevent the work from proceeding to the point I describe. But I think it was a slow start. In retrospect, I think our emotional balance and mutual schizoid tendencies brought us too easily in tune with each other.

In sum, I think schizoid coping styles in both participants make for a safe match in the short run but not necessarily a good one in the long run. The treatment is, in a way, too good a microcosm of both their lives. If they are lucky enough that something disruptive to their mutually coconstructed emotional balance occurs early on, the treatment may be very productive. But years can go by, with little happening, before this point. And if the disruption never occurs, two ships may pass each other in the night, so to speak, stay on their original course, and glide on. Personally, when I recognize this has been happening between a patient and me, I am likely to feel a potent brew of shame, anxiety, guilt, and regret. Time is so precious. Wasting it is so painful to me. Probably more than any other style, a cocreated schizoid pattern brings out my personal "not-me and bad-me" feelings. But each of these cocreated styles, from obsessive to paranoid, narcissistic, borderline, and schizoid, has the potential to elicit, in the analyst, a profound sense of professional and personal inadequacy.

Chapter 7

Bearing Isolation and Sorrow
Chronic Mourning in Clinicians

It is 10 minutes before the final session of a long analysis. Everything looks pretty much as usual. My chair sits in its place. The couch is crowned by its pillow, covered by a clean paper towel that demonstrates my attention to hygiene. I stare at a blank piece of paper. This is the last time that my patient and I will ever meet. Should I take notes? Generally I take at least a full page of notes, during every session, so I can at least glance at them before the beginning of the next time. But now there will be no next time.

I ask myself my favorite questions: What is the goal? What good can this session do? Is it enough to aim just to get through it? Given how I am feeling, perhaps it is.

What, exactly, am I feeling? Well, I know I feel sad about never seeing her again. But it is a sadness abbreviated by a sense of unreality. How can it really be true that we will never see each other again? Given where we have gone together, that is absurd. I almost wrote that it seems absurd. But, actually, it doesn't just *seem* absurd. It really *is* absurd.

If we were getting a divorce there would, at least, be some contact through the unpleasant proceedings. But a treatment termination severs differently. No property to split up, no silverware to fight over, no custody arrangements. It might be very useful to have something to fight about. A little anger would feel so good right now. Bracing. Relieving. Like a cold beer on a very hot day.

These thoughts won't help me. Let me get back to the only question that is important right now: What is the goal of this session?

I can't accept that the goal is merely to slide through it. That feels so anticlimactic, so empty. Unworthy of the work we have done up until now.

As I begin to focus on goals, I can think about the bind I am in. I want her to know how much she means to me. But I don't want her to take care of me. I don't want her to feel she has to stay put, to pay a debt. I don't want her to be distracted from herself. I want her to have all that this moment can give her. A clean break. Some of the joy of a graduation. A feeling of accomplishment, for all the years of hard work. We made it.

But did we? Is it really the right time to stop? Are we (still) avoiding something? Or is that question, itself, selfish? Is it a way of holding on to her, for my own sake?

I try to imagine what will happen in the last few moments. Will we shake hands, like politicians after a debate? A hug would take a stand that this is final. It would be such a break with our traditions. We have never touched. With a hug we are not "us" anymore. We are just two women now. Two women who knew each other, once, for a while. A hug seems to bring us closer but, in a way, proclaims us separate from now on.

Am I really thinking of what is best for *her*? Can I know anything about that? Who is this "clean break" really for?

Maybe it really *is* for her. I have heard about so many botched terminations and the wounds they can leave, like stitches ripped out instead of carefully attended to. There can be such a legacy of haunting, hurt bewilderment. When an analyst won't let go at the end, the patient can be left with painful questions that cast a shadow of doubt over the whole treatment. The patient wonders, "Did the analyst ever really care about me? Was it all fake, a sham? Did the analyst pretend to care about me, to collect the fee? If that is the truth, why didn't I see it? Am I that hungry for love? Am I that naive? Gullible? Where else have I let myself be fooled? Looking back, now, is everything I thought happened in the treatment null and void? Like the pile of canceled checks, are the 'insights' canceled too?"

I really believe it is important to terminate with grace. If the analyst balks, protesting there is still vital work to be done, the patient may come to feel, "My analyst just won't let go of me. He [or she] is not really interested in my welfare, but just wants our work to continue, for the sake of the money, or to keep the status quo between us, or for some other self-interested reasons. What personal need has my analyst been satisfying all along? What have I been blind to? How have I let myself be used?" This terrible feeling of betrayal and self-betrayal can be colored by the specific meanings it can recruit from the patient's earlier life experience. For example, let's say the patient feels that, as a child, he or she collaborated in being abused by a parent. Ironically, this insight might be one of the central accomplishments of the analysis. But then, at termination, if the analyst keeps claiming there is more to do, and the patient starts to question the analyst's motives, the situation can become profoundly confusing and demoralizing. Is a negative transference dictating the patient's suspicion about the analyst's motives? Or has the patient really (once again) collaborated in being abused? Furthermore, was the whole construction of the parental abuse genuine insight about the patient's past or a displacement of what was really happening in the treatment? Was it all too convenient (perhaps for both the analyst and the patient) to see the perpetrators as the patient's parents? Everything the treatment has accomplished may be called into question when the termination raises profound suspicion.

Of course there can be legitimate reasons for the analyst to object to a termination as premature. The wish to terminate, itself, may be an enactment, on the part of the patient, the analyst, or both. But, at least in my experience, I think what most frequently happens, when things go wrong at the end, is that the patient wants to terminate, the analyst protests, and the patient eventually does end the treatment, leaving with lingering questions about the analyst's motives.

Two minutes to go, and although I may be clearer about what I don't want to do in this session, I am no clearer about my hopes for it. Do I really have any? What do I want to be sure I have said?

Henry Krystal (1975) emphasized that each of us needs someone to bless our growing up and taking over our own emotional care. We need to get the message that the caregiver will be fine, so it is okay to be self-sufficient. Will I really be okay? Yes. Then, what does that mean about my relationship with this patient and with all my patients? What does that mean about me?

Like a quiz show signal, the doorbell tells me that my time for self-reflection is up. She is here. My goal is suddenly clear. I want this session to be a decent memory, for myself and for her. I want us both to be able to look back on it and smile a little. I really don't mind it if we cry. I would rather cry than wear a pasted-on smile. But I want the tears to tell us both something we can live with.

For me, I know that I can live with loss if it is overshadowed by something else that is really important. For example, when I have felt that patients must leave treatment because their lives are elsewhere, I am okay. The loss still hurts, but another feeling is stronger. Once again I have sided with life, not against it. I have gone with the current. The fullness of time has eclipsed the present moment. Its sting is not just pain. It is also a reminder that birth always hurts both people. The one thrust out bears the pain of sudden, naked exposure to the elements. The one giving birth goes from full to empty. They suffer differently, but each is willing to suffer, in the name of life.

TERMINATION AS THE DEATH OF THE TREATMENT

Nina Coltart (1996) likened treatment's termination to death:

> The totality of the ending, which seems to go against the grain of all our work on love, loyalty, object-constancy, and intimacy, is reinforced by the austere prescription of no social contact thereafter. Thus we create an arbitrary situation that has much in common with a death. (p. 151)

Over the span of a career, experiencing the deaths of numerous treatments can have a tremendous cumulative effect on the clinician. I think of myself as in a state of chronic mourning. Chronic mourning does not have the sharp jab of an acute state. It is dull, more like an ache than a pain.

Clinicians such as Aronson (2009), Langan (2002), and Marshall (2008) have contributed to the literature on the analyst's experience of the actual death of a patient. I also wrote a paper about my own loss of a patient in her 30s, who died suddenly over a weekend (Buechler, 2000). As I review these papers, I see they express some remarkably similar feelings. I describe a few of these striking similarities in what follows and reflect on the cumulative impact on the clinician of decades of losses of patients.

In describing what it was like to attend patients' memorials, Aronson, Marshall, and I used remarkably similar language for our feelings of being both intimately involved with the patient and yet profoundly outside the group of mourners. We were insiders, who knew the deceased in ways no one else could. We knew stories about most everyone present. We knew the patient's dreams, hopes, and profound disappointments. Yet we were, in another sense, strangers to everyone present at these events. As Aronson (2009) said about attending the funeral of his African American patient, "Perhaps many in the predominantly African-American church wondered, Who is this Jewish man wearing the skullcap? What is his connection to Patrick? To the family? Despite my intense, intimate connection to Patrick, I felt completely outside the circle of mourners" (p. 546).

In "Portals," his beautiful essay on the death of a patient on September 11, 2001, Langan (2002) said succinctly, "I knew his life so well yet stood outside it" (p. 477).

And Marshall (2008), at the memorial service for a patient who died in a car accident, seems to me to be crying out when she said, "Everyone seems isolated and detached. Hundreds of people are present, all strangers to me" (p. 221).

In my own paper about a patient who had suffered from physical and emotional difficulties most of her life, I described what it was like to attend a memorial service for her (Buechler, 2000):

> To see her die at such a young age caused me indescribable pain. Unlike others who mourned her, I had no one I could really talk to about these feelings. Her relatives and friends were not mine, and I would have felt it inappropriate for me to discuss the treatment with them. Some of the mourning of an analyst proceeds in solitude. (p. 80)

But there are other striking similarities in some of these comments of analysts whose patients have died. We are in shock and disoriented, and each, in his or her own fashion, denies the death. Marshall (2008) was up front about it: "I will not admit that she has died. A colleague says, 'A little

denial, eh?' I say, 'Not denial at all! A dual reality: gone but not yet gone'"
(p. 222). Aronson (2009), after his 20-year-old patient was murdered, said
of himself, "My inclination is to turn back the clock, to relive the days of
old: Patrick isn't dead; this can't have happened. ... I could not get my mind
around the fact that Patrick would not ring my buzzer on Friday at 1:45"
(p. 556). And in my own paper (Buechler, 2000), I reported, "I turn a corner
and 'see' the patient I mentioned earlier, who died years ago. I realize how
often this has happened in the many years since she has died" (p. 89).

I wonder if a tendency toward some form of denial of patients' deaths
might follow from our profession's more general attitudes toward death.
Shapiro (1997) wrote of the "extent to which the collective denial of death
permeates our field. Psychoanalysis, with its interest in psychosomatic diseases, gave weight to the belief that if we thought the right thoughts and
dealt properly with our emotions we could avoid a great many diseases"
(pp. 129–130). Later, she remarked that our field's attitude is especially
ironic, given that its founder, Freud, "lived with chronic pain and fear of
death for the last 15 years of his life" (p. 130).

The inherently interpersonal nature of all human experience suggests
that it is inevitable that we lose a bit of ourselves when our patient dies or
terminates treatment (Aronson, 2009). We lose the aspect of ourselves we
were able to embody with that person. Just as losing my child would mean
losing myself as his parent, losing a patient means losing myself as the particular analyst I was able to be with that person. I also lose the reflection of
me that I could find in that patient's eyes. The self I could be with him, the
person he was able to see in me, is now only a memory. I will never again
be exactly *that* kind of analyst. I return to this point later.

Loss challenges our notions of life's predictability in ways that can be traumatic. We need to believe planes don't crash into buildings, so September
11, 2001, shattered us. Similarly, I would suggest, clinicians need to believe
that this Thursday at 2:00 will not be entirely different from last Thursday
at 2:00. The doorbell will ring, and our patient will arrive. Marshall
(2008) put it succinctly when she said that after her patient's sudden death,
"My illusion of predictability is ruptured. I myself feel ruptured" (p. 225).

Because we are meaning makers, I think seemingly senseless losses are
especially traumatic for us. Sometimes we prefer the most painful explanations of a patient's death over profound uncertainty. After his patient's
death in the calamity of September 11, 2001, Langan (2002) searched his
notes for ways he could have predicted and prevented the tragedy. Aronson
(2009) and Marshall (2008) went through similar self-examinations.
Marshall was especially unsparing in her sense of responsibility. Wondering
if she could have prevented her patient's fatal accident, she conjectured,
"Maybe, after all, I am to blame for my blind confidence in the continua-
tion of life" (pp. 221–222). As clinicians we tend to believe everything that
happens has meaning. Human behavior makes emotional, if not logical,

sense. If we understand the meaning of events, we can more easily "resolve" and accept them. So what happens if we can make no sense of a loss?

Like a sudden death, some treatment terminations seem to make no sense and go against the assumption we need to hold that the process will be ongoing. In a way, each treatment is a vote in favor of life. It says that a better, richer life is worth whatever effort it will take. Treatment is, to me, an ongoing, steady statement on the part of two people that says, "Yes we can." In contrast, an abrupt, unilateral termination says, "No we can't." It violates beliefs that are essential to our work.

STATES OF CHRONIC MOURNING IN ANALYSTS

I have come to believe that as analysts many of us are in a chronic state of mourning for all the patients we have lost and those we will lose in the future. We are often largely unaware of these states, or we may not consider them as states of mourning. But this, I feel, is one viable way of explaining some of the pain analysts experience.

For example, the analyst constantly afraid his or her patients will terminate could be suffering a form of chronic mourning. Those forecasting the death of psychoanalysis can also be understood in this way. Some analysts act out aggressively, against each other, and against candidates. I think they are also, at least in part, reacting to the constant drumbeat of their losses. The analyst who burns out, relatively young, and has no enthusiasm for taking on new patients may be responding to a lifetime of terminations.

It is true that pediatricians, teachers, and others also lose all those they work with. Why am I emphasizing the impact on analysts of losing all our patients, sooner or later? I am not negating the idea that pediatricians and teachers may also feel their losses. But analysts are uniquely involved in patients' inner lives. We hear someone's hopes, dreams, successes, and failures, sometimes for many years. And then it is over, and we may never know what happened to them. To me, it would be remarkable if we *didn't* mourn, in some way!

Anxious, Ashamed Mourning

Jerry is a social worker in his 40s who has been trained analytically and is in private practice. Like so many others he has grown somewhat dependent on insurance companies to supply him with sufficient patients to make a living. Although he resents their intrusions into his treatments, with their challenges to his clinical judgment, incessant forms, and unpleasant, bureaucratic obstacles to overcome in order to be paid for his work, he feels he must "play ball" with them, so he is on a few panels.

Lately, Jerry has become obsessed with the possibility that his patients will terminate. As soon as one of them questions the treatment in any way, Jerry jumps to the conclusion that they have one foot out the door. He is in a state of constant anxiety about this. He feels terribly inadequate, too. He asks himself, and me, as his supervisor, why this is happening to him. Is he really clinically deficient so, naturally, patients don't want to pay for his inferior work? Should he be "taking the bull by the horns" and raising the issue of termination before the patient does? Or should he feign a blasé attitude about whether they will stay in treatment, waiting for them to bring it up and reacting minimally when they do? Would that signal that he is "strong" and "capable" and doesn't rely on them too much? Was there something missing in his training? Or is there something wrong with his character? Did something go wrong or get neglected in his training analysis?

Jerry enters a supervision session, with his usual agitated smile. In as matter-of-fact a tone as he can muster, he tells me that a patient he has seen for 2 years just didn't show up for his session last week. The patient didn't call either. The week before last the patient had raised the possibility of coming every other week, because finances were tight. Jerry had discouraged this move, but now wonders if he made a mistake. What if the patient just disappears and won't answer Jerry's calls? How much should he "chase after him"? Calling feels humiliating. It is as though suddenly the roles are reversed, and *Jerry* needs something from the *patient*. In a defensive tone, Jerry tells me that he really cares about this patient. It is not just about losing the fee. What if something terrible happened? Could it be that we will never know?

But then, Jerry seems to shift from anxious worry to glum depression. He wonders why he has been losing so many patients lately. Maybe he went into the wrong profession. Where did he get off, thinking he could help people? He certainly didn't come from the healthiest family background, and he certainly hasn't built the most balanced life for himself! What made him think he could help others with *their* problems?

Listening, I feel sad and concerned. Jerry *has* lost a lot of patients lately. The truth is that I don't know why that has happened. To me, it sounds like it would have been better to be more confronting with this last patient. Although Jerry did discourage a move to every other week, he didn't really explore what the patient felt about the treatment that played a role in his wish to cut the frequency of the work. Or, put another way, what was missing from their work that, if it were present, might have convinced the patient that, despite the financial difficulties, he wanted to continue weekly sessions? But Jerry was probably so afraid the patient might quit that he couldn't raise these issues.

Terminations have eroded Jerry's confidence in his clinical ability and, more generally, his confidence in himself as a sensitive, empathic human being. He constantly feels anxious that the terminations will keep happening, and he will "bleed" patients uncontrollably. Evidence of any ambivalence in his patients becomes a new trauma for Jerry. He reacts like someone going through PTSD. He freezes. He worries he will overreact or underreact to the patient's ambivalence. After the session he obsesses about what he *should* have said. Maybe he didn't pick up on the ambivalence enough, and the patient will act it out by quitting. Or maybe he focused on the ambivalence too much and inadvertently gave the patient the idea he should quit.

I would call this a form of chronic mourning because Jerry is *always* dealing with loss, even when no loss is actually occurring. He is poised for the next loss, like a tennis player ready for his opponent's serve. He feels as though losing patients is his doom, his fate, a foregone conclusion. It is just a question of when it will happen, not whether it will happen. Jerry is in a perpetual state of regret over the patients he has lost and those he is just about to lose. In his recurring waking nightmare, Jerry has to try to keep his patients in treatment, even though he feels he "knows" they will leave. The best he can do is to postpone the inevitable. And with the next abrupt termination, everyone (including Jerry) will have to admit Jerry is just no good as a therapist.

I know Jerry dreads our supervision, just as much as he dreads his work with patients. Will this be the day he is finally found out? It would be horrible but, also, a bit of a relief. Maybe waiting for the axe to fall is the worst part. He gets up the nerve to ask me. Do I think he is hopeless as a clinician? Once he finally asks, he does not leave room for me to answer. I think about Sullivan's (1956) distinction between false reassurance and real reassurance. False reassurance globally promises that everything will be fine. It reminds me of the description of the present as the "best of all possible worlds" in Voltaire's (1759/2005) *Candide*. But real reassurance points to an actual, solid basis for hope.

Aiming for real reassurance, I talk about Jerry's strengths as a clinician. I admit that I don't know why so many patients have abruptly left. I wonder whether Jerry now has such a bad "reputation" with himself that he doesn't see his own successful moments anymore. They don't add up, because there is no bank account, so to speak, to collect them. Jerry no longer has a category in his mind for moments he reached a patient emotionally or understood someone particularly well. All Jerry registers is repeated confirmations that he is a fraud as a clinician. He believes that patients *should* leave him, and if he becomes paralyzed with anxiety and a sense of inadequacy, this could become a self-fulfilling prophesy. He has to make a living, so he can't retire yet. I wonder if he has so thoroughly given up because he wants to spare himself the shame of believing in himself and being disappointed (again). Perhaps Jerry feels that this, at least, is a humiliation he still can be spared.

Sad, Depleted Chronic Mourning

We met very early in Dan's career as an analyst and in my career as a supervisor of psychoanalysis. Perhaps this partially explains why everything that followed had a kind of halo around it. We both felt that immediate click that told us we would work well together. There could be no question about whether Dan was talented. As soon as he graduated, he already had too many patient hours. Former supervisors, and many others, lined up to refer patients to him. As frequently happens to the young, he was given their hardest referrals. But, unusually, Dan *wanted* hard cases. He actually *liked* working with severely "borderline" and "narcissistic" patients. He felt he was doing vital work with them. It would really make a difference in the quality of their lives. He dedicated himself to his patients. No overentitlement was too annoying for Dan. No acting-out behavior was too irritating or anxiety producing. He could handle the suicidal, the self-mutilating, the boundary violating. He was never retributive. He was calm, fully present, always understanding.

After several years of supervision, we terminated, but Dan still called me, once in a while, to consult on especially difficult cases. Usually, I found myself encouraging Dan to be firmer and "put his foot down" a bit more. Sometimes I had the feeling he was listening politely, cognitively agreeing, but knowing, in his heart, that he would never follow my suggestions. Once in a while I voiced this feeling, and we made a joke of it.

Then came a long period of silence. After years of this, I got a call from Dan, asking me for someone's telephone number to make a referral. I called back immediately, eager to talk and find out how things were going for him. When he got on the phone, he sounded very tired and depressed. He told me that he wasn't seeing patients anymore. He didn't go into any details about why he had ended his practice or how he was supporting himself financially. I voiced concern. He said he would like to tell me more but couldn't just then. He said he would call again, soon. I knew he wouldn't call.

I could label this sad outcome "burnout." But what happened to cause it?

In 1986, Arnold Cooper issued a warning that clinicians who start their careers trying to be (in effect) too dedicated are likely to burn out. Although persuasive, his argument seems to me to be unlikely to have much impact. If you have ever known (or been) an idealistic, eager young clinician, you know how tenacious this attitude can be. In previous chapters I focused on the various stages of a clinical career and their long-term effects. For now, I will just catalog some of the forms of burnout I have encountered and suggest a few possible contributing factors.

For many years I advised all who wanted my input to "specialize" in a particular age range, or diagnostic group, or type of treatment, such as work with couples. More or less akin to the advice in the movie *The Graduate* to go into "plastics," I based this on the idea that specialization is the wave of the future. I reasoned that if a young professional could get his or her name associated with the treatment of a particular group, they could get enough referrals to make a living.

It may have worked out well for some, but it certainly backfired for others. Some clinicians who decided to devote themselves to helping the sexually abused, or severely disturbed, or medically ill, or drug dependent have since told me that they now feel specializing was a mistake. It fostered early burnout. Waking up, knowing they were likely to hear yet another horrendous story of the ravages of crack became too much to bear.

Of course these clinicians might have "burnt out" even if they had not been so dedicated and even if they had not chosen to specialize. But hindsight suggests to me that, for many, these two factors helped make their work, ultimately, too burdensome to bear. How many of us could survive if for most of our waking hours our minds and hearts were populated by perpetrators of horrifying sexual abuses and their victims? A friend of mine worked on a hospital unit that treated children suffering from severe burns. To explain why she was quitting the job, she told me a few of her most recent dreams. She didn't need to explain any further.

But burnout can happen in less dramatic circumstances. I have no data to help me answer the many questions that occur to me. For example, do clinicians with certain professional backgrounds (such as social workers or psychologists or psychiatrists) burn out more quickly? Of course *burnout* would be very difficult to define, much less quantify. Here I am using the term rather loosely to refer to those who stop practicing earlier than expected, feeling depleted and unhappy about their careers. Perhaps others would define it differently. I hope that writing about this encourages other clinicians to voice their viewpoints about how burnout should be defined and what its causes may be. Are there personal factors, in the clinician, that can help us predict the likelihood of burnout? For example, do clinicians who might be diagnosed as "narcissistic" tend to burn out more often than their less "narcissistic" colleagues? Are there reliable gender differences? Is it relevant if the clinician is a parent, or is trained analytically, or engages in teaching or supervising?

The relationship between professional burnout and physical health would have to be complex and multidirectional. Each could easily profoundly affect the other. I think it would probably be impossible to sort the "chickens" from the "eggs" and guess how much health problems are causing burnout or how burnout is having a negative effect on health.

Depletion, or burnout, can be expressed in more subtle ways and not just by permanently closing down a practice. Over time, we can become less involved in our work, less stimulated by its challenges, less willing to try something new. We fade out rather than abruptly exit. We avoid the harder patients. In our writing and teaching, we repeat ourselves, beating dead horses. When we give public talks we use the same, worn case examples to make the same, tired arguments. No one has quite enough courage (or is it insensitivity) to tell us to retire. But candidates steer clear of us, giggle about us behind our backs, and just manage to tolerate our presence.

In my opinion burnout can also take the form of exaggerated expectations that the field will die or has already died. For some, it might be easier to bear the idea of the field's demise than to face their own inability to sustain passionate involvement in their life's work. Of course the challenges are significant, and a good case can be made for the belief that they are more daunting than ever. But I don't think the need for help with "problems in living" (Sullivan, 1953) is likely to disappear.

In general, burnout seems to me to be a form of very severe depression. It is more than just a loss of all vital interest. It is a willed death. In a way, it is a career that has committed suicide. Out of profound pain it has taken its own life.

Like all other forms of depression, I think burnout can be (partially) a reaction to overwhelming loss. It is obvious that significant loss often precedes depression. Of course Freud (1917/1915) and, by now, countless others have dealt with the question of why some respond to loss with sadness and others with profound depression. Here I can offer only the idea that burnout, like depression, can sometimes be a more complex and extreme response to loss than sadness.

In a subsequent section of this chapter, I list some of the losses we sustain by the end of our careers. The loss of all the people we treat heads the list. With some of these people, we develop intense, long-term relationships. It would be rather amazing if we didn't have powerful responses to these losses. But why do some burn out, while others find a way to maintain vital connections with their life's work? Essentially, it seems to me, this is similar to the issue addressed by Freud (1917/1915) in his great paper on mourning and melancholia. After any substantial loss, why do some of us grieve but then find the resilience to go on with our lives? After losing hundreds of patients, why do some of us burn out and others find the strength to begin anew with the next patient and continue our careers?

Aggressive Forms of Mourning

Just as depression can take on an angry "masked" expression (Bonime, 1982; Buechler, 1995; Alan Cooper, 1969; Spiegel, 1967, 1968, 1980), I think burnout can have an aggressive guise. "Masked depression" describes "a hostile form of depression in the unwillingness to join in the reciprocal give-and-take of social interactions in friendship or work relationships" (Bose, 1995, p. 440). I believe that just as the individual's character shapes his or her depressive or nondepressive responses to loss in general, character patterns affect the clinician's burnout or nonburnout responses to the specific losses every therapist faces. Interestingly, in summarizing the literature on those who eventually show a masked form of depression, Bose (1995) suggested, "What characterizes depressive anger particularly is its imploding quality and the protean forms it takes as boredom, withdrawal, disgruntlement, and the like. These forms also lead to a particular depressive personality pattern that has been defined as 'masked depression' (Spiegel, 1967)" (p. 440).

Analogously, I think those of us who tend to respond with bored withdrawal when we are dissatisfied probably have a greater likelihood of developing aggressive forms of mourning losses in general, including aggressive forms of burnout.

What does this form of burnout look like? That is, if an analyst enters the field with a character type that leans toward boredom, withdrawal, and disgruntlement, when this analyst suffers countless losses and starts to burn out, how is this expressed? It is impossible for me to do more than make a suggestion about this. It is my hunch that this is one way we can understand some of the more painful aspects of our professional politics. More specifically, I am suggesting that the analyst who inclines toward aggressive forms of depression is the person who will become aggressive toward colleagues as he or she burns out.

Unfortunately, there are many easily available forms aggression toward colleagues can take. The literature on the history of psychoanalysis is replete with ways we humiliate and damage each other. But, to my knowledge, it does not link this behavior with losses and burnout. Once again, I am not ignoring the importance of character patterns in shaping the individual's responses to the stresses of a clinical career. But I think whoever we are, we each have to face saying good-bye an enormous number of times before we close up shop. I understand that for some of us, these endings may bring relief, or the joy of having accomplished something, or pride, more than any negative feeling. And, of course, every ending is unique, with its own complexities. But just as some of us react to the death of a loved one by becoming easily irritated, so can some colleagues, given their personality tendencies, react to professional losses with irritability. Elsewhere, I have focused on some of the expressions of the analyst's anger toward patients (Buechler, 2008, chap. 7). I explored instances of emotional withdrawal, sleepiness, impatience, and various forms of withholding. Chronic mourning might be one, among many, sources of this anger. Similarly, there might be many sources for our aggressive feelings toward our colleagues (see Chapter 5 for an extended discussion of this issue). Here I briefly describe some of the ways I think angry chronic mourning could be expressed toward colleagues.

Withholding Inclusion

Most of us can remember childhood and adolescent experiences when inclusion or exclusion from a group seemed crucial. Whether or not we were accepted by the "cool" kids really mattered. Chronologically we have left those years behind long ago, but emotionally how far have we come? There are still so many ways we hurt each other by denying each other admittance to our "exclusive" professional club. A colleague's case report is deemed "not analytic" or a candidate's progress is harshly reviewed. Of course there can be substantive reasons for negative evaluations. But some of us are not inclined to readily accept others into the fold. Again, our personal character traits are key components in shaping these attitudes. I am suggesting that chronic mourning also plays a role, at least for some of us. Time and time again, we may have invested all we could in a treatment, training, or course. As is natural, treatment, training, and courses end. We are left. Just as the sufferer in a masked depression registers complaint by angrily withholding himself or herself, I think some of us behave similarly in our professional dealings, taking out our disappointments and losses on more vulnerable colleagues. We, who have been left so very many times, can be too eager to close the door in a colleague's face. That door might be slammed shut, as when we vehemently denounce a conference member who dared to express disagreement. More often, I would suggest, we engage in a quieter (but no less harmful) form of withdrawal of inclusion or acceptance.

The Ravages of Boredom

Boredom can be devastating. In boredom the passion that animates curious exploration is defunct. Our deadened minds become barren, and we exist rather than truly live. I think we have all known boredom, but can it be a response to chronic loss?

My sense is that when we are bored, we are refusing to play. It seems to me that clinical data and theory provide endless possibilities for creativity. So if instead of rising to this challenge we become bored, I think we are saying "no" to an invitation. Why? When we close our minds, we are enacting a kind of cognitive suicide. Suicide can be an expression of rage, in fantasy meant to hurt someone else but in reality lethal to the self. Here, in my view, instead of closing the door to admittance to our "club," we are closing the door to admittance to our minds. Again, there could be many reasons. One, I suggest, is the constant drum of losses. After losing every patient and every trainee, as well as the less concrete losses we all suffer, some of us close up shop. An idea, like a ball, has been thrown our way, and instead of catching hold of it and putting our own spin on it, we just let it drop with a thud. Countless times we have reached toward another's thoughts and feelings. We have ventured out, left our own perimeters. And every time, whatever else happens, eventually the "other" is gone. Perhaps it is understandable that many of us succumb to the temptation to just curl up and cease effort. But when curiosity dims and we stop reaching out for new connections, a deadly boredom can follow.

Color Wars

Those new to the field can be bewildered, and sometimes terribly disillusioned, by the fierceness of our political infighting. The warfare between opposing viewpoints within institutes, between institutes, and among differing theoretical allegiances is extremely costly, in many senses. Our time and effort are spent in endless fruitless battles, instead of being dedicated to fighting for the continuance and health of the field. Like the adolescent "color wars" fought in the name of one's school flag, our battles can quickly devolve into something akin to name-calling.

Anger can be a last-ditch defense against dissolution (Sullivan, 1953). Do we fight so hard for or against classical approaches in part to avoid experiencing potentially debilitating sorrows? For me, although this is impossible to prove, it is a very persuasive argument. Once again, of course, there are many other factors. We express our envy, competition, greed, pride, and other motives in our warfare. But explanations that leave out sorrow have never seemed powerful enough to me. Perhaps we turn away from the endless losses that *can't* be prevented to fight for something we are convinced we *can* achieve. If I can't keep my next patient from precipitously quitting treatment, I can, at least, hold my institute's banner aloft. If I can't get many of my patients to commit to working long enough and often enough to make progress, it *is* within my power to fight for the theory or the training I think most effective. Perhaps I would rather feel self-righteous than bereft. It might be easier to play politics than it is to feel the pain of endless losses. We may feel more powerful when we are drawing a line in the sand, in the name of "high quality" (as we define it), than when we face the blank lines in our appointment books. We can't determine how many patients will leave us next week. Does that make us hungrier for power? Because we can't control our patients, do we try to control each other?

EMOTIONS THAT COMPLICATE MOURNING

In previous work, I explored some of the factors that can interfere in an analyst's capacity to mourn losses of patients (Buechler, 2000, 2004, 2008). Briefly, these include the following:

1. Prohibitions (stemming partially from the particular analyst's character issues, reinforced by the analytic culture) against fully experiencing the personal meaning of patients in the analyst's psychic life.
2. The absence of the opportunity to share memories, which normally helps mourners bear loss. Usually the analyst does not have a chance to reminisce about the patient with others who have known him or her.

3. There are no rituals for mourning a terminated treatment. There is no traditional pattern of bearing the loss. On the contrary, the analytic culture may foster and reinforce an analyst's denial of the depth of his or her feelings about losing a patient.

4. A wide variety of other losses occur in the ordinary experience of an analyst, and they may play a hidden role in intensifying the feelings of loss at terminations. For example, there are many moments when we lose hope about having substantial impact.

5. Some analytic cultures reinforce clinicians' personal inhibitions against incorporation or identification with the patient. These inhibitions may interfere in the normal mourning process.

Of course termination can occur in many different ways, and this is likely to have an impact on how it is experienced. The sudden death of a patient is hardly the same event as a planned termination. In addition, I think there is nothing else quite the same for the analyst as when a patient unexpectedly quits an extended treatment in a brusque telephone message.

I am assuming that sadness is part of the human experience of mourning any significant loss. And I accept the notion that mourning requires us to maintain, as well as let go of, our attachment to the object (Gaines, 1997). The Freudian vision of having to let go of the lost object in order to develop new ties was based on a mechanistic model that is now outdated. Because Freud assumed that we have a limited quantity of cathexis, he believed we have to decathect the lost object in order to have room to move on to new relationships. Decreasing adherence to this Freudian model has paved the way for theories that assume that *strengthening* the inner relationship with the internalized object actually enhances, rather than decreases, the capacity for healthy mourning. Both holding on to the internalized object *and* letting go of the lost external object need to occur during the mourning process. Here I examine the question of how this model of mourning can be applied to the analyst mourning the loss of a patient.

What can interfere with anyone's ability to mourn? Freud's seminal paper on mourning and melancholia (1917/1915) stressed unresolved aggression and ambivalence as key components of disturbed mourning or melancholia. My own belief is that *any* emotion has the potential to interfere in the ability to mourn (Buechler, 2000). That is, guilt, shame, anxiety, and other emotions can complicate mourning just as much as anger can.

Returning to the plight of the bereft analyst, I suggest that shame is especially likely to interfere in his or her process of mourning the loss of a patient. How our training heightens our vulnerability to shame is the topic of the first section of this book. Much of the rest of this book addresses how our shame is fostered by the analytic culture throughout our professional lives. For now, I concentrate on why unacknowledged grief and shame seem to me to be crucial aspects of the analyst's unresolved mourning for lost patients.

First, a word about the sadness or grief that is inevitable in response to loss. Sadness is a normal human reaction to any significant loss (Izard, 1977). Elsewhere, I have explored in greater detail how a variety of emotions, such as regret, guilt, and shame, can complicate our sadness (Buechler, 2008). Here, I would like to suggest that it is especially shame that can play the greatest role in hampering the analyst's grieving for lost patients. Ironically shame is the emotion Freud (1917/1915) specifically *excluded* from his understanding of melancholia. As already noted, Freud privileged anger as the emotion that interferes in the mourning process. He described the melancholic as suffering from a conflict between anger and grief. He said that in the melancholic, feelings of shame are lacking or at least not prominent. Freud was so emphatic on this point that it sounds to me like a charged issue for him. The melancholic, for Freud, couldn't *possibly* be ashamed and grieving.

> They are not ashamed and do not hide themselves, since everything derogatory that they say about themselves is at bottom said about someone else. Moreover, they are far from evincing toward those around them the attitude of humility and submissiveness that would alone befit such worthless people. On the contrary, they make the greatest nuisances of themselves. (p. 247)

But it may be more sympathetic toward mourners in general and, specifically, analysts mourning lost patients to see shame as a possible component of their feelings. In the *Nicomachean Ethics*, Aristotle defined shame as "pain or disturbance in regard to bad things, whether present, past, or future, which seem likely to involve us in discredit" (Hanson, 1997, p. 167). When a patient abruptly terminates, for example, it seems likely to me that the analyst could feel discredited. This could add shame to the analyst's sadness at having lost someone with whom the analyst may have felt connected.

Tomkins (1987) made an interesting comment about shame that seems to me relevant to the analyst's shame when a patient leaves: "In shame the individual wishes to resume his or her commerce with the exciting state of affairs, to reconnect with the other, to recapture the relationship that existed before the situation turned problematic" (Lansky & Morrison, 1997, p. 124). Probably every clinician has felt something like this at one time or another. A patient leaves, and we replay the events just preceding the departure, looking for what we could have done differently. Feelings of loss marry feelings of shame, as we wish for the "do over" that is granted in some childhood games.

Morrison and Stolorow (1997) seem to me to reach the heart of the matter when they write,

> Shame can seep into the very core of our experience of ourselves and thus constitutes the essential pain, the fundamental disquieting judgment that we make about ourselves as failing, flawed, inferior to someone else, unworthy of the praise or love of another, or falling short of a cherished idea. (p. 82)

When a patient commits suicide, we are especially likely to feel we have fallen short and contributed to the tragedy. Among others, I have written of the particular pain evoked by my patient's suicide (Buechler, 2008). This took place in a hospital setting. Just after I interviewed the patient, he hung himself in the bathroom. No one emotion describes what I felt, and still feel, about that event, but I am sure shame plays a significant role. And even when the cause of death is not suicide, clinicians comb their memories to see if they could have foreseen and somehow prevented the tragedies (see Aronson, 2009; Langan, 2002; Marshall, 2008, discussed previously). During these extensive self-examinations, they may have felt the sense of insufficiency that is one of the hallmarks of shame.

More generally, it seems to me that a truly interpersonal vision of profound loss would include shame as a likely component. An older patient of mine lost her husband after a rather prolonged illness. She deeply misses his companionship. She feels lonely, in their home, with only her cats to talk to. Her sense of loss is intense, as she imagines how they would have enjoyed holidays and vacations together. But along with losing her partner, my patient has, in a way, lost aspects of *herself*. She lost the wife she was to him. When she wakes up Sunday mornings, thinking to make them pancakes (as she used to do) and then remembering his death, she (once again) loses him, her urge to make pancakes, and the *self* she would have been preparing the batter. When we lose someone, our loss is double. We lose that other, but we also lose the aspect of ourselves that existed in relation to them. With this loss we might feel the barren diminishment whose name is shame. Elsewhere, I have written about the play *Rabbit Hole* (Lindsay-Abaire, 2006), in which a couple loses their only child in a car accident (Buechler, 2008). With the loss of their son, they also lose the parents they would have been with him as he learned football, went to college, and had his own children. They lose an aspect of themselves. Even if they have another child, they will never be exactly the same parents that they would have been with the son who died. Those parents died along with the boy who fell from his bicycle as the car hit him.

I suggest that the same is true for the clinician who loses a patient, no matter how the loss occurs. When my patient leaves me, I have lost that person who may have had great significance to me. But I have also lost the *analyst* I was when working with that patient. Furthermore, I lost the analyst I could have become with him had he stayed. These losses may well sadden me, but I think they often do more than that. I think they can bring me shame, in various ways. The most obvious way is that I may feel I mishandled some aspect of the treatment, resulting in the termination (if it was abrupt or ill timed, from my perspective). But in a more subtle sense, in that I lose an aspect of myself when the patient leaves, I think I have become poorer. I *am* less, and *will be* less, because I have lost this person. We could also say that I lost a "playing field" for the exercise of my analytic skills. But, I think more vitally, I have lost the Sandra Buechler that this patient and I might have coconstructed. What happens to all the "selves" we might have been? I consider it a legacy from my Interpersonal forebears to think of these losses as irreplaceable. That is, let's say I was developing a certain aspect of my human potential with my patient Abe and then he leaves treatment. The Sandra I might have become, with a year more of working with Abe, is different from the Sandra I will develop with a new patient. Each patient is unique, and together we create a relationship different from any other. With another analyst, my patient would have had a different analysis. He doesn't have a preformulated, unvarying set of internalized "object relationships" that he would play out with any clinician he worked with. Nor do I. Together, Abe and I forged an interaction that was unlike any other. This Abe/Sandra is irreplaceable. With my next patient I will develop differently than I would have with Abe. Interpersonal theory emphasizes that the sparks that flew between Abe and me are not just a replaying of sparks that flew in the past for each of us. They are not just the product of preprogrammed, invariant, internalized object relationships. They are the result of a specific, unique combination of human beings called Abe and Sandra. That combination no longer exists when we part. Of course we have our memories of each other. But that is not the same thing as having a live, potentially surprising, ever-changing, embodied relationship.

What is the impact of a lifetime of losses of patients, connections, and the selves we might have become? For one thing, I think this makes sadness and shame two of our occupational hazards, as I suggest throughout this book. Often, they take shapes that don't look like sadness and shame, at least as we usually expect them to appear. If you look around, you will see colleagues who find the (analytic and nonanalytic) world an impoverished place. Could their anticipation of the end of psychoanalysis, and their experience of the world as inhospitable, (partially) be the result of a *projection* outward of inner losses? Maybe those of us who have been practicing for many decades are primed to see an empty world, because we have sustained countless losses of treatment partners, relationships, and potential selves, so we feel empty *inside* but experience the emptiness as about *the profession*. I believe that our sadness and shame don't always take the easily recognizable shapes (that might facilitate understanding). We don't cry or blush on a chronic basis. And, of course, we are individuals, and we experience our losses in our own, personal, complicated ways. But thousands of good-byes are bound to leave an indelible stamp of *some* kind.

As already noted, pediatricians and teachers also say many good-byes. But, usually, they haven't shared as many dreams as we and our patients do. In analysis, at least as I see it, we formulate a different language, a set of customs, a nest of memories, with each person. Then, as might happen in a science fiction story, the jointly constructed planet, with its only two citizens, disappears forever. Sometimes the world ends in a violent explosion, and sometimes it gently fades out. But in either case, poof, and it is gone for good. Some of us develop an arsenal of weapons against sadness and shame. Some avoid any emotional connection with their patients. You can't lose what you've never had. Some hold themselves "above" the patient, so losing them can't have much sting. Some find an intellectual way of making patients interchangeable, so, even when they leave, the supply goes on. Some use self-disclosure to forge an immediate, egalitarian, "close" bond. Perhaps it is hoped (probably unconsciously) that sadness and shame will be counteracted by a very intense interchange. Some deny the sadness and/or the shame by focusing on fame and the exercise of power. It is as though they think that with an elevated status one can avoid ordinary pain and feelings of diminishment.

Some use chronic anger and contempt to ward off pain and shame. This can take many forms, including contemptuous criticism of the thoughtless youth of today, our superficial culture, the damages wrought by managed care, and the wickedness of individual patients. We can use interpretation as a shield against our own vulnerability. We can forge theories that position each termination as evidence of our pet theory rather than as a personal loss. We can see other clinicians' sorrow and shame as evidence of the inadequacy of their analyses or as evidence of their peculiar countertransferences. We can rail against the ungrateful patients who left rather than feel the pain and shame of being left. We can rationalize, theorize, why it shouldn't hurt. We can plunge into focusing on financial rewards, trying to reduce everything to the "bottom line." We can concentrate on theory rather than on people. We can focus on climbing social and professional ladders. We can narrow our vision in countless ways to try to avoid the emotional truth that, over a career, we sustain immeasurable losses.

A PARTICULARLY PAINFUL LOSS

For more than 30 years of doing supervision at a child guidance clinic and supervising at institutes and in private practice, I have heard versions of an especially painful story. A clinician treats a child and works long and hard to establish rapport. The treatment finally takes off. Some progress is made. Then the child's parents abruptly yank the child out of treatment, ostensibly for one reason or another. The clinician is devastated, for the child's sake and his or her own sake.

Here is a situation likely to recruit a complex emotional response. Of course there is the sadness of loss. And, as already noted, the losses are for what both the child and the clinician could have become by working together. They lose each other now, but they also lose all their tomorrows. It seems to me that lost opportunities are some of life's most poignant blows.

What is this situation likely to evoke in the clinician, besides sadness? I would suggest that a kind of angry shame is one possibility. First of all it is so easy to assume that it could have been otherwise. Clinicians ask me, "Did I try to go too fast? Did I focus too much on the child and not enough on the parents? Did I inadvertently threaten them? Did I act out issues against my own parents that are unresolved in me? What did I do wrong? Should I call them (again)?" These questions can elicit shame, that is, a feeling of insufficiency. The clinician feels that had he or she been more skilled, the termination could have been averted. Because it is unlikely we will ever be sure what happened, we are left with lingering questions.

For many, this situation calls forth extremely intense feelings. Especially for the young clinician, it can be easy to overidentify with a troubled child. What does it mean, then, to lose the opportunity to help that child have a better life? This can take on great significance. Many of us entered the field looking to "cure" versions of ourselves (at least in part). Dropping the ball, so to speak, can feel like a big letdown. We have failed a child (the patient, and, in identification, ourselves as children, and, in addition, ourselves as adult clinicians). We had a chance to make a difference in the quality of a life, and we blew it.

Many of my supervisees have been especially perplexed by this situation. How ardently should they continue to try to make contact and persuade the parents to bring the child back to treatment? Technological advances have multiplied the questions. Should they call, e-mail, text, or write? Send the bill, with a note or without a note? It is frequently easier to get caught up in obsessive debates about strategies than it is to mourn.

I have often thought that this situation can elicit a particularly intense combination of sadness, shame, and anger. It can seem to the clinician as though the parents are being retributive, but this can never be proven accurate or false. The clinician may feel stymied. Confronting the parents could further alienate them, diminishing chances they might return the child to treatment in the future. But failing to confront can feel cowardly. The clinician can see this failure as yet another missed opportunity to have an impact. I think shame can result. The clinician feels inadequate, as though a better therapist would have had a better result. But, along with sadness and shame, there may also be anger. We can feel set up to fail or deliberately struck down. It can seem as though the parent has played a trump card. We were making headway, perhaps "winning," in some sense. We know it isn't a race, and yet the triangle of child, parents, and clinician can feel like a contest to all concerned. Suddenly (from our perspective) we are put in our place, or, rather, we are dismissed, without a place at all.

Perhaps saddest of all is the question of how to say good-bye to the child (if given any opportunity to do so). Especially with younger children, it can feel unhelpful to explain that the parents are responsible for the termination. No matter how hurtful the situation, the child still has to find a way to live with these parents (unless abuse warrants official intervention). Yet, should we stay silent and, perhaps, let the child believe that termination of the treatment was our choice? This can also have damaging consequences. To the extent that we feel the parents are deliberately, unnecessarily, and/or retributively creating the situation, we are bound to feel some anger, but it is likely to mix with other potent and painful feelings.

I can recall some of my own feelings when I left the child guidance clinic and had to terminate with all my patients. Here it *was* my choice. I remember a little girl, about 7 years old. She simply couldn't believe it. She kept asking, "Why?" I found words, but they didn't bring either of us much comfort or clarity.

In some ways numbers numb. I think it is impossible to mourn numerous losses at once. When I left the guidance clinic, I terminated with dozens of children and families. Since then, in my supervisory work, I have helped clinicians end their practices for geographic moves or because they were retiring. Even when the loss is temporary (e.g., when the clinician is going on maternity leave), it can be extremely difficult to bear for the clinician and the patient. I think we often resort to a kind of mental and emotional shutdown. We "place" patients with referrals. We try to turn people into tasks. Sometimes there is meaning to giving a patient the telephone number of a "covering" therapist. But what is being "covered"? I think "covering" is most often really "covering up." We are trying to cover up the emotional truth of what it means to sever a tie, perhaps just for a while or, perhaps, forever.

Whether the patient (or the patient's parents) leave or the clinician leaves, eventually all treatments end. Does our training prepare us to bear a lifetime of endings?

Perhaps the most painful loss of all is the loss of one's identity as a clinician. This includes, but goes beyond, the loss of any particular patient. At least for me, it is much rehearsed. With a shifting mixture of longing, relief, and sorrow, I often think about what it will be like to give up my practice. Of course, to format the loss this way is hopeful and, in a sense, presumptuous. I am assuming that ending my practice will be a *choice* I will make on a conscious basis. Life may have other plans for me.

Like many losses, my passage from doing clinical work to retiring as a clinician is mostly unimaginable. Given that doing treatment has been a major part of my life for so many years, without it, who would I be?

It is very hard to picture my life (or myself) without my practice. Although I have functioned in widely differing settings (inpatient, child guidance clinic, college, analytic institute, private practice), the one constant is my identity as a therapist. Without this role, would I regress and revisit qualities I thought I left behind long ago? Would I flounder, rudderless, lost?

In contradictory ways guilt keeps me working but also leads me to question the wisdom of this choice. Ending my practice seems like an abandonment of the many people I work with. I imagine thinking about retirement as immersing myself in a sea of indecision. When is a good time? How long before that point is it still okay to take new patients and supervisees? Should I just cut down gradually? How would I do that?

At first glance, it may seem like another in a long line of choices about whether to privilege my own needs or the needs of my patients and supervisees. But I think it is much more complicated than this would imply. What, exactly, is in my self-interest?

Often, lately, I have a guilty and somewhat ashamed reaction when I listen to newly minted therapists worry about beginning their practices. Will they get enough patients to pay the rent and become viable professionals? In contrast *I* have *more* than I need. Should I be cutting back, sharing the wealth?

I am reminded of one of my favorite poems, Robert Frost's (1971) "Two Tramps in Mud Time." Although there are obvious, great differences between its protagonist and me, the psychological parallel is so strong that this poem has come to represent the dilemma of the older practitioner of any passionately loved occupation. Frost's protagonist has lived a life of self-control, storing up energy he still wants to expend. Enter the two strangers who want his job. Frost said the sun was warm, but the wind was chill. Is that an allusion to an outwardly calm but inwardly shaken state of mind?

The oldster knows that the young tramps want to take his job, but he won't give it up. In fact, although he had loved his work well before the tramps came along, he loves it even more after he sends them on their way. Although the tramps said nothing incendiary, the older man knew that their very presence would fill his head with guilty thoughts. How can he hold on to his work, merely out of love for it, when they were in dire need of work in order to survive? What selfishness! Fair-mindedly, he admits,

> My right might be love but theirs was need
> And where the two exist in twain
> Theirs was the better right-agreed. (p. 114)

It seems simple, but is it? Should their need automatically trump his love?

Frost resolved the poem in a fascinating way. He asked about the best set of motives for hard work. His answer is that only when we love *and* need an activity is it done for the right reasons. When work is done out of love and need, it can *both* sanctify us and provide for the next generation.

So stepping aside to leave room for the younger and hungrier is not necessarily noble. But there is, I feel, something unseemly about still being greedy as one ages. I am reminded of a very troubling image from early adulthood. I was a member of a group that organized parties in residential homes for the severely mentally disabled. As we brought out toys to give away, I remember one older, developmentally disabled woman pleading for one of the dolls. It was certainly not my first experience of being shocked, but it felt like a new and bizarre kind of shock. Aside from the age disparity of an older person desperately wanting a child's toy, I think it seemed unseemly for someone that age to vie so openly. Perhaps I had unconsciously assimilated an image of older people demurely nodding and sipping tea in a rocking chair. Whatever my stereotype might have been, this woman with raw desire didn't fit it.

When is it time for us to give up all raw hunger, including our desire for referrals? When does it become unseemly to grab with sharp, unfettered need? When does all wanting (a referral, a status, and so on) become shameful, as though we have exposed inappropriate sexual longings?

For me, it is T. S. Eliot who best expressed the position of the old who still want, much to their shame. In "The Love Song of J. Alfred Prufrock" (1930), we have a perfect representative of aging desire as mortification. Having already measured out his life in coffee spoons, how can he dare to presume anything? Perhaps, after all, it is better not to venture out. What if he has let himself desire, only to be told, by someone settling a pillow by her head, that he has misread the situation and what he is thinking is not at all what she meant. What utter and complete humiliation! No, he can't take this chance, for he is already sometimes "almost ridiculous" (p. 15). This is the time when he shall wear the bottoms of his trousers rolled, giving in to aging. Any effort to still enjoy the pleasures of the young brands him as a fool. To dare to eat a peach in the open shows that he is unaware that peaches are for the young, and he is no longer young. Although he has heard the mermaids sing to each other, he knows they will not sing to him. I imagine him accepting this with sad resignation. Resignation, and not peaches or love songs, is appropriate for a man Prufrock's age.

What format can desire take, as we age, without exposing us to ridicule? Or should maturity make society's censure unimportant? Should we continue to live, work, show ourselves, however long we like? Is it the job of the aging to practice a nonchalant disregard for society's stereotypes?

Of course, this view of aging is only part of the story. Some younger practitioners welcome the input of their elders. Some are happy to see that an active, vibrant enthusiasm can accompany analysts as we age. Some view the referral we still take not as a loss for them but only as a good sign about their own futures.

Along with so many other issues, what it feels like to age, and still want referrals, is rarely discussed in public, although it may be a focus among friends in the field. Just as desire itself can feel shameful as we age, still needing help to get referrals can feel stigmatizing. We imagine everyone will see us as failures. After all, other analysts our age have waiting lists. Some of us find ourselves caught between our desire to keep working and our pride. If we show we still want new patients, we may feel humiliated, but if we don't show our desire, we may feel (and actually be) overlooked. In between a rock and a hard place, it can be easy to slink off, give up, and blame external factors, such as the sagging economy, the "dying" profession, managed care industries, pharmaceutical false promises, and so on. It is not unusual to hear older colleagues recall the good old days, with their once glorious but never to be recaptured respect for psychoanalysis. I often wonder how much this is a projection of one's own burnout and despair and how much it is a genuine observation of changing times.

If still desiring is seen as shameful, how can the aging clinician stay vibrant? Here is yet another challenge, built into the analytic life, that requires resilient self-esteem. Surely, we had better start out our careers bolstered by an "internal chorus" that is supportive and stimulating. Surely, if we still want to work, after the mermaids have stopped singing to us, we need perspective, solid personal and professional self-esteem, and, perhaps, a well-developed sense of humor.

Part 4

Sustaining Practice

Chapter 8

The Ordinary Tragedies of an Analytic Life

In the previous chapter, I discussed how patients and analysts disappear from each other's lives. It is not hard to understand these experiences as losses. Here I extend discussion of their cumulative impact and then highlight some more subtle but even more pervasive shortfalls in the analyst's work life. Loss is woven into the fabric, in many senses. Previously, I wrote about the lapses of hope, faith, and connection that commonly thread their way through sessions (Buechler, 2008, chap. 6). But, even more commonly, some diminishments are built into the very nature of the analytic way. The frame of the relationship, its focus, and its inevitable limitations intimately acquaint us with loss. The ubiquity of these experiences makes them hard to discern, but I have no doubt about their tremendous cumulative impact, at least for me.

In her early teens Maisy was a somewhat overweight, intensely emotional, strikingly beautiful teenager with a flare for the dramatic, a ruddy face, and an infectious laugh that would sometimes relieve her usual scowl. The scent of Maisy's presence in my office was unmistakable, long after she left our session. She loved animals and considered dirt her natural habitat. In a way, dirt was her religion, and she certainly maintained a fervent belief in her absolute right to dwell in it. Objectors were small-minded, fussy, beneath contempt.

I am a petite person, but I always felt smaller than usual in Maisy's presence. On the surface we were opposites. Maisy shattered quiet contemplation. Her red-blooded exuberance made me feel anemic, not just delicate.

Maisy appeared, disappeared, and reappeared in my office for several decades. I got to see the adult she became, a young woman who was somewhat subdued but still vibrantly alive. The last time we met, about 8 years ago, much was still up in the air about her career choices and relational life. I have no idea how she is, where she is, or, even, whether she still exists.

What should I do with Maisy? Is she a "file" I ought to "delete"? Would that make room for others? After all I may never see her again, and, surely, I will never again see the Maisy who exists in my mind.

In one sense the question is meaningless, because I can't delete Maisy. My Maisy, with her red cheeks and full, husky laugh, cannot be erased. But that is fine, because I don't believe her absence would confer any advantages. The idea that we must "de-cathect" lost "objects" to have room for new ones has never appealed to me. Elsewhere, I have written about how we can be misled by this conception of mourning (Buechler, 2004, 2008).

In the heart and mind of an analyst, countless stories remain unfinished. I suppose this leaves me free to imagine an ending of my choosing, but this is unsatisfying. I will still want to know whether Maisy has passed on her exuberance, and her dark eyes, perhaps to a child of her own. Has she found a good place for herself, where she is welcome to be her whole self and not just a truncated version?

Maisy's story is unfinished, perhaps permanently. In this, it has much in common with the losses I described in the previous chapter. Why is the loss of Maisy particularly painful? Maisy stands out, in my experiences, partly because I knew her over a substantial period of her early development. Because of that, as well as the vividness of my memories of her, the loss of Maisy weighs heavily. Unfinished stories are unsatisfying in different ways. Sometimes therapists are left in suspense, sometimes in dread. Often we wish we could share in a joy we believe was imminent. We are shut out of sorrows just as often, and that, too, leaves us in a peculiar limbo. What happened to a patient of mine who had been diagnosed (years earlier) with a serious illness? Did it recur? Is she alive? What about the one locked in a fierce battle with her sister? Our work helped her understand her part in their warfare, and they seemed better able to help each other bear the burdens of advanced aging and other difficulties. Or was this just a temporary truce?

And what of a patient I last saw as Alzheimer's finally truly claimed her life? She had slid into a state of such forgetfulness that maintaining sessions was impossible, and she wanted to terminate. I made some follow-up calls and then let go. Did she now wish I would have tried harder? Was her termination because her shame over her handicaps overtook her connection to me? If I had fought harder for the treatment, would she have felt respected and wanted and gladly held on?

Elsewhere, I have written that there is no funeral for a terminated treatment and no prescriptions about how to mourn (Buechler, 2000). I don't know anyone who knew my patients, so I can't find out about them or share a memory with someone who knew them. In some cases, I don't even have the (frequently consoling) thought that they are free from whatever misery they had. They are gone from my life but not from my memory. In my mind's eye they are younger than they must be in reality. They form rows and rows of permanent question marks. Aside from satisfying my curiosity, what could they teach me?

But I, unlike some of my colleagues, have a strong belief I should not initiate contact with them. To my way of thinking, some aspects of treatment are not reciprocal, though many others are. Treatment is mainly for the benefit of the patient, who, we hope, increasingly knows what he or she desires. If the work has been at all successful, patients should have a clear sense that they have the option of returning, but it is their choice.

So, most of the time, the questions remain unanswered. Not unlike in the rest of life, uncertainty must be accepted, and we must learn to bear our losses.

In clinical practice loss is so pervasive that it can be hard to notice. We are aware of it when patients leave, of course. We sometimes seem to over-react to these endings. This subjects us to the suspicion that our motives are mercenary, and we want to hold on to patients to keep getting our fees. Although this can be true, it is not the whole story. An array of losses weaves into the fabric of the clinician's professional life. The actual loss of a patient crystallizes them into coherence, allowing us to experience loss on a conscious level. So we "overreact" to termination because when a patient leaves treatment, we are free to react to all our more subtle, accumulated losses, as well as the actual loss of the patient. The nature of these accumulated losses is the subject of much of this chapter.

What do I mean by "clinical losses"? Obviously I can answer this only from my own vantage point. In this chapter I am making a personal statement about my own losses and the experiences I have heard about in supervisions and consultations.

What seems most striking is how much we take most of our losses for granted. We expect ourselves to bear them without complaint. Much of the time they slip under the radar, so to speak. I believe we are emotionally affected by all our loss experiences, but many are not clearly labeled, making them harder to mourn.

I am highlighting the losses inherent in many ordinary moments in a clinician's workday. Included are the simplest, most temporary cognitive losses, like the loss of the ability to think clearly. These can be jolting but are usually momentary and may pass so quickly into oblivion that we never really assess their meaning or personal impact. More complicated are the losses of illusions about who we are. The clinician frequently encounters what Sullivan (1953) called the "bad-me" and the "not-me" aspects of himself or herself. It can be hard to hold on to cherished illusions. Hard-won self-esteem can be endangered by the clinician's evident failures, limitations, handicaps, and lapses (for more examples, see Chapter 5).

Our losses of hopes, dreams, and fantasies can be subtle, implicit in clinical exchanges, or quite explicitly part of the work with specific patients. Of course every loss I feel is colored by who I am as a person. But throughout this book I am suggesting that the record of my losses is more than just an autobiography. I think what I have lost, and what my supervisees have lost, has some overlap with what other clinicians experience. But that supposition on my part will be tested by my readers.

Losses of connection occur on many levels. *Every moment in a session can be seen as a retreat from connection or an advance toward greater connection.* I sometimes think of the 45 minutes as a dance, with two partners constantly moving toward and away from each other. Greater intimacy seems possible, evaporates, and emerges again.

TIME LOST

A clinician I supervise sees a connection that now appears obvious and wonders, "Why didn't I see that before?" Or clinicians report a passage in a session where their experience was that they couldn't think at all. They wish I could give them a mantra to help them through the next baffling clinical interchange.

Therapists regularly encounter moments where we can't think, or remember, or make connections that normally would be easily available. I am calling these experiences "losses" in the sense that we count on having these faculties, but with a particular patient or in a particular hour, they are missing. Some of the examples in this section are ways people seem to me to refer to these losses in supervision. These clinicians are puzzled at their own behavior. Reporting a session with a patient, they wonder what happened to their usual capacities for thinking spontaneously, remembering, and connecting one piece of material to others. As I listen I am reminded of similar dysfunctional moments of my own.

Contagion, or the idea that we are less able to forge "links" with patients who have similar handicaps, probably accounts for some of our cognitive lapses but not, I suggest, for them all. There are times when the patient seems perfectly able to think, remember, and make connections, and it is the clinician who is feeling nonfunctional.

A patient bitterly criticizes her analyst for every aspect of the frame. Why can't they meet outside the office, have a physical relationship, or plan a future life together? The analyst, who is in training, struggles to keep thinking. He becomes less and less able to concentrate. As he later describes it, it is not that he becomes distracted and thinks about something else. It feels more like he doesn't think at all but then becomes aware that time has gone by. They end the session on a disquieting note. The patient questions the value of their work together, and the analyst privately joins her, though outwardly staying quiet and waiting for the hour to be over.

We could imagine various explanations. The analyst is anxiously anticipating the patient's next move, and this anxiety causes him to lose cognitive capacity. Or he could be angry, perhaps with both the patient and me (his supervisor). Together we are "sandwiching" him into a bad spot. The patient is demanding that he depart from the frame, and I am expecting him to (mainly) adhere to it. But he and I also hope he will keep the (training case) patient in treatment. So he could be anxious and/or angry and, therefore, have trouble thinking, because in effect he is expected to accomplish what may be impossible.

But what I am asking is, regardless of the *cause* of the candidate's lapse, what is the *effect* on him of having the lapse? And what will be the cumulative effect of thousands of these experiences, as his clinical career continues to unfold? I would suggest that the emotion of shame may be part of their legacy.

Working with this material in supervision reminds me of my own treatment of a middle-aged professional woman. We have worked together for many years, and the depression for which she originally sought help has somewhat lifted. But there is another experience that has not changed at all. Once in a while, during a session, she stops hearing me. That is, the patient hears that I am saying something, but she cannot make out what it is. She hears words, but they don't have any meaning to her.

At first I was quite puzzled and startled by this phenomenon. Because it has happened many times, by now I am more used to it. Occasionally it feels deliberate, and then it sometimes annoys me. But mostly, I am focused now on its impact on my own cognitive functioning.

The sequence always starts with my saying something to the patient. We have figured out that the content of what I say usually has some negative meaning to the patient about her worth as a person (whether or not that is the message I intended). Because the patient is on the couch, I don't see her facial response. Usually what comes next is silence. After a few minutes the patient then tells me she couldn't hear me. Sometimes she asks me to repeat whatever I last said.

Here is the part most relevant to this chapter. Sometimes I can't remember what I just said. Of course we can imagine many possible reasons for that. As was true for my supervisee (discussed previously), I could be angry or anxious. Or we could imagine a kind of contagion between the patient and me where her temporary cognitive "impairment" spawns mine. No matter how we understand *why* I can't remember, my focus here is on the *effect on me* of my not being able to remember what I last said, as well as the effect on me of how I handle it.

The moment feels potentially shaming for me. Although I am no longer as startled as I used to be, I still sometimes get caught up, momentarily, in the question of whether to admit I don't remember. My reluctance to admit it seems to me to reveal that I would like to avoid the potential shame in admitting the truth.

There are many times I have told the patient what was going on, for me. But this sequence has occurred at other times, and I have stayed silent and felt ashamed, both of my not remembering and of my silence about it. These miniscule brushes with shame are what most concern me, for myself, as well as for the patient. I just go along, as though no rift in our communication had occurred. My focus here is on how this may affect me, in both the short term and the long term.

I think the reader can understand the multiple sources of shame for me in this material. I feel shame when I don't remember what just occurred between the patient and me and more shame if I failed to have the courage and honesty to realize what happened and admit it to her. Because of this behavior on my part, the patient and I will lose an opportunity to explore something that might have been useful.

I am reminded of my own previous writing on shame, where I suggested that shame is the only negative feeling that usually intensifies when it is pointed out (Buechler, 2008). That is, when someone interprets to us that we must feel sad, we may or may not feel sadder. But when someone points out our shame, we generally feel more ashamed. This comes to mind because I am aware of some shame as I write this.

What are the likely long-term effects on me of repetitions of these episodes? Like my supervisee (discussed previously), I may lose a bit of self-esteem and, maybe, attachment to the work. Of course who we are in relation to shame plays a significant part in what we each lose. Elsewhere, I have discussed how by the time we enter adulthood, each of us has a rich store of self-experience with each of the fundamental emotions (Buechler, 2004). So, by now, I have a whole personal history of what it has been like to be Sandra Buechler-when-angry, and Sandra Buechler-when-sad, and so on. The effect on me of a brush with shame will depend, in part, on my personal history of experience with that emotion.

Another cognitive "loss" that, I suspect, is very common is the clinician's inability to see a connection between material presented by the patient now and material presented previously. In supervision when I think I see such a connection and I point it out, the supervisee's reaction often includes the question, "Why didn't *I* see that?" Similarly, in my own clinical work, when I make a connection, patients often ask, "Why didn't you see this before now?"

It's a good question. What kept me from connecting "c" with "q," that is, for example, an event from the patient's early history with an event in his or her present life? Elsewhere, I have written extensively about how to train people to make these connections (Buechler, 2008). So what would prevent me from making them in my own clinical work?

But, in this chapter, I am less focused on *why* a clinician fails to make a connection than I am on the impact of the failure. Sometimes when my patients ask why I didn't see something earlier, I feel they are accusing me of not working hard enough. The implication is that I could have made the connection sooner if I were really trying. But, at least for me, that often doesn't jive with my experience. I feel I *was* trying, and I just didn't think of it before. The phrase that often comes to mind, perhaps in self-defense, is that I am "dancing as fast as I can."

In other words, why do we think of what we think of when we think of it? More to the point, why *don't* we think of it before then? What part does each participant, clinician and patient, play in the timing of connections? And, even more to the point here, what is the impact on us of the repeated experience of having failed to make vital connections for long stretches of time?

My hope is that readers will compare their clinical experiences with mine. I know my reactions reflect who I am as a person. For myself, I can say that when I realize that, at least in theory, I had all the material to make a significant connection months or even years ago, I feel a very wide gamut of emotions. Sadness is often, for me, a major component. Personally, I am especially sensitive to the issue of time lost. I know this colors my response, but I wonder what other clinicians tend to feel.

With several of my patients, I have had another "cognitive" loss. In sessions, sometimes, I can't remember something I feel I "should" be able to recall. For example, with one patient, after many years of work together, when she mentioned a close family member, I couldn't remember who he is. Or, another time, with the same patient, I couldn't remember anything about our previous session.

Perhaps it is relevant to mention that I generally have a pretty good memory, and I take fairly extensive notes during every session. So these lapses are unusual for me. I imagine that this augments their impact on me, because they counter my expectations about my abilities (see Chapter 5 for further discussion of challenges to the clinician's sense of self).

I could speculate about why I have these lapses (and, of course, I have done so, sometimes with the patient and sometimes on my own). But more relevant to this chapter is the question of their short- and long-term effects on me.

Years ago, I gave some thought to the experience of "getting through" an hour. I reflected on how demoralizing it can be to slog through 45 minutes, longing for a session to end. When this happens to me, I feel profoundly empty, dulled, out of joint. I hate the feeling. It reminds me of agonizingly slow days on inpatient wards. The dazed patients, shuffling across the day room, seemed to adapt more easily to the crawling pace, whereas I felt like any moment I would have to jump out of my skin.

I often think of these hospital experiences during sessions when I can't recall something that seems vitally important to remember. The first decision is whether I should hope it will come back to me if I just listen for a few minutes longer. Or I could immediately ask for help (see the similar quandary in a previous section of this chapter and in Chapter 5). Each choice may be preferable in some circumstances, and, once again, we have to make that call for ourselves. There are potential pitfalls no matter what we do.

SPONTANEITY TAMED

For 45 minutes, three times a week, Lynn and I think together. We are the only inhabitants of a miniature community, with its own time-honored rituals, respected roles, and established customs. For example, we rarely interrupt each other. Waiting for the other to finish her thought is particularly significant in our world. It means to us that we value each other's minds, which is very important to us both. It also expresses our wish to treat each other with consideration.

We have a language. In one sense, it is English, but it is also particular to us: *our* English. Sometimes we need few words to get an idea across, because the referents are so familiar to us both.

Most days, Lynn doesn't have to speak at all for me to have a general idea of how she feels. The set of her mouth, and the muscles around it, tells me as soon as she enters the room. Sometimes her rigid muscles are barely holding back a torrent of words.

Analysts are often so accustomed to the peculiar limitations and rigidities of the analytic relationship that we no longer fully register them. Thoughts of each other may occur to Lynn and me often, but we are physically in the same room for prescribed 45-minute periods at scheduled hours of the week. If she desperately needs to talk to me on a Tuesday, theoretically she could call me. She never has. If I thought I suddenly understood something important about her on a Saturday, theoretically I could call her. I never have.

We both obey the rules of the frame of treatment. We start and stop sessions on time. It does not matter if the most significant moment occurs after 44 minutes. We still stop on time. It doesn't matter if an overwhelming tragedy has hijacked my heart the hour before Lynn's time slot. I still start her session on time.

What are the human benefits and costs of this arrangement? For both participants, one benefit is that it allows treatment to be a laboratory for learning to bear life's "terminations," some of which make some sense, and some, from our point of view, are painfully arbitrary.

I think most of us resist awareness of how much in life is ruled by chance and seems arbitrary. Why did some people miss their train on September 11, 2001, and get to work too late to be a victim of the disaster? As one of my patients constantly asked me, why was Sandra Buechler born with two good legs while she had to spend her life trapped in a motorized wheelchair?

The frame of sessions has just the right arbitrariness, from my point of view, to be a microcosm of much of the rest of life. Why 45 minutes? We can make a theoretical argument for the use of the couch and the number of sessions per week, but it is hard to find airtight arguments for (or against) other aspects of the arrangements. Fees, for example, vary widely, with seemingly little rhyme or reason. Certain policies about paying for missed sessions can also feel somewhat arbitrary, although the need for an articulated policy is clear to most.

In her astonishing paper, Melitta Schmideberg (1947) blithely dispensed with most aspects of the analytic frame. If a patient "rang," she would see him or her that day, even asking someone waiting for an established session to yield the slot to the more troubled caller. She described running from one consultation room to the next, conducting two sessions at once, sometimes also talking with people in the hall. When I assign this paper to candidates, they are, at first, delighted by it. It seems so liberated and so profoundly empathic. Here was an analyst who cared more about her patients' needs than about following a set of dusty old rules.

But then some of them think further. She must have thought she was indispensable. No emergency could be handled without her! And how could she believe in her own omniscience enough to calculate who needed her most?

At this point, some candidates begin to express appreciation for the usual, somewhat arbitrary frame. At least with that, both analyst and patient know the routine. No hocus-pocus about the analyst divining whose needs merit attention most. Perhaps "to each according to their need" is idealistic in theory but, at least in therapeutic settings, hard to translate into practical reality.

Arbitrariness is something you can count on. Lynn knows that it is very likely that there will be times when she needs to talk to me more on Tuesday, when she does not have an appointment, than on Wednesday, when she does. In the same way as she knows that her grocer won't lower his prices in the months she is strapped for cash, she knows that her analyst's presence or absence does not vary according to the degree of her urgency. I think this is a crucial aspect of the frame, in that it declares that to live in this world, a human being has to come to terms with arbitrariness. Of course it is arbitrary only from one vantage point. From inside Lynn, my availability is arbitrary because it does not correspond to the intensity of her feelings. *It would make more emotional sense to Lynn if I were most likely to be present when she most needed my presence.* From inside Sandra, however, the regularity of the schedule makes more emotional sense.

Edgar Levenson (1982) made the significant point that the "frame" is not established, once and for all, at the outset of treatment but continues to be negotiated throughout the work. From his point of view, the frame includes the expectations each participant has of the other and of the treatment. Expectations constantly shift, get redefined, are disappointed, or are gratified. The bar raises and lowers all the time. This is another way that treatment parallels other relationships and, therefore, can serve as a microcosm. When one of us feels shocked by the other's incomprehension, unreliability, insensitivity, or any other major jolt, can we recover? Like any other relationship, the treatment partners frequently face the challenges of the "morning after." Can we forgive and/or forget? Must we forget in order to forgive? Can we will ourselves to forgive? Because recovery is as relevant in treatment as it is in the rest of life, treatment can serve as a microcosm.

Like so much else in life, treatment is a deal struck between two people. Each has something the other wants. The arrangement is based on bartering. But what, exactly, is exchanged, aside from money? Fundamentally the clinician offers his or her attention for a circumscribed period of time per week. In other words, we rent out our minds (and hearts). The terms of the deal obviously differ from those of most other intimate relationships. But the barter system is, I would say, similar.

Certain issues, that we can call "oedipal" if we wish, recur inside the frame. The only way I have been able to make sense of the oedipal issue is that it is a language for unsatisfied human longing. We are always wanting more than we are strictly owed. So a central human challenge is learning to negotiate the feelings this elicits. In this sense treatment's limitations and arbitrary qualities form the perfect microcosm for discovering one's handicaps in learning to bear this aspect of life. Through living within the treatment microcosm, we (both) have an opportunity to repair our equipment for dealing with this universal human challenge.

Shakespeare's *King Lear* (1633/1972) poignantly expressed this human quandary. Lear's daughter Goneril has just disputed her father's need, not just for the large retinue he demands but for any retinue. Lear cries,

> O, reason not the need! Our basest beggars
> Are in the poorest thing superfluous;
> Allow not nature more than nature needs,
> Man's life is cheap as beast's. Thou art a lady;
> If only to go warm were gorgeous,
> Why, nature needs not what thou gorgeous wear'st,
> Which scarcely keeps thee warm. ... (Act II, Scene 2,
>   Lines 453–460)

"Reason not the need" is, in my way of thinking, a brilliant expression of one of the play's central themes. Need can't be understood from reason alone. Give a human being only what he or she, strictly speaking, reasonably needs, and you reduce him or her to an elemental "beast."

Interestingly Cordelia, the daughter Lear renounces, makes the same error. When asked, in Act I, Scene 1, to express her love for her father, she answers,

> I love your majesty
> According to my bond, no more nor less. (Lines 93–94)

Told by her father to mend her speech, Cordelia, nevertheless, remains resolutely reasonable.

> Good my lord,
> You have begot me, bred me, loved me. I
> Return those duties back as are right fit,
> Obey you, love you, and most honour you. (Lines 95–98)

Perfectly reasonable and, for that reason, in a way, heartless. Cordelia sticks to the "frame" and, by so doing, is the first of the three daughters to break her father's heart.

Reason would dictate the size of the retinue Lear needs, just as it would limit each of us to love our parents only according to the bonds of parent and child. The wild, reckless love of a child who wants to "marry" a parent is out of bounds. It is not reasonable. It must be tamed. The treatment frame makes the same demands. That makes it a good microcosm of much of life. It requires analyst and patient to accept a limited relationship, so we can have all that *is* possible. In a sense, the price of having what is possible is forgoing demanding the impossible. "Resolution" of the oedipal issue means, to me, coming to terms with this aspect of life.

Just what does that elicit in each of us? I would say that for some people, in treatment, it elicits a consummate acting job. One or both participants behave as though the possible was also acceptable, because that allows the work to go on. Whether or not this is a good outcome depends on one's point of view. It is good as a rehearsal for much else in life. But it is bad in that it does not get at the whole truth.

Oedipus had to learn the hard way that appearances can be deceiving. A man you take to be a stranger turns out to be the father you are doomed to kill. Our capacity for knowing reality (through our senses and our powers of reasoning) is limited. Oedipus had to lose the faith that he knew what he was doing. Eventually he recruited physical blindness to advertise this new awareness.

From my point of view, the treatment frame expresses some of life's (and Shakespeare's, and Sophocles') basic lessons:

1. One of the most difficult human challenges is finding a truthful way to live within limits, whether these limits are imposed by our own fallibility, the needs of others, or societal dictates.
2. We often don't know what we are doing until it is too late. We may be dividing our kingdoms between our daughters before we are really ready to retire. The next stranger we kill could be our father. For this reason, we must have rules that will seem arbitrary, because they *imperfectly match felt experience*. But they also protect us from acting impulsively before we are aware of possible consequences.

3. Even the most intimate relationships can be seen as deals of some kind. You give me this, and I give you that. Lear wants a show of love and honor in return for his kingdom. Oedipus wants to be a hero for solving a riddle with his superior powers of reason. Analysts and patients agree to a swap enacted and symbolized by the frame.

4. Surprise can be traumatic. Ritual constraints, however arbitrary they may feel, can safeguard us from some surprises.

Too late, Lear's fool warns him:

> He that keeps nor crust nor crumb,
> Weary of all, shall want some. (Act I, Scene 4, Lines 188–189)

In other words, life can surprise you (e.g., by making you sorely miss what you once longed to give away). In a storm of upheaval, Lear (and Gloucester) has to turn his every verity on its head. The "good" offspring is really evil, and the "bad" is really saintly. Traumatic surprises are equally central to the tragedy of Oedipus. He, too, is shocked into an entirely new perspective.

By prescribing the limits and extent of the analytic relationship, the frame eliminates some surprises and, I think, facilitates others. The surprising leaps that connect childhood events to current experiences are made possible, in part, by the protection from surprise that the frame provides. Unlike Lear, Gloucester, and Oedipus, in analysis the partners can take much about the process for granted. Analytic rituals dictate a nonsurprising sameness about the room, the analyst's behavior, and the "deal." Because these basics can be taken for granted, a kind of creativity becomes more likely. Limited choices concentrate effort and bring out creative variation. For example, painters of the Annunciation in the 1400s had to obey certain restrictions. Some surprises were off limits. This focused them on a moment, out of all possible moments: the moment when the angel Gabriel reveals Mary's fate to her. Focusing on that moment, some brought out Mary's shy gaze, whereas others emphasized Gabriel's intensity.

Analysis has been aptly understood by Irwin Hoffman (1998) as an effort to integrate ritual and spontaneity. He described "a continual struggle with the tension between spontaneous responsiveness and adherence to psychoanalytic ritual" (p. 235). My own way of saying this is that by prescribing rituals, such as the setting, the frame eliminates some surprises, *which potentiates others*. Because we know we won't physically touch, we have to concentrate all our tenderness in our words. Because we won't dance, we have to create other ways of partnering each other. By making some things off limits, the rituals engender a specific kind of creativity. We can't turn our schedules around, so we turn our ideas around. For example, we ask what if "B" caused "A" rather than the other way around. Another way to think about this is that in most intimate relationships, many kinds of projects are possible. For some of us, there are many potential ways to collaborate with work partners. Some personal relationships include the joint raising of children. Study groups can decide to write something together. But analysis concentrates all our creativity into one project. The limited format forces us to find creative ways to express our individuality and to reach each other emotionally. Physical hugs between people are fairly similar, but verbal hugs differ and can take a good deal of creative effort.

In sum, the treatment frame challenges us to find creative ways to express the basic emotions within its bounds. Given all we are not allowed to do, how do we still care for, create, enjoy, encounter, argue with, and forgive each other? But then, isn't that really a microcosm of all of life? Within the boundaries of fleeting opportunity, how do we nevertheless forge a life that is satisfying, rich with love, work, and play?

LOST IDOLS AND IDYLLS

Before I further explore the frame as an exercise in bearing loss (for both participants), I would like to make clear that I have taken from my reading of Winnicott (1971) the idea that whatever traumatizes us has such a severe impact because it repeats an earlier trauma. In a parallel sense, I am suggesting that when the frame of treatment is experienced as a tremendously painful loss, it is partially because it (usually symbolically) repeats a significant previous loss.

So far I have suggested that the frame serves as a microcosm of some of life's limitations and that the two people in a treatment cocreate the particular ambience of their frame. Each couple lives the frame in its own way, just as each married couple lives the institution of marriage in its own way. We can point out patterns and aggregate some marriages in a category, such as "very competitive" or "collaborative," but this does not completely capture the lifelong love affair between two particular people, who may have had three children, loved to go bird-watching together, frequently fought over money issues, and so on.

What are the human losses that treatment often repeats or, in a sense, confirms? That is, what aspects of the limitations inherent in human experience are easily recruited by the frame? At this moment I am not distinguishing between analyst and patient, although my primary focus is the clinician. Although their experiences of the frame may significantly differ, for both it asserts certain similar prohibitions. What everyday human tragedies are both analyst and patient likely to (re)live?

LOSS OF BELIEF IN MAGICAL HARMONY

Treatment demonstrates and confirms that we can't expect magical harmony between others and ourselves. By the frame's very existence, it negates the hope that the analyst will appear just at the moment he or she is most needed. Similarly, for the analyst, the frame confirms that rules are necessary to ensure that the patient will attend sessions, pay the fee, and generally refrain from the behaviors it prohibits. In other words, the magic of two people in perfect synchrony, automatically knowing and fulfilling each other's needs, is not to be expected. For most people this is not news. But I don't think that means it isn't experienced as a loss and, sometimes, a traumatic loss.

Similarly, the frame confirms that the magic of being perfectly understood will be a rare occurrence, if it ever happens. As always, I am using the word *frame* in a Levensonian sense (see above) to mean the establishment of what can and can't be expected from the treatment.

LOSS OF CHILDHOOD

Adolescence has been considered by some to be a protracted period of mourning for the end of childhood (Kiel, 1964). Of course it can mean other things, including a protracted period of *celebrating* the end of childhood! But I think there can be a significant loss integral to this moment in life (whenever it occurs chronologically). Whatever loving care we have or have not received when we were not yet fully formed and still brimming with promise, there comes a time when childhood's opportunities end, or, at least, it seems to most like they should end.

Treatment's frame naturally reminds us (analysts and patients) of that moment and replays its particular personal meanings for each of us. It can provide a medium for remediation of our difficulties with the transition from childhood's privileges and interpersonal expectations to adulthood. That is, aspects of the frame can serve as repetitions of the (relatively) limited way adults take care of each other, as compared with how parents (we hope) take care of very young children. This can occasion reliving mourning childhood's end. For example, after years of seeming relatively emotionally unconnected to the treatment, a patient of mine became very agitated about a scheduled break. The frame, in the sense of its regulation of contact between analyst and patient, has (finally!) come to symbolize his previous traumatic experiences of the unavailability of care.

The frame does more than merely symbolize *previous* limited care. It also provides a template for a *new rendition* of the issue in the treatment. This can be especially painful (and potentially valuable) for those who were insufficiently nurtured in early life (as I elaborate more fully later). For many patients, the meaning of the frame is more than just the limitations in what they can expect from the analyst. The meaning extends to the feeling that this is all the analyst *wants* to give. For some this brings back, in full force, the feeling of being thrust out of childhood dependency, perhaps before they felt ready to take care of themselves. For others it replays the feeling of never having been taken care of at all.

The frame can represent and concretely provide loss experiences for the analyst and for the patient. What can't be lived out between them is often as vivid for the analyst as it is for the patient. Everything about the therapeutic relationship depends on what must be left out of it, as well as what can be included. Obviously, any sexual contact is prohibited. But so much more than that is (at least for some analysts, including me) out of bounds. Although sharing of countertransferential responses and information about the personhood of the analyst is much more common than it used to be, the treatment is still, mainly, about helping the patient have a richer life. Prioritizing this means to me (among so many other things) that no matter how much my patient who is a stockbroker might be of personal use to me, I will never ask him for tips on the market. The moment when I realize this provides a chance for *me* to relive my own transition from childhood dependency.

It seems important to emphasize that although I have focused on the losses inherent in the frame, I do not mean to imply that loss is the only way the frame is experienced. It also, at least potentially, provides a firm basis for what *can* be expected. This can be very reassuring to many (patients and analysts), especially those who suffered from parental unreliability or neglect.

We hope that in childhood we can feel entitled to have basic needs met. If we profoundly need attention, there is a way to get it (at least in relatively good familial circumstances). I think that for many, the frame relives the time in our lives when we first consciously recognized that we might not get attention when we most need it. An adult has to be able to bear this. Something else, or someone else, may be the priority. For some the frame crystallizes this aspect of adult life. In a sense, both participants have to accept, as we all do at some point, that sometimes it is not our turn. It is someone else's. No matter how much we need, or want, it to be our turn, it is *still* someone else's. In earliest childhood we are not expected to understand the concept of taking turns. But at some point this changes. For many, I think, the frame is a reminder of that change, a reiteration of it, and an opportunity, in a sense, to relive and rework it. How do we each bear learning that it may not be our turn at our moment of most intense need?

LOSS OF WHAT NEVER EXISTED

I have already alluded to the pain, for some people, of reminders of the childhood care and security that they have never had. I think this can be experienced as an acute loss, seemingly in response to the frame of the treatment. But how can we lose what we have never had? This is a very important question, to my way of thinking, and it is much broader than I can address here. But I suggest that the losses of what never existed form some of the most painful losses in many lives.

People often look around at what (they imagine) others have and feel intense envy, rage, competition, and jealousy. It isn't fair. How come he (or she) has a partner, when I am just as deserving? How come they have children, money, opportunities for a more varied life experience? Why do they have better parents than I had? Even in comparison to their own children, some people feel cheated and go through what I would call mourning for the advantages they never had themselves.

The frame can bring this home in a vivid way. Sherby (1989) wrote about a patient who protested that her analyst should have been her mother. The satisfactions and limitations of the analytic situation made clear for her what she would never experience. She *could* have a very able, responsive analyst as her analyst but not as her mother. The patient demanded to know why others (in Sherby's family) could have Sherby as a mother and she would never have that experience, no matter how much she needed it.

I am suggesting that these losses (of what never existed) are sometimes made palpable by the frame. The treatment helps some patients (and analysts) know what truly attuned relating feels like, perhaps for the first time. The absence of such attunement in past or current life partners, parents, or others stands out against this background. Of course it can also go the other way, and the treatment partners can be *less* attuned than others in both participants' lives. But I am emphasizing what happens when treatment acquaints patients with warm, empathic attunement for the first time or one of the few times in their lives. Clinicians are generally familiar with the phenomenon of patients who begin to feel unsatisfied with their partners after individual treatment has gotten well under way. This can occur for many reasons, including triangular dynamics. But certainly one possibility is that the patient is beginning to profoundly understand what has always been missing in his or her primary relationship. Through what it permits and prohibits, the frame makes the significance of these losses clear for both participants.

The pain of never having had some satisfactions recruits different emotions for different people. For some, it evokes feelings of having let oneself down. One patient feels if only she would have gotten treatment earlier, more of life's joys would have been hers. In a sense her feelings include guilt toward herself. What she has never had, and believes she will never have, feels like her own fault. She experiences some shame (a sense of inadequacy) about this, too. But mostly she lives in a state of guilty regret. This is the shape of *her* pain. For others it easier to blame those who they feel have failed them, rather than themselves, for what they never had. I want to emphasize that good treatment relationships can engender guilty regret in either or both participants.

SPECIFIC FANTASIES DISCONFIRMED BY THE FRAME

Probably there are endlessly varying fantasies that are disconfirmed by the existence and terms of the frame. Here I list several, but I imagine they will remind clinicians of others they have encountered. I suggest that these fantasies can be precious to patients and analysts alike. Their disconfirmation can be met with many forms of mourning, including very angry protests.

The fantasy of the perfect soul mate. No doubt there are many forms of the fantasy of the perfect soul mate. One, with which I am familiar, has an intellectual flavor. It is the fantasy of someone who would think in perfect tandem with us and whose interests exactly match ours. Our curiosity would focus on the same subjects at the same time. Our values and emotional reactions would also jive. The same aspects of culture and the arts would most appeal to us both, and we would want to share them. In treatment patients and analysts can fantasize that they have found that soul mate in each other and then experience the frame as blocking the perfect fulfillment that would be possible as lifelong partners. This fantasy may contribute to the high incidence of boundary violations between patients and analysts that are being made public today.

The fantasy of dispensing with the need for self-interest. In this fantasy there is no need to assert self-interest, because the two people have each other's interests as uppermost priorities. Making sure one's own needs are met becomes unnecessary. The other person will reliably see to that.

The fantasy of words being unnecessary. The wish to be understood magically, without exerting any effort, can take the form of a fantasy of words being unnecessary or an idealization of nonverbal forms of communication and devaluation of verbal communication. It is interesting to me that some children seem to hold on to this wish more strongly than others. Perhaps many of us still harbor it, in some form, as adults. In any case, clinicians are familiar with protests against having to speak in order to be understood. Some patients (and analysts) wish other avenues of communication, such as touch, were possible in treatment.

The fantasy of having all needs met by one person. This wish has obvious roots in the maternal relationship (or its absence). I have encountered it in other areas of life besides treatment. Some people seem to insist on finding a partner or a friend who satisfies all their needs. This issue can be played out in relation to work as well. The search for the perfect job or career that satisfies all emotional, intellectual, and spiritual needs can be endless and endlessly disappointing.

The fantasy of perfect agreement. Perhaps this fantasy can be described as a wish to control the mind of the other person. In any case, the wish is for a partner who will never see things substantially differently. This can be expressed as a desire or demand never to be criticized in any way. One can always cite a theory that explains why this wish should be granted.

The terms of the frame can clash with any one of these fantasies, or all of them, depending on how the frame is lived by individual analysts and patients. Probably all analysts and patients cocreate their own variation of the frame, which meets some of their individual needs but not all.

We can also consider how theory shapes the terms of the frame an analyst prefers. Of course the analyst's character plays a role in the theory he or she adopts, so all these variables are related. And the same analyst probably lives the frame differently with different patients. But overall, the "classical" frame, with its ideals of neutrality and abstinence, seems likely to create clashes with some patients' and analysts' fantasies more than others. Similarly a Kohutian might more comfortably fulfill certain of the patient's (and his or her own) wishes that an "interpersonalist" doesn't, and so on. Frames are built from varying materials, including the character styles of two people, their (associated) values and beliefs, and their characteristic ways of dealing with emotionally charged issues.

The frame's lessons about what is unavailable can be crystallized at termination, when unavailability becomes palpable and permanent. In the next section I describe one potentially painful consequence of this. I have found that sometimes it has seemed to me as though patients terminating have stripped me of aspects of my *own* self-experience.

THE ULTIMATE TEST: TERMINATING RESPECTFULLY

Once again, I am expressing some thoughts and feelings that, for me, accompany the reality that clinicians lose every treatment partner we ever know (see Chapter 7 for further discussion of this topic). This is obvious and yet shocking. How does this incredible accumulation of lost relationships affect us as human beings? What impact does it have on our ability to invest in the next (therapeutic or personal) relationship? How might these losses contribute to burnout?

Among the most peculiar aspects of emotional life as a clinician is the subtle injunction not to "make a fuss" about these losses. It would be unseemly, maybe even unprofessional, to mind terminations, except, perhaps, when they are unplanned. Although, at least in the current therapeutic climate, we are encouraged to respect the power of the relationship between the clinician and the patient as a vital aspect of treatment, it seems as though its *loss* is not supposed to have a major impact on *us*. We expect ourselves to magically transform our involvement with one patient into an involvement with the next.

My former patients are frozen in time, never aging, like pressed, dried flowers marking a memory. I hold the story of their early history; I hold their dreams. I shared their hopes. I learned so much about them. I remember so many tiny details and have no one to tell them to. I am alone in an echo chamber, my recollections reverberating only with each other. There is no way to be more alone, more cutoff.

LOSING MYSELF

To describe how I lose aspects of myself when patients leave treatment, I focus on Barbara, a middle-aged woman I treated three times a week for many years. How did losing her affect me? When I was with her, I almost believed in God. God was one of the few explanations of her radiance that made any sense to me. Her face had its own light. It had, in fact, a whole complement of weather conditions. Brief showers would sometimes magically give way to sunshine. No matter how long clouds prevailed, I always knew the sun would eventually shine through.

I couldn't look at her face without believing that there had to be a God. In her presence I found myself smiling, though I'm not sure why. I firmly asserted what her future held, as though I saw it clearly. I *knew*. I allowed myself brief fantasies of growing old beside her.

I was quite aware that I was different from my usual self when I was with her. But it didn't really feel so much like I had changed. Rather, the world seemed different, and I had just responded naturally to it.

Barbara's lively beauty was a secret from herself. I found it astonishing that she thought she was plain. It gave persuasive testimony to the power of the unconscious. Looking in the mirror Barbara could only see herself through her mother's eyes. I let myself hate her shadowy monster mother. This, too, was an unusual self-indulgence. But it seemed necessary for me to hate the woman who fed on Barbara's life so greedily. Hating Barbara's mother helped me feel I wouldn't let myself do something similar.

In some ways, Barbara reminded me of other strong women whose self-esteem has been battered. Barbara was too old to start her life again but not old enough to accept her tally of joys as final. She was in her 40s, newly self-aware enough to realize she should have married a soul mate but too spent to start looking for one. She found me instead.

Barbara was an accomplished, beautiful woman who often saw herself as an unintelligent, ugly nobody. Shame was her lifelong companion.

When I was with Barbara, I was sure of myself. I knew my job as well as I knew my name. It was my job to help Barbara push her mother out of the way when she looked in the mirror. I needed to introduce her to her own smile, and how it radiated aliveness, and the pinpoints of light dancing in her eyes.

Losing Barbara includes losing the person I could be when I was with her. I focus on this loss here. I hope to understand what I have lost, besides her presence. Who could I have been if Barbara hadn't left us to create herself elsewhere? For her sake, I am glad she left. A new life awaited her, full of professional and personal opportunity, in a rich intellectual environment well suited to bring out her gifts. I am genuinely happy for *her*. But what about *me*?

I used to believe that losing patients, and others, was bearable so long as we cut our losses to their minimum. If we could retain the inner object, we could bear the loss of the external object. In other words, if unresolved anger, regret, guilt, or any other negative feeling didn't keep me from having a good relationship with the internalized Barbara, I should be able to bear losing her actual presence in my office. This thought used to comfort me more than it does now. Experience has led me to two unavoidable conclusions.

1. I miss Barbara's body. No "inner object" has her fragrance or fills a chair the way she did.
2. I miss becoming all the Sandras I would have become for her sake.

Rilke (1934) told us that loving is "a high inducement for the individual to ripen, to become something in himself, to become world, to become world in himself for the sake of another person; it is a great, demanding claim on him, something that chooses him and calls him to vast distances" (pp. 69–70). Thus, the child takes her first steps toward the arms of someone she loves who also loves her. I don't believe that she takes her first steps toward the idea of someone but, rather, toward that person's arms. Throughout life, we become a world for the sake of another person. When I do treatment, I count on this. Over time, I have become a more convinced interpersonalist. Growth is always interpersonal. At least partially, it is both *toward someone* and *for someone*. Although at times it may be possible, I think it is less likely for us to grow for the sake of the idea of someone. When a loving mother holds her arms wide open, she invites her toddler to brave first steps. Excited joy carries the child forward, forgetful of past bruises and brushes with pain and fear. I believe this never changes. Only love gives us the courage it takes to cover the vast distances between our first and our last steps.

In treatment the two of us create a world with its own phrases, memories, rituals, and jokes. It is fully alive so long as we are together. We hope that when we part something remains, but it is not the same. Barbara won't surprise me tomorrow. I won't change for her sake tomorrow. We won't invent a new phrase. We won't look forward to being together next week or think about what we should work on in the future. I might try to grow, some, for the sake of the *idea* of her, but it is not the same high inducement as it would be if she still brought her unmistakable ambience to my office. What is the cumulative effect on the analyst of losing so many selves?

WHILE SOMEONE ELSE IS EATING

About suffering they were never wrong,
The Old Masters: how well they understood
Its human position: how it takes place
While someone else is eating or opening a
Window or just walking dully along

—"Musee des Beaux Arts" by W. H. Auden (Young, 2010, p. 3)

Many have commented about the incongruity of loss against the backdrop of others leading their daily lives, unaware of the tragedy next door. We have the urge to shout, to break the silence and disturb the peace. It feels sacrilegious that everyday life continues unbroken. It seems an offense, an affront to the dead.

Yet, when Joan Didion's husband, John, died, and the doctor was hesitating about telling her, the social worker said it was okay to tell her, because "she's a pretty cool customer" (2005, p. 15). As she left the hospital, she "wondered what an uncool customer would be allowed to do. Break down? Require sedation? Scream?" (p. 16). I think that in general society gives us conflicting injunctions about our responses to death. It's wrong to look too cool, but it is also wrong to lose control entirely. Of course the expected response differs a great deal, depending on the nature of the situation. But, often, it seems inappropriate to be unaffected but equally inappropriate to be totally unhinged.

But for us, as clinicians, when we lose a patient, how are we expected to act? And what are our own expectations of ourselves? Speaking for myself, I know I feel obligated to keep confidentiality so that I would not discuss with the next patient the termination of the patient who just left. Even if the two know each other, in some way, I would never say, "Boy, I am going to miss her!" It is precisely this problem, that confidentiality requires us never to talk to one patient about another, that convinced Ferenczi (Dupont, 1988) he had to abandon his experiment with "mutual analysis." We may choose to disclose other aspects of our lives, but we can't talk about our experience with one patient to another.

I think the pull, here, is to be a kind of "cool customer," in Didion's sense. But this can come at a cost. Perhaps the feel and meaning of it is different for each of us, but I will try to describe my own experience. I remember a last session with a patient I had seen for more than 10 years. It was a "good" termination in that the treatment had been helpful, and we were able to spend some time looking back and reflecting on our work together. Still there was the inevitable sadness, along with many positive feelings. In the midst of actually saying good-bye, the buzzer sounded, announcing the next patient's arrival. I remember having a brief moment of embarrassment, as though I had been caught at something. Later, I questioned myself about this reaction. What was there to feel ashamed of?

I think, for me, buzzing in the next person before the departing patient left felt like I was being too "cool" a "customer." I was transitioning too smoothly. In Auden's language, I was "just walking dully along." I was resuming ordinary life before the body was cold, so to speak. Perhaps it also felt a bit like showing off, as though I were demonstrating that I can just move on. We are back in elementary school, and someone is painfully taking her leave, and I am smugly announcing that I already have someone else to sit with in the cafeteria.

THE SHOCK OF EXPECTED LOSSES

In summarizing some firsthand reports of responses to a death, Joan Didion (2005) suggested, "The most frequent immediate responses to death were shock, numbness, and a sense of disbelief" (p. 46). It seems very meaningful, to me, that human beings often respond to a death with surprise, in some sense, even when it has been long anticipated. Similarly, the termination of a treatment can have a surprising impact on the clinician, even if it had been planned well in advance. Perhaps the surprise is a reaction to grief's unexpected intensity. Or, maybe, when we are anticipating losses, we are thinking about them in the abstract, but when they happen, their concrete meanings become evident.

No matter how well planned a termination may be, I might still feel a shock when Monday morning 10 o'clock rolls around and, for the first time, no one is at the door. Yes, I knew about the termination of the patient who used to come at 10 on Mondays. But what I knew was the abstract *idea* that he was gone. It is only at 10 on the first Monday after termination that I am shocked by the *actuality* of his absence from my life.

For me, the aspect of a treatment termination that is hardest to realize is its impoverishment of my own self-experience. It is far easier (though it may be painful) to understand the loss of the patient. What is most difficult is to comprehend that because of this ending, I, myself, am diminished. Some of my selves are gone. Persons I was becoming may never exist. This can be extremely hard to grasp, let alone accept. Returning to the subject of Maisy, the patient I described in the opening of this chapter, I want to express that by the time I retire from practice, I hope I have learned more ways to hold on to my Maisy.

Chapter 9

Transcending Shame and Sorrow

THE EFFECT OF WRITING ON THE CLINICIAN'S EMOTIONAL BALANCE

There are times when clinical work alone does not provide enough to rescue us from the shame and sorrow it can engender. I need to be transported to a plane where time stands still. At least for me, writing provides one avenue for this transformation. On this level clinical moments that, in themselves, may have been fraught with pain can initiate contemplation that doesn't have to obey time limitations or any other requirements. I can allow myself to get lost and roam around in my thoughts, much as I love to get lost in a city that is new to me. Of course, in theory I could experience this transformation within sessions, and not just in writing about them, and in actuality this does sometimes happen. But when I am doing clinical work, I can't stray endlessly. Also, in my writing, for example, the patient who leaves me becomes an instance of a phenomenon rather than John Jones, who felt he wasn't getting enough to make it worthwhile to stay in treatment with Sandra Buechler. At least for me, writing most easily brings me to a *higher level of abstraction*. This reminds me of something Levenson (1982) wrote about supervision. He said that clarity is easier to achieve in supervision than in clinical work, because in supervision we deal with a *class* of patients rather than one person in all his or her (sometimes confusing) particularity. Furthermore, I would say that both writing and supervision have in common the absence of the moment-by-moment press of a live transference–countertransference exchange. This limits them in some ways but also removes them from some of the painful immediacy of acute shame and sorrow.

Another way to put this is that when I write, clinical experiences that could bring me shame and sorrow find uses that transform their meaning (at least to some degree). In an emotional sense, the arithmetic has changed. Subtraction has given way to addition. Moments of loss of self-esteem have been transmuted into moments where enhanced curiosity changes the balance of my emotions, and new understandings can add to my capacities. For example, clinically, I may have experienced a patient's abrupt termination as (partially) my failure. For the moment, that may be its most vivid meaning to me. But when I start to write about it, the termination becomes an event that can help me self-reflect, learn, and teach. Of course, once again, in theory the termination could take on these functions without my having to write about it, but I think the act of writing facilitates this jump to a higher level of abstraction. In writing, I experience a jolt that knocks me into a new self-consciousness. Similarly Jacobs (2008) sees writing about clinical work as providing an opportunity to take one's personal analysis further:

> Writing and rereading, then, offer surprises, and with those surprises the possibility of new knowledge, new insight. They continue, I believe, to add to the process of reawakening and reworking old conflicts, old solutions, old images of self and other that begins in one's analysis, inevitably continues in our own clinical work, and is given impetus when we turn our hands to writing about the deeply stirring experiences that we share with our patients as we engage with them in the analytic process. (p. 517)

In an article on "forging an analytic identity through clinical writing," Palmer (2008) used Winnicott's concept of transitional relating. Palmer reminded us of our privileges in Winnicott's transitional space. In that realm we are never asked the question, "Did you conceive of this, or was it presented to you from without?" In the magical dimension of the transitional, this question is never formulated. I suggest that this is *precisely* the relief the analyst most needs. As analysts we spend most of our waking hours intent on differentiating what is coming from outside versus what we have injected into the situation. In other words, the differentiation of transference–countertransference from *non*transferential–countertransferential perception is crucial to our work. We are always trying to grasp the part we have and have not played in the patient's experience of us. We are constantly doing the work of deciphering interpersonal from intrapsychic experiences. I believe this necessitates frequent forays into transitional space. I, personally, frequently crave the relief of a kind of time-out. When I write, at least in the first phase, I simply try to put my feelings, thoughts, and perceptions into words. Later in the process I may make more distinctions, but in a first draft, I allow myself the freedom to wander in transitional territory, to graze, and to explore. I let words happen, without subjecting them to judgment or scrutiny about their origins. Perhaps the freedom I allow myself in writing is available to others in their clinical work, but, for me, each has its own permissions, responsibilities, and limitations. When I write I depend on the existence of a "delete" button that is missing in much of the rest of life.

Another way to understand the relief of writing about clinical encounters is to refer to emotion theory (Izard, 1977). As I have frequently mentioned, concepts from emotion theory have often informed my clinical work and its formulation (Buechler, 2004, 2008). In emotion theory terms, every moment of our lives we experience an array of shifting feelings. In that the emotions form a system, any change in the level of intensity of a feeling affects the intensity of all our other emotions. Thus, for example, if I become more anxious, my curiosity level is likely to change, as will the strength of my joy.

Joy and curiosity seem especially important in trying to understand how writing can affect the author's emotional balance. Elsewhere, I have explored the healing powers of joy (Buechler, 2002b). In a general sense, human joy can be understood as "a sense of harmony and unity with the object of joy and, to some extent, with the world. Some people have reported that in ecstatic joy they tend to lose individual identity, as in the case of some mystical experiences associated with meditation" (Izard, 1977, p. 271). In other words, joy can be a product of shedding our usual sense of separateness and unique individuality. We have probably all experienced magical moments of losing ourselves. In my paper on joy (Buechler, 2002b), I wrote of times where "I lose myself in the feel of the work. The patient and I are not bound by our histories and self-definitions. We are two instances of life" (p. 617). As analysts we have countless opportunities for time and space travel, and in some senses, this is even more true when we write about our clinical work. We enter the worlds of others, trying to see through their eyes and know them through their yearnings. Of course I am always myself, but, in unmoored joy, my awareness of these limitations is intermittent.

As analysts and writers we have access to another source of joy, the enjoyment of appreciating our individuality. Writing, in particular, can facilitate forging a professional point of view. Often contrasts teach us who we are. Noticing details about how each of us experiences life can help us articulate our own, unique perspective on being human. I think of writing as, in part, a voyage of self-discovery. I get to investigate how my ways of thinking, feeling, and behaving are different from, as well as similar to, the patient's. I also get to identify commonalities between other clinicians and me and, at the same time, cultivate and recognize my individual analytic voice.

In my paper on joy, I concluded, "Heightened awareness of the profoundly human and the richly idiosyncratic provides some of the potential joys of an analytic life" (p. 621). To me, joy is the universal antidote to all the negative feelings in life in general and in treatment in particular. Moments of joy make the painful aspects of life bearable. Another way to express this is that joy improves our emotional balance, regardless of what has rendered us off-kilter. In 2008, my way of expressing this was as follows:

> If anger is fundamentally a response to an obstacle, joy frames what cannot be overcome with what can. If anxiety and shame are ways of feeling insufficient, joy says sometimes I can be enough. If sadness spotlights loss, joy that exists alongside it makes figure and ground out of losses and gains. (Buechler, 2008, p. 120)

Many opportunities for joy exist for the analytic writer. Through reading and writing we can discover, or rediscover, our common humanity and our particular individuality. When I read Maroda (2005), Mitchell (1993), or Zeddies (2002), I feel less alone. I recognize fellow travelers. The more the writer reveals of his or her own process, the clearer are our similarities, as well as our differences. I can access the joy of feeling at one with them, as they describe their clinical travails. I can also discern differences in our styles. Sometimes I can say something like, "That is interesting. I don't think I would have said that to the patient, but I can see why it might be helpful." Sometimes as I read or write, I become unusually aware that one of my analytic ancestors is looking over my shoulder, pointing out the places where an "interpersonal" orientation differs from a "classical Freudian" or other theoretical affiliation. In other words, reading and writing help me define my analytic identity through contrasts.

Partially because of their level of abstraction, I think reading and writing enable us to experience a joyous triumph over the shame and sadness inherent in working clinically. To write we have to see something clearly enough to express it verbally. Although it may be true that in our best writing we evoke more than we (consciously) know, I think writing requires a level of mastery of experience way beyond many moments in sessions. A treatment hour can leave me speechless, utterly overwhelmed and lost. If I tried to write at those moments, I wouldn't know where to begin. By the time I feel able to put words down on paper, I have a better sense of what I am experiencing. I am, I would say, less likely to feel the insufficiency of being swamped or, as Harold Searles (1986) once wrote, outnumbered by the patient. I am, therefore, less likely to feel the total helplessness of shame combined with anxiety. (I explored the combination of shame and anxiety more extensively in Buechler [2008]; see also Chapter 3.) The combination of severe shame and anxiety can create a traumatic experience. If something happens in a session that makes the clinician feel totally overwhelmed, it may not be possible to learn from it or, at the worst, even remember it. As Sullivan famously said (1948, 1953), anxiety operates like a blow on the head.

Writing is often my way of trying to make sense of my experience. When I write I may not be consciously choosing to try to decrease my shame and anxiety, but that may be the result. In the most successful attempts at finding words, I have the joy of transcending an obstacle, overcoming personal limitations, feeling more emotionally connected with the patient and with myself, and, perhaps, (once again) recognizing my idiosyncratic personal idiom, to borrow a phrase from Bollas.

When we change our focus from the analyst's feelings of shame to the sorrows of the clinician, I think we can see that there are few outlets aside from reading and writing. There are no rituals for mourning a lost analysis. Unlike society's and religion's established rituals around death, our grief cannot be public. We can talk to no one who knew the patient. Even when we find colleagues to commiserate, we don't have the satisfaction of being able to say something like, "You remember how he always used to ..." No one, besides the patient, shares our memories. There is, in a way, no death as final as the death of an analysis. No loss is as complete or as ironic given that, most of the time, both people are still alive. Yet, at least in my way of working, I would not initiate contact with a former patient. I may never know what happened after we last saw each other.

In that what we write about a patient is always disguised, this format for remembering and reworking has its own limitations. But it may have to suffice, as the only monument we can erect, to commemorate the work we have done. It may be the only concrete marker of where we have traveled together. Writing about a patient may modulate the sorrow of loss in that I gain something from thinking, formulating, and expressing my experience. So what I have lost is modified by my gains. If I can use the writing to teach, I feel my memories are serving a purpose, which somewhat shifts my emotional balance in a positive direction.

For me, however, it is not as simple as this may sound. I don't always feel a notch less shame and sorrow when I write about a patient. Sometimes, through writing, I discover limitations in the treatment, at a point where it may be too late to address them, because the patient may have terminated. Sometimes, in remembering someone, I realize how much losing that patient means to me. Perhaps it would be more accurate to say that writing may make me more consciously aware of shame and sorrow about the limitations of my work. It is also true, at least for me, that when I write about someone, I feel that I am making new use of our experience together. This can be a positive feeling, adding to my sense of our joint gains, as noted previously. But it can also have a negative tinge. I can feel as though I am exposing something private, for my own aggrandizement. My choice to write about someone is unlikely to benefit him or her, but it may bring me rewards. Of course, it is possible that my enhanced clarity might benefit the treatment, if it is still ongoing, and it is possible for me to share what

I have written and thereby give the patient something of use. But, most of the time, I am the one to profit from the writing, in several senses.

One form this can take is that writing can enhance my curiosity. Writing transforms clinical events into something akin to marvelous blocks with which children can build anything imaginable. Many clinicians have explored the significant role curiosity plays in analysis (Buechler, 2004; Levenson, 2003; Stern, 2002). Here I consider its role in writing about treatment. Although curiosity can be defined in various ways, I come back to James's (1890) description of mind as "a theatre of simultaneous possibilities" (p. 288) and Izard's (1977) statement, "Our interest makes us want to turn things around, upside down, over, and about. This is because we see some possibility in the object or person or condition that is not immediately manifest to the senses" (p. 225).

I would suggest that writing about clinical work allows us to be actors and audience members in a theatre of simultaneous possibilities. What occurred in a session becomes just one of the countless examples of what could have happened. In a session I am constantly choosing a course of action (e.g., whether to remain silent or to speak). In thinking and possibly writing about it later, I can, in Izard's words, "turn things around, upside down, over, and about." To the fullest extent of my own imagination, I can exercise curiosity. The real clinical moment is transformed into a magical building block with limitless functions. Just as the block might gird a castle or a barn, the clinical moment might contribute to a study of defenses, a deeply personal exploration of my own countertransference, or a piece of writing on relational psychoanalysis, among endless other possibilities.

Thus writing transforms actual clinical moments into theatres of simultaneous possibilities. If I was silent in the session, I can imagine what might have happened if I had said, "What are you feeling, right now?" If I made inquiries I can imagine what might have happened had I been silent. In the theatre of my mind, the cast members are always ready to improvise their lines. A script exists, but it can be considered just a first draft. Like a child throwing a ball for the sheer pleasure of seeing what happens, I can wonder what might have happened if I had made different choices. Giving free reign to my curiosity, I can play with ideas, imagining what my own analyst might have done. In my mind, I can ask her to rewrite the script. Or I can call upon one of my former supervisors. Elsewhere, I have written about the "internal chorus" of teachers, supervisors, analysts, and others that the clinician internalizes in training (Buechler, 2004, 2008). When I write I can deliberately focus on what I imagine each of them might say, if I could consult with them about the clinical moment I am studying. Or I can wonder what Sullivan, or Kohut, or Mitchell, or anyone else might have done differently from the way I responded. The possibilities are endless.

But the actual clinical moment is a limited experience. Although, of course, it can be revisited, the patient and I made certain choices and not others. Thus, for us both, it may evoke shame and sorrow about the personal limitations it exposed and the opportunities that were lost. But later, as I prepare to write or as I merely reflect, the time-bound clinical moment is freed of all constraints. My shame and sorrow are not merely forgotten, they are transcended. Whatever limited me in the actual clinical encounter is transformed from a liability to an opportunity. I can use it to understand myself better, to write, or to teach. It morphs from a sample of my limitations into stretching equipment. It helps me focus on the clinician I might become in the future. My writing frequently brings me joy, in that it reminds me how I am "more human than otherwise" but also uniquely myself. It also stimulates my curiosity about the clinical instrument I might become tomorrow.

A paper I wrote in 2000 gave me an especially vivid experience of the struggle to use writing to transcend my own limitations and sorrows. In this paper I tried to convey my experience of the death of a patient I had treated for over a decade. My patient, who I will call Helen, was in her mid-30s when she died, suddenly, over a weekend. Although Helen had struggled most of her life with a crippling disability, we had no awareness of the immanence of her death. The poignancy of this loss was exacerbated by my feeling that Helen was finally overcoming the psychological obstacles that had prevented her from forming intimate relationships. I felt something like, "Oh, no! Not now! We have worked so hard, and, at last, she is ready to live her life with more love and joy. It isn't fair! She has fought so courageously, against so much hardship. How can it all end, now, and in an instant?"

My sorrow was for Sandra, as well as for Helen. Looking back, I think I understand more fully that working with Helen was a watershed for me. I sensed that she changed me, in more ways than I could formulate. As I write this, I am still trying to find words for her impact.

From the beginning, Helen challenged me, in many senses. I don't think I have ever felt so deeply hated and envied by any other human being. In no uncertain terms, Helen hated me for having legs, for the ease with which I could go to the bathroom, for being able to leave a session without anyone else's help. She hated me because of the childhood she imagined I had enjoyed, running, skipping, taking my body for granted. She hated me for the carefree adolescence she fantasized I had relished. In her mind I had always been able to be and do whatever I wanted. In our first years together, her heart hardened toward me. She wanted my life, but she couldn't have it. Although she knew this wasn't rational, she felt I was withholding it from her. I was too mean to let her have a piece of my freedom. The one power she had, the only weapon she felt she could wield against me, was her ability to leave by committing suicide or just terminating treatment. Helen frequently reminded me that because taking good care of herself was an arduous task, it would be easy to let herself slip away. Her threats had their intended effect, if her intention was to frighten me, make me think about her between sessions, and take away some of my peace of mind. In fact, for more than 10 years, Helen certainly possessed a piece of my mind!

Much changed, over the course of the treatment. I came to believe that her envy of me expressed how profoundly she wanted life. In fact, the depth of her rage at me was (partially) a reflection of the power of her life force. It took us many years for her to come to cherish her own life. She even got to the point of truly wanting to share what she called her "disabled life" with a partner. And then it was over.

Since her death, I have wondered if she had had premonitions of it. For many of our last sessions, she seemed to me to be making sure I knew how much I had helped her. Casually (I thought), she dropped phrases I recognized as my own into our conversations. I wondered if she was aware that she was quoting me. I never got around to asking. But now I believe that using my language was her way of giving me the gift of mattering. Over our last years she had admitted me into the realm of her rich, sarcastic, witty way of looking at life and the denizens of her world. I got used to the music of her laugh. In so many ways, I felt forgiven. An ache told me how much I had longed for her forgiveness. She died on a Saturday night. On Sunday, a relative called all the telephone numbers in her address book. He didn't know I was her therapist, but he knew, only, that I was important enough to Helen to be listed.

I didn't write about her right after her death. I don't think I could have. But, gradually, a paper took shape, with the title "Necessary and Unnecessary Losses: The Analyst's Mourning" (2000). This paper was my first public attempt to find a way to bear losing Helen. I thought maybe I could tame grief by calling it names. I thought that words, my old friends, might rescue me. Can they?

What transforms and therefore transcends an experience for one person may not have that power for another. But it seems to me that an altered focus is often part of the process. Writing has frequently transfixed and thereby "fixed" something for me. Fixating on words alters figure and ground for me. I am centered on adequately conveying my inner experience. That is, when I try to communicate what losing Helen means to me, *my attention shifts from the loss itself* to the expression of its meaning to me. I can never see Helen again, but I might be able to conjure up what it is like to miss her.

For me, writing sometimes changes my focus enough to lift me. My perspective shifts away from the unattainable. As I write this, I add to the pile of what Helen has given me. Nothing will ever bring back the musical sound of her deepest chuckles and that slow smile of hers. Remembering them is not the same. She will never again surprise me by casually, slyly, deftly quoting me and making me feel profoundly known. I will never again wonder whether to ask her if the quoting was deliberate and whether she wanted me to recognize the Sandra in the mirror. I will never again wonder whether today's words will come back to me next year, like determined homing pigeons. All these losses are irretrievable. But I know *I might be enough* to find a way to tell you about losing Helen. I might find words that get you to see her a little or, at least, to feel what it is like for me to remember her.

Joyce Carol Oates, who wrote a book about the death of her first husband, and Meghan O'Rourke, who wrote about her mother's death, discussed why some people turn to writing after such experiences. Joyce Carol Oates said, "The act of writing is an act of attempted comprehension, and, in a childlike way, control; we are so baffled and exhausted by what has happened, we want to imagine that giving words to the unspeakable will make it somehow our own" (2011, p. 4).

Meghan O'Rourke (2011) emphasized the interpersonal nature of much grieving, saying that grief reverberates among the living in shared laments. I am struck, as I have been in the past (Buechler, 2000, 2004, 2008), with how alone I am in my grief for Helen. For me, there is no way to share my laments with others who knew her. Writing (including writing this) is the only way for my grief to have a chance to reverberate at all, and it will never be shared with others who remember Helen. O'Rourke so poetically described the power of shared lamenting to offer consolation. She described how mourners "burn through the days, passing from one person to the next the lit match of memory." Writing is the only way I know how to pass the "lit match" of my memory of Helen.

Thus writing performs a magic that I suggest the analyst especially needs, as well as forms of magic we all need. Writing allows the analyst to share her mourning with the readers in her imagination, as well as those who actually exist. In many of the previous chapters of this book, I described the clinician's ever-expanding losses. Here I suggest that through writing we can, at least, sorrow out loud.

Writing may also spare the analyst some of the shame I described in previous chapters as the lot of the clinician. Sometimes, it is possible to find words that adequately convey our experiences when we write. Unlike our words in a session, the written word can be (endlessly) tweaked. As I am sure we have all discovered, this has its disadvantages and advantages. But it does give us a way to feel some sense of mastery over experiences that are inherently baffling, as Joyce Carol Oates suggested.

Writing performs another feat of magic. It stops time. For me, as for others, when I write, I often have no awareness of the passage of time. It quite literally and concretely doesn't consciously exist. But in another sense, writing is like a photograph. It takes one moment out of the flow of experience. Time is constantly carrying whatever is happening away from us. Someone's beautiful face will never, again, be exactly as it is right now. Time will (eventually) take everything I have ever had. We are all subject to its power. But the clinician has, in a sense, more to lose than most. As I have tried to express in many of the previous chapters, loss is our constant companion.

SPEAKING AND TEACHING AS ANTIDOTES
TO SORROW AND SHAME

On the way to a first class or conference, I often try to articulate the main point I would like to communicate. This is (in part) an effort to get beyond any nervousness I might otherwise feel. If I focus on a purpose, and on something of great interest to me, I am less likely to become anxious about how well I will do.

There are many potential joys in going public, in one form or another. Speaking to colleagues provides much that can heal the wounds of a clinical life. "Shameful" clinical failures and painful losses can become sources of a potentially fruitful theory, which can be passed on to a new generation.

For me, personally, I worry less about the impact of my own narcissism when I teach or speak than I do when I treat, even though I know quite well that it can hurt people in all of these roles. But when I write and teach, my own exhibitionism causes me less (conscious) guilt. In fact, it often feels like an asset. I can enjoy the spotlight and still feel I am fulfilling my role. Nevertheless, although I feel less guilt about narcissistic gratification in public roles, I am quite aware that it can lead me astray there, too. I am sure we are all painfully familiar with the discomfort of sitting in the audience, or on the podium, while a colleague shamelessly panders for audience approval. Perhaps most of us can recognize that desperation because we have felt it ourselves. In countless moments I have cringed at a colleague's display of self-promotion, wondering how many times friends see me as behaving similarly.

I would suggest that some of our prideful public misbehaviors stem (partly) from the constant drubbing our egos get when we are doing treatment (see Chapter 5 for a more extensive discussion of this connection). A patient treats us like we are of no worth, and the next night we rip a colleague's paper to shreds. Although I cannot prove that these two events are related, it is certain that they are painfully frequent. In the play *My Fair Lady* (Lerner & Loewe, 1956), Eliza Doolittle suffers hurt pride and vows to "get a little of her own back." I wonder how much conferences provide opportunities to "get a little of our own back" at our colleagues' expense. I address this danger more fully later.

When we teach we have some of the same chances for narcissistic gratifications and wounds as we have speaking at conferences. In each, the situation itself implies that we can say something worthwhile. Although some of our patients that week may have made it clear that they don't think we have anything of value to offer, when we go to class we are (sometimes) greeted by a group of colleagues assembled, waiting to take in our precious insights. Of course we are sometimes greeted by colleagues who feel quite differently, but I think teaching fosters the feeling, or, at least, the illusion, that people believe we have something valuable to say.

In speaking and teaching, I can *feel like* the only person potentially damaged by my narcissism is me (although, again, I know this is not always true). If I make a fool of myself, I feel like I will be the only one who will suffer. If I act wiser, or smarter, or better than I am, I may be humiliated, but, at least, I am the only one to suffer the consequences. The situation is very different in clinical work, where it is more obvious that the patient and I, as well as countless others connected with each of us, may experience the fallout of my deficits.

Again, I know that this distinction (between the fallout of our narcissism in our clinical work and the fallout in our other roles) is not entirely true, and people can be as seriously hurt in the classroom as they are in the consulting room. I have seen it happen. In this book's second chapter, I suggest how severely damaging some training experiences can be. For whatever reasons, when I am teaching or speaking, I am most aware of my own pride being on the line, and I am not as focused on the vulnerabilities of my listeners, as a rule.

But in the consulting room, the opposite is the case. Consciously, I am more often thinking about my patient's pride than my own, even though, as I have said, jolts to my self-esteem often occur.

The public arena combines some of the solitary joys of writing with some potential interpersonal fulfillments. Preparing to speak or teach, we get to discover our point of view in private (rather than with a patient watching us). Then we get to share it with candidates and other colleagues, who have probably been in similar clinical conundrums. We have a chance to feel that someone may share our vision of the situation. This may diminish some of the clinician's loneliness. Elsewhere, I have expressed my feeling that one difference between a peaceful aloneness and a painful loneliness is the sense in loneliness that no one will ever see the situation quite the same way as we see it (Buechler, 1998). The misery of loneliness stems, at least in part, from the feeling that the isolation is permanent. When we are alone with our patients, I think we have ample opportunities to feel truly lonely, in that no one besides ourselves will ever see the situation exactly as we do. But when we teach or speak and share our experiences with a group of other clinicians, we can feel there is a chance others will identify with our viewpoint. Other clinicians may, literally and figuratively, know where we are coming from. I have written elsewhere that we share a culture with others in the field, with its own language, values, mores, and sensibility (Buechler, 2004). This can lead us to expect that those from our culture are more likely to understand what we were trying to do with a patient, whether or not it was successful.

Thus there are many potential gratifications from speaking and teaching. At least in my experience, when I speak and teach people seem to feel they should show appreciation of my willingness to share my experience.

Obviously this can also occur in the clinical setting, but, at least for me, it seems less "built in."

I am suggesting that my own ego has been stroked by my teaching and speaking in a way that sometimes heals the narcissistic injuries I experience in the clinical arena. I am very aware that the opposite is just as plausible, and clinical work can narcissistically gratify, whereas speaking and teaching can narcissistically injure. But, to me, there is one difference. When I ascend the podium, I am clearly *looking* for the spotlight. I am claiming attention and embracing an opportunity to go public with my views. I don't think the same can be said when I enter the consulting room. If anything, there it is the patient who has claimed the right (or need) for attention. He or she is "going public," with much that may have been private, up until now. Most of the time, the patient is in the spotlight, although there may be many moments when the spotlight is shared.

So, when I speak and teach, I am, in effect, saying, "Listen to me, look at me!" I am risking shame but also asking for attention and respect. I am subjecting myself to the possibility of humiliation, ridicule, or merely disregard. I am also vying with others, in a sense. I am putting my reputation on the line and publicly declaring, "This is what I stand for; this is what I think."

Although these declarations may well figure into our clinical work too, there they are generally less prominent and public. In sessions with patients, we are *primarily* there to explore their inner worlds, although mine will also play an important part.

As I grow older I am increasingly aware of the wish to pass something on. I feel this need in many settings now, including sessions with patients, but it is most palpable when I write, speak, or teach. My own hope to communicate something helpful to younger clinicians can keep me motivated even when my physical stamina is running out. A generative need, along with narcissistic investments, can motivate me to forego relaxation. It is easier for me to gratify these needs through writing, speaking, and teaching than it is through practice. Speaking and teaching allow me the illusion that I can communicate without the interference of a transference and countertransference matrix. Again, I am aware that this is an illusion, but it is a tempting one. In a classroom I can believe I am getting to speak to other therapists without going through any filters. They are not hearing me as though I were their mother or father. They are listening to *me* and taking in *my* words and *my* thoughts. Whatever may have frustrated my generative impulse in the clinical setting can (at least in fantasy) be compensated for in teaching and speaking. Once again I "get a little of my own back."

At least in my experience, there is often an unspoken deal in teaching and speaking. I put forth the effort to pass something on, as honestly, directly, and forthrightly as I can, and the audience rewards me with compliments and gratitude. Again, I am very aware that this description of the "deal" in teaching and speaking is my subjective experience and may not be representative of others. But perhaps it is common, to varying degrees.

If that is true, I think we can see how teaching and speaking can help to heal the narcissistic injuries clinicians incur and protect us from some of the losses inherent in doing treatment. Unlike patients, students and audience members sign up for a specified time period and usually remain for that time. Although some may walk out early, a mass exodus in class or at a talk is highly unusual. Even bored participants generally put up a good front while, perhaps, unobtrusively checking their cell phones, doodling, or zoning out. A clinician can be fired in any session. Losses of all kinds occur, as we have seen in previous chapters, including losses of pride and tangible losses of income, as well as the more complicated losses of connection. I think that in speaking or teaching there is some protection against the most painful losses. Usually the "relationships" are temporary and not terribly close. Although there may be complexities, they are generally less complicated than relationships in treatment. We might say that, generally, in "educational" contexts, as opposed to clinical contexts, less is at stake emotionally. For both participants less is likely to be gained and less is likely to be lost. Once again, I am aware that this is not always the case, but I think it is usually true.

These contexts give me some of the pleasures of emotional connection, with fewer of its dangers than would be the case in a treatment setting. Two of the central sources of human joy are available to me (Buechler, 2008). That is, I can feel my oneness with other human beings and, at the same time, sense what makes me uniquely myself.

In short, I think teaching and speaking can provide a "cure" for some of what "ails" clinicians. Accumulated losses of pride and connection can be momentarily healed. Wounded self-esteem is soothed. Emptiness is filled. The abrupt and planned terminations of patients multiply in the "loss" column, but when I speak or teach, I feel there is another side to the equation. I hope that if I have said anything helpful, it will have a positive impact on listeners' clinical work, and I can feel I have done something worthwhile.

A NOTE ON THE DARK SIDE OF CLINICAL TREATMENT, WRITING, SPEAKING, AND TEACHING

Breaches of Confidentiality and Other Boundary Violations

Why are violations of confidentiality and boundary violations so common? With every year I practice, I hear more stories of analysts having affairs with their patients or engaging in other clearly unacceptable behavior (see Burka, 2008, and Dimen, 2011, for two poignant examples). Does this happen just as frequently in other fields? Or are clinicians especially prone to misbehavior, because of our character issues and/or the intimate nature of the treatment process?

Certainly our character issues and the potential closeness of the treatment relationship contribute to the causes of these abuses. But I am suggesting that we consider another aspect. Our roles demand that we pay exquisite attention to the needs of another person, most of our waking hours. That other human being can precipitously leave us, berate us, or humiliate us, among many other possibilities. Let me be clear: I am *not* excusing boundary violations. They should never happen. But I think we should try to understand as many of the reasons why they occur as possible, so we can work to prevent them.

I am suggesting that some of the demands of our roles may contribute to the reasons boundaries are so frequently violated. It may not be the case that the analyst abuses the patient who demands the most. I suggest that when analysts abuse their privileges, they are, in a sense, acting out against *the field* and not just against that particular patient. They may be frustrated with the constraints of living within the therapeutic frame, hour after hour, day after day. For some, a boundary violation may be a kind of vengeance or, perhaps, a grandiose assertion that "these rules don't apply to me." The repeatedly narcissistically wounded analyst might become taken with an opportunity to feel special and not subject to the limits imposed on others. Of course, there are many factors, including the analyst's patterns of defense, fundamental character issues, and personal situation, that might play roles in this behavior. But I believe that we are more vulnerable to temptations to violate boundaries because of the inherently narcissistically injuring nature of our work (see Chapter 5 for an extensive illustration of this).

Grandiosity in the Classroom and at Conferences

When I entered graduate school, I expected that a faculty of clinicians would be an especially upright and empathic group of people. Although I recognize this meaningfully reflects my personal psychology, I don't think I was the only one who began training with this expectation. I understand that clinicians are not the only professionals to violate ethical rules. We have only to open a newspaper to see examples in other disciplines. But, by definition, ours is the only field expressly dedicated to enhancing psychological health. Yet there are so many instances of gross misconduct, in the consulting room with patients, in training with candidates, and at conferences, with our colleagues. Why is this so?

By now I imagine it is clear that I am suggesting that, in part, we injure each other's pride so much because of the humiliations and sorrows of the clinical life. Examples of colleagues grievously hurt by being considered outside the fold are too numerous to enumerate. From the charge "This is psychotherapy, not psychoanalysis; surface, not depth" to the invective "You were not completely analyzed," many extremely productive analysts have been branded inferior. We have only to think about Ferenczi, Bowlby, Sullivan, Winnicott, and countless others who were deemed unworthy, in some sense. We may still be suffering from the legacy of the pain this caused. Each outcast, scarred analyst may perpetrate similar implacable judgments on the next generation, perpetuating a cycle of trauma.

In the second and fifth chapters of this book, I suggested some of the unfortunate consequences of the frequency of acts of shaming candidates in training and shaming colleagues at conferences. I expand this discussion here. In effect, I am saying that narcissistic injury begets more narcissistic injury. Our conferences abound with grandiose self-displays, competitions for status, name-calling, pointed exclusions of "outcasts," mocking contempt for "alien" orientations, exaggerated claims for our own, and many other clearly narcissistic behaviors.

Untold damage results. Whoever has served as a discussant is very likely to have experienced frustration when other panel members share their papers at the last moment, giving the discussant insufficient time to do an adequate job. I have been a discussant of papers I never received at all or papers where the conclusions professed on the podium were the exact opposite of those in the draft I received before the conference. I remember once being the discussant of a very well-known author and being told by him, at the dinner just preceding the event, that he had decided that the draft of his talk I had received had many errors, and he was going to take a completely different approach in the talk. So, instead of declaring the value of theories A and B, he was going to deride them as lacking any value. Everything I had prepared, every carefully created argument, would be confusing to the audience, at best. When the speaker said, "Theories A and B lack value," if I read my prepared comments, I would be speaking as though I differed with him, but I would in actuality be agreeing!

Shaken and perplexed, I went into the bathroom of the restaurant where we were supposed to be enjoying the preconference dinner. I told myself I could spend the rest of the dinner hour in the bathroom, revising my remarks so they would make sense to the audience, or I could have dinner and "wing it." I had dinner. I don't remember exactly what happened in the discussion, but, obviously, I survived. But I do remember thinking something like, "Did he just happen to change his mind, right before this evening? Is he making sure I am off balance and can't discuss his work effectively? Am I being paranoid?"

I can't answer these questions, because I didn't have the courage to ask them at the time. But this incident happened about 25 years ago. Since then I have served as a discussant many times, and similar events have occurred, though none so dramatically affecting my preconference meal!

At the very least, this speaker failed to treat me with the consideration that would have dictated his warning me well before dinner that he was having a change of heart about the paper. Whether or not he was engaging in deliberately competitive or hostile, sadistic behavior, he was certainly inconsiderate.

I would bet that many of us have similar stories. We may never be certain of the intent, but we have feelings about the impact of these experiences. For me, they have left a kind of sour taste. I still serve as a discussant, at times, because it is actually a role I like. But I am much more selective about the panels I join.

I suggest that one of the most damaging effects of these experiences is that they discourage some from any contributions to the field. Some colleagues get so dumbfounded and demoralized by how they are treated at conferences that they simply won't attend or participate. Although we can never know the extent to which this occurs, we can be sure our field cannot afford these losses. Now more than ever before, we need to nurture talent and cultivate each other's contributions. Recycling and perpetuating our narcissistic injuries will not accomplish this end.

My own naive assumptions in graduate school (described previously) about the level of secure self-esteem in the members of a clinical faculty points to a significant problem. Less-experienced colleagues may assume that their elders "have it together." They may therefore fail to recognize the importance of registering appropriate and genuine appreciation. Whether or not it is ever consciously formulated, they may think something like, "Dr. X is so established. He doesn't need to hear what I gained from his class." I would suggest that, on the whole, this is not true. Dr. X may still profoundly need recognition of his generative achievements. It may be true that feeling he has contributed to the professional growth of younger colleagues could encourage Dr. X to further invest in the next generation. Investing in the future is one of the ways we can transform self-esteem needs, from their more damaging to their more positive potential. When we care passionately about what we are passing on, we create a win–win situation. We "get a little of our own back" from the enhancement, rather than at the expense, of colleagues.

ANALYTIC POLITICS

Thus far in this chapter, I have considered some examples of what I see as potentially successful efforts at transcending the clinician's shame and sorrow through writing, teaching, and speaking. I have also described some negative outcomes, where our grandiosity prevails in these arenas. Finally, I will mention the very broad domain of analytic politics, where I think instances of playing out unresolved grandiosity are often painfully apparent, although examples of transcendence also clearly exist.

The term *politics* itself covers a great deal of ground, from leadership roles within institutes to governing positions within the field's various organizations and conferences. Here I am not distinguishing between serving at a local level and functioning in positions on the national or international stage. I am suggesting that regardless of the size of the arena, politics can offer the clinician an opportunity to work on unresolved shame and loss. The reach and impact politics afford may heal some of the clinician's injuries, but a more negative outcome seems to me to be equally likely.

In other words, when patients leave us, or attack us, and managed care humiliates us, one option is to try to balance the scale, or "get a little of our own back," by asserting power in a political context. The analyst who takes up politics may have a significant effect on the field's present and future conditions. Politics can serve as an outlet for constructive, generative needs. This can benefit everyone. But all too often the result is more complicated and less rosy.

I find the complexities of analytic politics daunting to engage in and equally overwhelming to write about. Many others have attempted this task. Here I will mention just a few who have had a significant impact on my own thinking. Emmanuel Berman (2004) wrote a superb description of the process of change in an analytic institute in Israel. Richard Raubolt (2006) gathered together some sharply critical essays on the potentially damaging impact of "power games" in training institutions. When I put together a special issue of *Contemporary Psychoanalysis* (2009) on the "ideal" institute and training, many contributors touched on political processes. Some directly described the negative impact of institutes gone awry, whereas others focused more on what could make the process of training more helpful.

While immersed in this writing project, I had the opportunity to think long and hard about the problems that arise in analytic institutes. I came to believe that unmet narcissistic needs, on the part of participants at all levels, play a highly significant role. I spell this out more specifically shortly, but what I am suggesting here is that the narcissistic injuries and losses inherent in a clinical career can exacerbate any personal proclivities toward intense shame and sorrow, which can predispose us to act out needs for power in settings like institutes.

What forms might this acting out take in the setting of an institute? The following are some possibilities, drawn from the contributions to the 2009 project.

Bonovitz (2009) wrote of how supervision can heighten the candidate's "bad analyst feelings." Bonovitz cited Epstein (1999), who suggested that supervision can exacerbate feelings of inadequacy in the supervisee. But why would this happen? I am pointing to the possibility that supervisors may unconsciously compensate for their own feelings of falling short by acting superior to those they teach.

In a particularly trenchant essay, Donna Orange (2009) referred to institutes as "somebody-nobody hierarchies of domination, submission, bullying, and humiliation" (p. 354). This suggests that in training we may instill something beyond a feeling of falling short clinically. At times, those in power in training institutes engage in dominating, humiliating behaviors. We might understand this as a repetition of the humiliations in their own training. I believe this occurs with distressing frequency, but this is not sufficient to explain the phenomenon Orange described. For me, the only plausible way to explain the prevalence of these processes is that, as I have suggested in each of the preceding chapters of this book, loss and shame haunt the analyst at *every* phase of his or her career. In part, we humiliate candidates not only because we have been humiliated in our own training but because, in addition, we have been humiliated in all the subsequent phases of our posttraining clinical careers.

Karen Maroda (2009) pointed to another set of problems in training. "Disagreeing with a powerful training analyst can lead to being blackballed and, worse, being assumed to have a pathological reason for disagreeing. As a result, candidates routinely conceal their own and their patients' actions, and tailor case reports to the supervisors' needs and wants" (p. 317). To me, this goes beyond the shaming and humiliating discussed previously. This speaks of a pressure on candidates to barter away their integrity for the sake of their success. Thus, in addition to feeling shown up and humiliated by faculty, candidates may be induced to feel they have actually betrayed themselves.

Although we can hope these phenomena are not too frequent, I think we should consider the reasons they occur as much as they do. Why would training analysts exert pressure toward coerced conformity and tempt candidates to lie about their work? Why would we need candidates to become flag-waivers for our own brand of analysis? Perhaps we recruit candidates into roles as our followers in order to shore up our damaged self-esteem.

Lionells (2009) wrote that the training system "turns candidates into acolytes, attaching themselves to powerful senior people to ensure career benefits and referrals" (p. 312). And lest we feel that, at least, after graduation analysts are able to recoup, Crastnopol (2009) wrote that institute life, for both junior and senior graduates, can be a "narcissistic mine field" (p. 359).

What can we take from these reflections? These are the statements of substantial leaders in our field. We cannot write them off as the "sour grapes" of individuals who failed to forge successful careers. I suggest that we must hear, in these poignant pleas for change, the voices of colleagues who hope to halt the damaging repetition of narcissistic injury each generation of analysts has visited on the next. Can we enhance our empathy for our colleagues, and for ourselves, as we bear the losses and humiliations of an analytic career? Can we balance our own pain with fulfillments, so that we are capable of sincere generosity toward the next generation of analysts? In other words, can we transcend our own shame and sorrow by caring less about our own egos than we care about the future of our field?

OTHER OPPORTUNITIES FOR
TRANSCENDING SHAME AND SORROW

My supervisory experience has generated another idea about how clinicians can transcend our painful clinical experiences. I have supervised many clinicians who conduct treatment in other languages and translate sessions into English so we can discuss them. I have had many similar experiences speaking and teaching abroad, where clinicians present clinical material that is then translated into English so I can comment on it. Many of these experiences have had a special quality for me, unlike any of my other work. I have given much thought to wondering why this is so, at least, for me personally. Is this merely my own, idiosyncratic reaction to this kind of adventure?

I am sure my own psychology plays a significant role, but I think it is not the only factor. I think there is something *inherently* transformative about the act of translation. Here, I am not differentiating translations from Japanese to English, poetry to analytic interpretation, and unconscious dream content to conscious insight. I am suggesting that all translation from one voice to another has something in common. All translation offers us opportunities for transcending painful shame and sorrow.

Perhaps it is clear why there are opportunities for transcendence in translations from poetry to analytic interpretation or from dream language to everyday language. Let us consider the poem "One Art" by Elizabeth Bishop (2010). I have mentioned this poem several times because I find it extremely moving and relevant to the sorrows of the clinician. Essentially, Bishop tells us that we can practice the "art" of bearing loss. I hear a glittering, angry edge in her/my voice, as she/I/we declare,

> The art of losing isn't hard to master;
> so many things seem filled with the intent
> to be lost that their loss is no disaster. (Young, 2010, p. 215)

How would using this poem clinically help me transcend my shame and sorrow? First, as I tried to indicate previously in describing the poem's voice as Bishop's/mine, the poem opens up a Winnicottian transitional space. In this space I can luxuriate in a holiday from differentiating what comes from outside versus what comes from inside me. For example, I hear sharp-edged anger in the three lines just quoted. Where is the anger coming from? Is it "in" the poem, or have I added it? I don't have to know. I believe that in my work with patients, it is often crucial to distinguish the contribution of each of us, but when I read a poem, I can take a break from this effort.

How can this help me as a clinician? I had two exceptionally difficult sessions yesterday. In the first, someone I have worked with for a long time told me she feels ready to terminate. I agreed but immediately began missing her. In the next hour a patient tried to express what the abuse she suffered as a child has cost her. What could she have experienced? If her father had treated her as a vulnerable child instead of a convenient sexual slave, would she have had her own children? Would she have had a different life?

Loss is everywhere. As the first person terminates, we lose each other, with a completeness that would be unfathomable in most other walks of life. I don't feel it would be right for me to call her after we terminate. I won't know if she is well, happy, thriving.

The sexually abused patient and I are squirming around, trying to find a way to bear the lives she has lost. She looks into the face of a neighbor's child and wants to feel delighted but, instead, chokes with sorrow. She is awash in a sea of what could have been. For a while, so am I.

As I look at loss with Bishop, she forces me to widen my lens. Bishop wrote of her loss of keys, time, places, objects, homes, and people, all with the same light yet provocative tone. She treats losing as an "art" that can be practiced until it is mastered. In a tone I hear as flip, she tells us to lose deliberately so we can learn to lose well. Is she mocking grief? Is she telling us to pull up our socks and just move on? Or is she saying that small losses may be very painful because they remind us of the greater ones?

I find the ending of Bishop's poem extremely evocative:

> Even losing you (the joking voice, a gesture
> I love) I shan't have lied. It's evident
> the art of losing's not too hard to master
> though it may look like (Write it!) like disaster. (Young, 2010, p. 215)

I hear a fight within herself in these lines. Write it! Face it! It *does* feel like a disaster to lose someone's every gesture, the sweet familiarity of a special smile, a merry eye you have met for years. It is, in a sense, a disaster. But, then, if we widen our lens, isn't *all* of life a series of losses? Aren't "life" and "loss" equivalent? Didn't I just lose the moment in which I had this thought?

I have to bear the sorrow of losing the person terminating, the sorrow I feel for the abused patient, and the sense of inadequacy about my own limitations in my work with each of them. The first person and I are fast approaching a kind of final tally of our limitations together. Whatever we were unable to do will, at least for now, remain undone. Letting go of each other means letting go of the hope for more. Can any of us really let go of that hope?

My mind switches to a picture I have imagined many times. I see the first scene in Dickens's novel *Oliver Twist* (1837). A child, hungry and frightened, dares to ask for more food, sensing the danger he is in but, nevertheless, willing himself to march forward. Don't we all, always, want more of something? Isn't that why senses of loss and inadequacy are ubiquitous? Life is so competent at returning us to our most vulnerable moments when we have been wide open to our losses and pleading for more.

I see it as part of my job as an analyst to *translate* Bishop's poem into an interpretation I can use in my work. Bishop can both broaden and deepen my capacity for experiencing loss as a clinician (and as a human being). She highlights my own flickering between feeling the termination will be a disaster and feeling it is painful but bearable. Similarly, I can use Bishop in my work with the sexually abused patient. Bishop throws intense light on the ubiquity of loss. She puts me in touch with a vast array of my own lost opportunities. In a sense, the poem forms a bridge between the patient's experience and my own. I can see her/my/our losing as "one art." The art of losing is inseparable from the art of living. If I try too hard to hold on to this moment, I may keep hold of it, but by doing that I will lose the next moment. No matter what I do, I will lose something and want more.

To my mind translating from Bishop's poem to a moment in treatment is no different from translating from a patient's dream to her waking experience or from Spanish to English. Each requires the *recognition of a commonality*. Each builds a bridge, widening our perspective. A word in Spanish translates into a word in English because there is enough overlap in their meanings. Similarly, a thought about a patient's dream connects with a thought about her waking life because there is overlap, at least in my vision. And Bishop's poem overlaps enough with my clinical (and personal) experience to provide useful insight. As Bishop flickers from a sense of utter disaster to a sense of ongoing tragedy, I ask myself to recognize that flicker. When have I known it before? The flicker connects me with moments I have been able to turn disaster into an ongoing tragedy. What gave me the strength I needed then? How can these memories help me now, with my terminating and my sexually abused patients? Where does Bishop's capacity to flicker come from? Can I borrow her strength? Can I lend it to my patients? Can I keep some of it for tomorrow? Bishop has helped me access personal resources ("arts" I have practiced) that can help me bear moments with patients.

BUILDING OTHER BRIDGES

I have found that experiences other than reading poetry can also fortify me as a clinician (and person). From my perspective, each strengthens a "clinical value" I hold (Buechler, 2004). In the 2004 book I described the clinician's (and the patient's) need for hope, curiosity, kindness, courage, a sense of purpose, the ability to bear loss, integrity, and emotional balance. I think that whatever enhances these strengths can help us bear the shame and sorrow of the clinical task. Much that inspires these values for me comes from nonclinical interpersonal and intrapsychic experiences. I gather hope from watching the young become stronger and surer. Rembrandt enhances my emotional balance by adding infinite pleasure to an otherwise dull

Saturday morning. A friend's dogged determination to regain her health strengthens my own courage.

Ultimately we each find personal wellsprings. My curiosity may be nurtured by reading about exciting scientific discoveries, whereas your breath may quicken while traveling to a new continent. But some experiences are likely to enhance anyone's strength. The wise supervisor who passes up evident opportunities to show off may teach us something about kindness, as well as something about sturdy self-esteem management. Hearing about a colleague's committed political activism may help me forge my own greater integrity.

I have certainly learned from colleagues, patients, and others I have encountered who relish the truth as an end in itself and not as a means to an end. My own training analyst exemplified this quality and showed me that it is essential for the patient to be able to trust in the clinician's absolute allegiance to the truth. I have come to believe that no meaningful treatment exists without this faith.

Like the characters in *The Wonderful Wizard of Oz* (Baum, 1900), we may recognize our courage, intelligence, and heart in the course of our life's adventures. Anyone we grow to love potentially shifts our whole emotional balance. By loving them, we give them this power.

Each of these values is vital to the clinical endeavor. Each helps us live our shame and sorrow more fully, more transparently, and with more evident grace.

Chapter 10

Analytic Resilience

What allows us to bounce back, after a difficult moment, or session, or a longer stretch of time? What helps us regain our emotional balance, after we have been knocked off-kilter? Where do we find the strength to learn from our mistakes and move on? More generally, how can we understand human resilience? Is it something that can be nurtured, in training and in treatment?

Life is constantly renewing itself, in the miracle of resiliency. Some artists have used images of spring to comment on this capacity. We could think of the human fantasy of eternal life, or eternal spring, as a wish for boundless resilience. As analysts, I would suggest, boundless resilience is more of a job requirement than a wishful fantasy. We require ourselves to "bounce back," to be ready to relate to someone different every 45 minutes. Even within some sessions, we may need to call on our capacity for emotional resilience. Defeated, we may nevertheless look for a way to go on.

Long ago, Piaget (1954) supplied me with one way to understand resilience. In his thinking, there is a point in childhood when we can imagine that in order to get to a goal, we may have to temporarily head directly *away* from it. I think that this is a lesson we must learn many times throughout our lives. For example, a couple has a searing, emotionally draining argument. Each feels that continuing to fight will only draw them further apart and leave dreadful scars. Resilience may depend on the ability to focus *away* from trying to understand each other's points of view. Talking about something else, seeing a movie, or just taking a 2-hour "vacation" from the issue may facilitate returning to it more productively.

This can tell us about one of the profound problems in the life experience of an obsessive person. When obsessive-compulsive defenses are central to functioning, vacations are hard to come by. Like a broken record, the person is stuck replaying the same point. Unable to take even a 5-minute pause, the obsessive-compulsive wears down, vulnerable to depression from the tedium of endless repetition.

Analytic resilience takes several forms. It is the elasticity we call upon to recover from an emotionally trying session and enter a very different psychological space with the next patient. But it is also a capacity to keep working with someone, even during stretches of seemingly endless stasis. The work suffers a setback, the person who "recovered" from alcoholism has an unexpected binge, the teenager cuts herself over the weekend, and we may well feel discouraged, but we keep working.

BOUNCING BACK FROM FRUSTRATION, RAGE, SORROW, AND SHAME

Sometimes I have compared myself to a certain kind of prizefighter. You can knock me down, but it isn't easy to knock me out of the ring. I have had a few patients whose considerable intellectual powers have been devoted to trying. Was I just issuing a willful dare when I told one patient something like, "Look, I'm hard to defeat. Discourage, maybe. But I'll be back."

This patient, Bob, and I had a pretty consistent pattern. Sessions would start pleasantly enough, with a bit of banter. Then he would bring up one of his favorite topics, like the absurdity of psychoanalysis. The Tuesday Science section of the *New York Times* often came in handy for him.

But Bob didn't need any extra ammunition. He was extremely logical and verbally fluent, and he came to sessions well prepared. I remember feeling constantly challenged. Continuing to treat him proved (in his view) that I was a fool, a fraud, or both. But what would it mean to each of us if I gave up?

Of course, being trained in Sullivanian inquiry, I asked him why we were playing this particular game. He said he needed to figure me out. I said he was paying a lot for the privilege. Not just the money but also forfeiting chances to work on other things. He seemed unimpressed.

I kept my promise. No matter how fierce Bob's attack, no matter how contemptuous his diatribe, he sometimes knocked me down for the moment, but he never knocked me entirely out of the ring. But now I wonder. What enabled me to keep bouncing back?

Was it because he never really defeated me? Or because anything other than resilience in myself was intolerable to me, personally? Was there something about this patient that kept me in the ring? Did I sense that a part of Bob was rooting for me, wanted and needed me to be able to keep coming back? Was I rising to his challenge out of my own competitive needs? Or did I care about him too much to let him defeat me and defeat us? Is there some kind of tensile strength in me that he and I tapped into? Should we call my behavior therapeutic determination or resilience, or was I just being stubborn? Is there a difference?

I have found that at some point, in most treatments, I have to call on my ability to bounce back. But, for me, questions about the nature of resilience are too broad. I need to narrow them down by making them more emotion specific. For example, what does it take for me to bounce back when I am primarily feeling rage in a session? What does it take when I am very anxious, or terribly sad, or achingly lonely? When I feel very ashamed of my behavior in the previous session, is there anything I can do to nurture my resilience? Although I am never just lonely, or just anxious, I think it can be helpful to identify the predominant emotion I am feeling. For me, that is often the first step in working with my countertransference. I think bouncing back from feeling awash with grief takes something different from bouncing back from other states of mind, heart, and soul.

With Bob, a man whom I treated three times a week for more than a decade in a fairly intensive analysis, I frequently struggled with feelings of shame. As he flashed his superior wit and logic and used his keen intelligence to make a fool of me, he often succeeded in making me feel inadequate. The following sequence is not a verbatim account, but it is typical of our interactions.

BOB: So did you see the *New York Times* this morning?
SANDRA: No.
BOB: I guess that's why you can still charge money for showing up here.

I feel a sinking sensation in my stomach, a kind of dull dread. Here we go, again. It is going to be one of those sessions. Can I be on my toes today? Did I get enough sleep? Am I up to the challenge?

SANDRA: Is that all I do, just show up?
BOB: Well, if *you* don't know what you do, things are even worse than I thought. But, according to the *Times*, psychoanalysis is inferior to evidence-based therapies. It is immoral and, maybe, unethical to practice it. I could sue your ass off.

My mind is a blank. Maybe I can get away with just being quiet. He is so provocative. I hate this. I hope he quits the treatment. Finally. God, it would be good to start my week without thinking about what new tortures he will devise for me! I am remembering a phrase from a song, something like "Freedom is another word for nothing left to lose." So what is the worst thing that can happen? He will quit. Well, let him. Fine with me. Fuck you, Bob! No wonder you have no one in your life! Who would stand for this? Wow! I *am* mad. Why does he get to me so much?

SANDRA: Uh huh.
BOB: Is that really all you can say, "Uh huh?"
SANDRA: Uh huh.
BOB: Oh so now you are starting a war of attrition. Is that what they taught you to do in your fancy analytic training?

The phrase *war of attrition* is interesting. Bob got so little from his psy-chotically depressed mother and sadistic father. Come to think of it, I feel a little depressed, and he's got a lot of dad in him today. Though, at some moments, the roles reverse, and I feel like being his sadistic father with him. Boy, just a minute ago I wanted to get rid of him. Hated his guts. Now I mostly feel ashamed. Maybe he is *right* about psychoanalysis or, at least, about me. Do I do anything more than show up? What, exactly, am I giving him or, at least, trying to give him?

SANDRA: No, Bob, I am not trying to starve you out. I just couldn't think of anything to say. You are so harshly critical of me. Sometimes it leaves me speechless. You think it is deliberate withholding on my part. It could be, since I was feeling angry, but, consciously, it wasn't a delib-erate strategy.

BOB: So you really *are* as dumb as you look! Who would have thought it possible?

His tone sounded gentler to me, though his words bristled with the usual sarcasm and cynicism. But I think I will focus on the tone.

SANDRA: I wonder if you have any choice about attacking me. Could you stop, if you wanted to? What would happen?

BOB: Good question.

SANDRA: Thanks.

Working with Bob required me to continually bounce back from feeling an enraged, inarticulate inadequacy. Although the rage was fierce, at times, I think the shame was ultimately the strongest emotion for me. I often felt he was sharper, faster, wittier than I will ever be. I felt intense shame that he could engage me in these contests. Sometimes I felt that by becoming competitive with him, I was proving his point. Maybe the treatment had no meaning. Maybe I am a fraud. Maybe we were wasting his time, money, life. But, then, something he would say would catch my attention, like the phrase *war of attrition*. It would feel as though the phrase knocked me into a different self-state. Suddenly I would wake up and remember that he is a patient with severe problems relating to other human beings, and I am his analyst, trying to help him become able to lead a richer life. And then what I call "radical honesty" would come to our rescue. If I could only reach into myself and tell him what I thought my predominant motives were, it might ease his paranoid fears, and we could touch again. I could refind my therapeutic purpose if I didn't get too hobbled by shame. In effect, at a moment that he accused me of being worthless to him, and I *actually felt* foolish for getting drawn into another argument, I had to find the strength to be self-exposing, not just self-disclosing. I had to affirmatively choose to hand him ammunition he could use to further ridicule me. I knew he would probably criticize me for my admission that my mind had gone blank. But only this truth had a chance to convince him that, generally, I am not being deliberately withholding. What I trusted was that he would recognize the truth when he heard it, and some part of him would feel relieved, joined, and grateful. Although he might not admit any of these feelings to me, they would soften him and make him more emotionally accessible. Another way to express this is that he recognized the blankness I described as similar to what he and his mother had frequently felt when under attack by his father. In other words, Bob and I were reenacting the family drama but, most of the time, with him in the powerful role of the ruthless sadist and me in the role of the overcome, enraged, shamed, silenced victim. It was as though his phrase *war of attrition* evoked just enough curiosity in me to get me to begin to think again and remember us. His phrase called me back from a temporary blank. I remembered that he is attacking me for a reason. I was restored to feeling that how poorly I was looking, as an analyst and as a human being, was less important than the treatment itself. Success and failure were less important than Bob and Sandra.

What facilitated my recovery? Those of you who know me might think of a phrase I have often used: "No one can hurt me by calling me too tall." That is, because I know that I am definitely not too tall, I will not have too much trouble dealing with this criticism. Similarly, I think, I am generally fairly secure about my overall therapeutic intentions and intelligence. For Bob to keep me in an ashamed state, I would have to buy his arguments more than I really do. He can temporarily provoke self-questioning in me, but, ultimately, I bounce back to a primarily good sense of myself as an analyst.

Generally, I believe that shame is an interpersonal event. We have to agree with the low estimation of us in order to really be ashamed. In my heart, although I know I can temporarily hate Bob and want to get rid of him, I also love him, want to help him, and am willing to sacrifice my pride, momentarily, if that is what it takes. Elsewhere, I have called this becoming a "fool for love" (Buechler, 2010). I think the willingness to privilege therapeutic purpose over pride is what can sometimes afford us resiliency. When the going gets rough, I had better have a reliable friend in my own superego. No matter how inadequate I can momentarily feel, no matter how blank, useless, fraudulent, I have to basically see myself as generally well intentioned, thoughtful, honest, and courageous enough to be able to help people. So if, at a particular moment in time, with a particular patient, I draw a complete blank and feel defeated and worthless, this state is unusual enough to make me curious. I wake up from my blank state. I wake up from feeling like a fraud. I find myself interested in his phrase *war of attrition*. In that moment of curiosity I recognize Sandra, and I feel glad I am back to being a committed analyst. I had a moment of feeling stymied and ashamed. But that blank, beaten-senseless moment contrasted with my more usual states of mind and heart. I know me. I usually love my work. I even usually love Bob. Bob reminds me of some of my experiences as a middle school substitute teacher in Bedford Stuyvesant. There would often be a kid in the class, a wiseass, who would issue a snide challenge, in effect saying to me, "You have nothing I want." With Bob, and with that kid, I eventually hear his adamant, fierce hopelessness and old grief. I eventually hear Bob saying that he *won't* need anything from me, because I have nothing good in me, and he won't be fool enough to expect anything he won't get. I hear hope deadened by years of bleak disappointment. I hear that the only way to preserve pride has been to slash and burn everyone in sight. And then I am ready to fight my way back to being my more alive, curious self, to fight for hope, for Bob.

Whereas my rage at Bob came with a generous admixture of shame, my rage at my supervisee, Jane, had a different kind of purity. I would like to hit the pause button here, to comment about my feelings while doing supervision. It seems to me as though our field has not yet fully discovered that supervisors have feelings, about the patient being discussed and about the analyst presenting the work. I see the literature on supervision as one generation behind our literature on treatment. Apparently it will take time for us to come to grips with the subjectivity of supervisors. I am using the terms *supervision* and *supervisor* for clarity, even though they have unfortunate hierarchical connotations.

Jane, an analytic candidate, was presenting her three-times-a-week treatment of John, a 30-something unmarried teacher. The supervision, which has taken place once a week for more than a year, is under institute auspices. For me, it has a repetitive quality. That is, many weeks, Jane reports a session in which John found a new way to challenge the treatment's frame. John is, from my point of view, endlessly creative in this pursuit. One week he decides to pace around Jane rather than sit in a chair. The next week he moves his chair uncomfortably close to hers or sits on the floor at her feet. Or he brings her food or other small gifts. Of course he also takes advantage of the electronic age we live in, sending numerous e-mail and texts about feelings too intense to hold until the next session. He leaves phone messages that he can't come for the next session because it is too frustrating to be Jane's patient rather than her lover. He brings her letters and cards, written with special names for each of them, about how wonderful their relationship could be. He refuses to listen to interpretations and will not participate as "the patient." He researches subjects to lecture about to Jane during sessions. When Jane tries to remind him of their agreement to do analysis, he protests that although he knows that was their original contract, he has fallen madly in love with her and cannot possibly honor it.

I really like Jane, which makes my intense frustration harder to bear. As she tells me about John's latest frame-bending efforts and asks me whether, perhaps, it wouldn't be so bad to go along, just this once, I feel framed and not just focused on frames. I have to be the heavy, the bad guy, once again. I am so very familiar with the scenario where the supervisor criticizes the candidate for being too indulgent. I can hear some of my colleagues on the institute's training committee, shouting that this is not analysis or that the candidate is too soft and is not sufficiently confronting the patient's resistances. I have occupied several roles in that scenario, at one time or another. I have been the chastised candidate myself, and I know what that feels like. I don't like being the supervisor, telling Jane how she should have handled John's provocative behavior. And I especially don't like the feeling that Jane is really being provocative with me. Should I be saying something like, "Oh, come on, Jane, not again! Don't tell me you really don't know what to do here! You aren't really confused. You are being rebellious with me, just as your patient is provocatively, obsessively rebelling."

As I listen to Jane's slow rendition of the week's sessions with John, my impatience grows almost uncontainable. I feel like shouting, "Get to the point, Jane!" When I start imagining folding paper into airplanes and throwing them at Jane, I know I am in trouble. Why am I getting so enraged? Sure, I feel baited. I wish Jane would see her own rebellious streak, as I do. I believe it would make her a better analyst. I don't wonder why I am annoyed, impatient, or irritated. These reactions seem unavoidable, because we have gone over the same ground countless times. But why is my rage this nearly out of control? Why do I have to keep telling myself to calm down?

In this situation, it seems to me that bouncing back, or resilience, requires me to find a way to use my rage rather than worry about having it. I also need to access feelings other than the rage. Probably, there is something I need to embody with Jane, so Jane can live it out more fruitfully with John. There is some integration of following rules and remaining compassionate that I need to be able to model. Curiosity cuts a chink in my rage, as I really wonder *why* I get so mad. Is it that hard for me to be the bad guy? Am I afraid of what the training committee will think of me, when I eventually present this supervision to them? Is my own character so similar to Jane's that I can't stand seeing my obsessive traits, perhaps writ large?

What helps me most with Jane is humor. Perhaps it gives my rage an alternative, more acceptable expression. In any case, Jane and I have found funny ways to describe our own stalemates. Here we go again! Once upon a time, there was a kind woman, who was loved by a handsome prince, but a mean, nasty, old hag would let them talk for only 45 minutes a few times a week …

Humor does not rescue me when Barbara, a patient I have known for a very long time, tells me that her cancer has come back and spread. Barbara is what I would call a trooper. I very much identify with troopers. We had hoped for more time before cancer, our mutual enemy, took up her life again. There was still so much to say, so much to do! Barbara was in her late 60s, and her professional life was really just taking off. She was finally making it. She was sought after, at last, a recognized expert in her field. It was so unbearably unfair. No! Not now! No!

Barbara said the words I was thinking. Could we just pretend it wasn't real? Run away? Barbara had already been through ghastly chemotherapy that sucked the life out of her, in addition to costing her hair and a portion of her dignity. She swore then that she would never go through that again. Never! Maybe it made sense to just have the days, or weeks, or months left to her in peace. Without the endless hours suspended in waiting rooms, without the endless tests, the unbearable hope it will work and dread it won't, the waiting by the phone for test results, meanwhile pretending to go on living. The trying to believe it will be all right, the failing to believe it will be all right.

In this situation I don't have any illusions I can maintain equanimity, neutrality, or any other ongoing state of mind and heart. I fight tears as I find, lose, and regain some sort of composure. I try to think, too, and not just feel. I know Barbara will, ultimately, make up her own mind about what to do. But she needs something from me. What does she need most? My presence, so she isn't so alone? My willingness to bear this with her, to hear whatever she has to say, even if it terrifies me? Some sort of infusion of strength, courage, love for life, despite its outrageous blows? Love for Barbara?

I listen as she tries to decide whether to sign on to take part in a study and possibly get an experimental new drug. She might get the drug or be in the control group. She wouldn't know which group she was in. She would be taking a tremendous chance either way. If she got the drug, there is no guarantee it would work or even that it is safe. In any case her cancer might spread further rapidly. She reasons that she will get a good deal of attention if she participates in this study. Suddenly I feel tremendously anxious. I think I hear unresolved narcissistic issues, possibly blinding her. Would Barbara make the wrong choice, because she and I have not sufficiently worked on her lifelong need to be special? Have I, inadvertently, failed to confront her self-esteem issues effectively enough, so that this crucial decision could be made purely on medical grounds? Dare I bring this issue up at a time like this? Am I, quite literally, adding insult to injury?

I decide I can't live with myself if I don't bring it up. I tell her I am so afraid her need to get special attention will cloud her judgment at this monumentally important moment. I can't describe my relief when she actually smiles and says that she has already thought about that possibility. I feel like I wasn't breathing and can breathe again.

Barbara decided not to participate in the study but to be treated with more standard chemotherapy and radiation. Of course I wonder, out loud and silently, how I influenced this decision and, more important, what will be its outcome.

Here I had to bounce back from terror and sorrow. Fears of regret, shame, and guilt played important roles as well. If Barbara had decided to be in the study, and she grew rapidly worse and died, could I bear the thought that maybe my inadequate treatment played a significant role? Aside from this issue, I felt such terror and sorrow that life is so very, very hard. We have to make these huge decisions, mostly blind, ultimately relying on instinct. Barbara's decision about her medical treatment, as well as my decision about what to say, resulted more from anticipated feelings than from logic. Telling Barbara I was worried about the role of her narcissistic needs was less frightening to me than not telling her and facing the possibility that my silence would contribute to her following the wrong course. And Barbara decided she could best live with herself if she went through with a conventional treatment protocol. Sometimes we each have to settle for knowing what we can bear rather than pretending to ourselves that we can figure out which choice will bring the best result.

In this case, "my" resilience sprung largely from Barbara's insightfulness. When she told me she had already thought about how her needs to be special might be influencing her, she let me off the hook, so to speak. I had feared I would have to bear the responsibility for bringing this issue up, all alone. But her response told me I wasn't alone. The work we had already done, over the years, had made us better partners than I knew. "Oh ye of little faith," I said to myself, and not for the first time. Sources of resilience can be interpersonal and not just intrapsychic. How long has it taken for me to learn this?

The point is that resilience comes in different flavors. Bouncing back from shame, rage, terror, and sorrow are not the same, at least for me. But they do have some commonalities. They all prioritize something over something else. Essentially, they all vote for life. What gives us the strength this takes? For me this is the eternal mystery, for which I have no final answer. Like Winnicott's (1971) infant who finds herself in her mother's eyes, sometimes we can take strength from the mirrors we offer each other.

What enabled me to bounce back, with Bob, Jane, and Barbara? Thinking about this brings to my mind the differential emotions theory that has been so useful to me over the years. According to this theory (Izard, 1977), our feelings always exist in a system, so that a change in one emotion affects the intensities of all the others. For example, heightened curiosity tempers my shame and rage with Bob. The joy of playfulness rescues me with Jane. Fear of regret helps me access the strength I need with Barbara.

Elsewhere, I have spelled out my view of empathic relatedness as a struggle to regain emotional balance (Buechler, 2004, 2008). An intense feeling, such as acute shame, throws the analyst off-kilter. But then access to another feeling facilitates bouncing back. Resilience is often born out of a marriage of curiosity and love. Referring to curiosity is my way of talking about Schafer's (1983) "analytic attitude." While we are engaging in an interpersonal interaction curiosity can help us look at the exchange, at the same time as we are living it out. Access to this attitude is as important for the patient as it is for the analyst, in my judgment. Both participants need to cultivate their capacity to be curious.

Love is what can inspire fervor for life itself and for a particular patient's richer life. It is sometimes manifested in a sudden intensification of emotional availability. For example, with Bob, his use of the phrase *war of attrition* reminded me of expansive, loving feelings I have had for him in the past. We could say it kindled a more responsive self-state in me. Overcome by rage, regret, loneliness, shame, fear, or sorrow, our responsive range is narrowed, and we can't access other emotions, with their rich affective resources. For example, in a state of intense rage, I can't fully resonate with sorrow. But just as a strong emotion can temporarily throw the balance off, so fervent feelings can restore it. Resilience, for me, is a regaining of access to a wide range of feelings, including the two that most open my mind and heart: curiosity and love.

I have always been fascinated by artists who seem to me to express some of emotion theory's central tenets in what they create. For example, in his image of melancholia, the 15th-century artist Albrecht Durer portrays this state as an imbalance of the "humours." I think he captured a vital truth. Emotional balance is an essential aspect of healthy living.

In countless mythologies, human beings and gods are rescued by love. I believe that as analysts, we, too, can be restored to our full resourcefulness by curious love. Adam Phillips (1994) described the conjunction of knowing and loving in psychoanalysis. I quote from his witty and wise essay "On Love":

> "Transference," "repression," "fetishism," "narcissism," "the riddle of femininity"—all these key psychoanalytic concepts confirm the sense that in psychoanalysis love is a problem of knowledge. That lovers are like detectives: they are trying to find something out that will make all the difference. (p. 40)

In the Bible, to know someone is to have sexual intercourse with that person. An example can be found in Genesis (4:1): "And Adam knew Eve his wife, and she conceived." Knowing, like love, is a potentially fruitful form of penetration. In psychoanalysis knowing is the form of loving that allows both participants to conceive themselves anew. Heinrich Zimmer (1948) wrote, "The true *dilettante* will be always ready to begin anew" (p. 6). To me, beginning anew is a way of describing resilience, the capacity to recover emotional balance. In that sense the analyst must be a true dilettante, ever ready to begin again, to love through curious knowing and know through profound love.

Emotional resilience is at the heart of empathy, from my point of view. I differentiate empathy from sympathy. The sympathetic listener feels something similar to what she is hearing. But the empathic listener goes further.

She feels in tune with the other person, recovers her balance, and learns something potentially useful from this process. To illustrate, it is generally not empathic to join a child having a tantrum by having one of your own. Empathy requires us to feel the edge of the tantrum, so we emotionally reverberate with it but then right ourselves and, finally, understand something potentially useful about what happened, so we can help ourselves and the child grow from the experience. Resilience comes from our own need to recover balance. Perhaps we have felt intense, contagious rage or anxiety or sorrow in a session. Being available for this mutual experience is the first stage of a healing empathy, but by itself it is not enough, in my judgment. Curative empathy requires us to dig deeper into ourselves than that. We need to call upon all our emotional resources to come *back* to a curious holding. Once we have done that, we can wonder about the whole journey and, we hope, learn something about the patient and ourselves. Sometimes in living through an unbearable sadness, we may better understand the patient's losses and our own. If the process stopped there, it might be comfortingly sympathetic and, therefore, alleviate loneliness in both people, although certainly not a bad outcome that is often not enough, in my judgment. I agree with conceptions of analysis as a process of structural change and not just amelioration of painful feelings. That is, analysis aims at changing how people function and how they process their experiences and not just what those experiences are. In analysis it is not enough to help someone feel better today. We aim to help them know life differently, to take it in differently. Structural change means to me hearing with new ears and seeing with new eyes. We don't just help people hear or see something more positive today. We help them hear and see more life today and forever after. They no longer waste one ear and one eye in trying *not* to hear and see, that is, in defensiveness. They spend less of their resources defending *against* their experiences and more of their resources *having* their experiences. Through bearing something along with patients, we feel how they take life in. And then we use whatever we have inside to regain the capacity to wonder and to connect. And then both of us stop, look back, learn, and maybe change. Engaging empathically takes tremendous emotional resources. Every positive feeling, from joy to hope, to curiosity and love must be recruited, and it is necessary to have a capacity for bearing every negative feeling, from loneliness, to anger, to fear, to sorrow. This work requires us to be human beings who can think feelingfully and feel thoughtfully.

The two emotions that have dominated my thinking in this book are shame and sorrow. At each stage of our careers, from training through early career, midphase, and late-career experiences, what enables us to bounce back from the blows we are dealt? Both shame and sorrow are ultimately, partially, about loss of self. In shame, we lose a sense of our own adequacy. In sorrow over a patient's abrupt termination, for example, we feel we have lost a relationship that might have brought us to new self-states. When we lose anyone, we also lose who we could have become with that person. Although shame and sorrow have different focuses, they have commonalities as well. Both implicitly compare what is with what could have been and, in some sense, should have been.

For a clinician, moments of shame often meld with moments of sorrow. The patient who terminates over the phone elicits both emotions. We wonder if the patient left because of our clinical inadequacies, so we feel a sense of shame and loss. What strengths allow us to bounce back? How can we understand the mysterious miracle of resilience?

Perhaps resilience can best be understood by looking at moments when it is absent. I have already touched on this, with comments about the stuck position of the prevailingly obsessive clinician. For whatever reason, the clinician who has burned out lacks the resilience to bounce back from a troubling experience.

BURNOUT

Just as sadness profoundly differs from depression, exhaustion is fundamentally different from burnout. That is, just as depression usually includes some sadness but is more complicated, depletion is just a component of burnout. By itself, depletion is not powerful enough to burn us out. In other words, when we are burned out, our "tanks" *are* on empty, but this, alone, would render us temporarily drained rather than burned out. When do we burn out rather than merely need to pause to replenish ourselves?

I suggest that burnout is one way to describe the loss of resilience when we no longer feel a sense of purpose in our clinical work. Elsewhere, I have discussed the clinician's sense of purpose as a necessary ingredient in treatment (Buechler, 2004). The sense of purpose is not about any particular goal but, rather, a general expectation that the work will be meaningful. In this type of burnout, despair has displaced hopeful expectation. In other words, we can be seen as suffering from burnout if we have lost the ability to believe in the inherent worth of our chosen field.

How can we tell when we, or a colleague, have burned out, and a vacation will not restore commitment to the work? And what causes this total collapse of belief?

In 2004, I suggested that burnout can be manifested in exaggerated pessimism about the future of psychoanalysis. Rather than face our own failure to create a personally meaningful and viable career, we may project this failure onto the field as a whole. Of course, I am aware that there are many realistic concerns about the health of psychoanalysis. Challenges to our profession come from many quarters, including managed care, a bottom-line-driven culture, and the unrealistic claims of a greedy pharmaceutical industry. But the burned-out analyst has lost the courage and determination that are necessary for us to continue to fight for the field. Personal character issues must play some role in determining who burns out. Throughout this book, I have suggested that formative experiences in training and beyond can make us more vulnerable to intense shame and sorrow. It seems likely to me that burnout can result from the cumulative effect of these painful experiences. Sometimes, when we have suffered extreme shame and sorrow, we might prefer to locate the failure in the field as a whole rather than in ourselves.

What follows is a composite profile of an analyst burning out. I have collapsed my experiences supervising several people who have left the field relatively early in their careers. In effect, I am sketching a portrait of one of the ways clinicians can permanently lose clinical resiliency.

Seeds of Burnout

A little older than most candidates, Mary entered the field truly dedicated to helping people cope. For her, this was a second profession. She was candid about her personal motivations for needing to facilitate therapeutic change. Her own childhood was littered with family members whose refusal to seek help had disastrous consequences.

As Mary's supervisor I had the impression that Mary respected and liked me, but her patients came first. If she thought my suggestions might compromise their treatments, she would find a polite way to avoid implementing them. Usually I feel some relief when I spot this attitude. It indicates that the candidate has confidence in her clinical judgment, which helps me feel less alone. Because she is on the "front lines," in direct interaction with the patient, I am glad that she is exercising her own judgment and not mindlessly following my ideas.

Starting a practice is much more difficult now than it was for me. A full caseload is pretty hard to come by. It is almost always necessary to rely on managed care to supply patients. Many clinicians promise themselves that this is temporary, and they will get off panels as soon as they build enough of a practice to pay the bills. But "getting off" managed care can resemble "getting off" an addictive drug. Trying to go "cold turkey" feels too hard. In theory, weaning seems more manageable. But in practice this, too, can be very difficult. Essentially the clinician must take a leap of faith and get off the panels even though she does not have a full practice yet in order to make enough room for new, non-managed-care patients.

But Mary didn't feel she could afford this luxury. She didn't have any savings, so paying the office rent each month was an exercise in financial juggling.

Mary's analytic patient came to treatment because he is running out of time. Of course, that is not what the intake says. In the intake, John complained about his unemployment and loneliness. Paying lip service to any personal responsibility, John railed against an unfeeling world. Recently the love of John's life had broken up with him. She got involved with someone else. John wondered if she left him because he was out of work. His voice turned bitter as he described how his parents blamed him for everything. In their view he had failed at everything he tried. John avoided his parents and younger sister as much as possible.

In supervision, Mary worried about whether John was at risk for suicide. Although John had not mentioned suicide, it did seem to me that this concern was warranted. I saw John as narcissistic. I have always believed in Miller's (1986) dictum that the other side of narcissism is depression. My understanding of this is that narcissists eventually run out of time. In other words, people who have trouble starting from scratch, because they feel entitled to start (careers, relationships) at more advanced levels, often get stalled. Eventually they watch peers moving ahead with their lives, and then they may succumb to depression about their unlived lives. To capture this familiar sequence, I say that time is the enemy of the narcissist.

Mary and I differed predictably about John's treatment. When John complained that the jobs that were available were beneath him, I would have confronted his entitlement, but Mary saw her goal as empathizing with his predicament. Of course these aims are not mutually exclusive. Mary and I got into something of a power struggle, partly because we both couldn't fully embrace the possibility of empathizing *and* confronting.

So Mary gave John all the understanding she could muster. And it was truly sad that a nearly 40-year-old man had so little to show for himself. No career, no relationship, no family to speak of, and only one "friend," who was really more of an acquaintance. John was poor in every sense. Hobbies eluded him, because there, too, he found it impossible to start at the beginning.

Let's pause for a look at my countertransferences. In retrospect, I think I had some strong reactions to both John and Mary. It is probably already clear that I felt impatient with both. With John I felt frustrated much of the time (although recognizing that I might feel differently if I actually met him). Why wouldn't this seemingly intelligent man choose the possible over the impossible? Why won't he see that his life will go nowhere unless he more gracefully bends to time?

I have very strong personal feelings about wasting life. When I am in the grip of them, I can lose sight of the point that what I deem a "waste" of life might not seem like a waste to someone else. However aware I am of this issue, my feelings in a (treatment or supervisory) session can be quite powerful. I would say that their intensity is both an advantage and a liability in all of my work. It lends me passion but also an urgency that can foster unhelpful enactments.

My countertransferences to Mary are more complicated. I like her. No doubt my liking and my negative feelings are both partially due to the fact that I *was* Mary, in a sense (and still am). Many years ago, my own supervisors tried to caution me about my therapeutic zeal. I know what it is like to be told that I am too identified with my patients and am trying too hard to ease their burdens, at the expense of honestly confronting their defenses and character issues.

But I can also feel thwarted and irritated by Mary. I want her to see how she (like Jane, discussed previously) won't directly differ with me but is passive aggressively "not understanding" how to be more confronting with John.

Time passes, and some things change, whereas others don't. John gets a job. It is way beneath his potential, but it will pay the rent, and he takes it. Mary is elated and more than willing to "go the extra mile" and change her own schedule to change his three appointments to evening hours. She doesn't mention raising John's minimal fee, even though it was set while he was unemployed, and his financial situation is somewhat improved. I comment on this, but, perhaps attempting to check my own aggressive feelings, I follow as Mary and John focus on other topics. Not surprisingly (from my point of view) John rapidly gets into a power struggle with his new boss, feeling that his talents are insufficiently recognized and rewarded.

Meanwhile John is finding it harder and harder to get to his sessions. He is late, or fails to appear, but calls to explain that he was exhausted from work or unable to leave on time to make it to his appointment. He also fails to keep up with all his bills, including the money he owes Mary. When Mary brings this up, John rather indignantly wonders why she isn't hearing how he is struggling with his boss's impossible demands. When he does appear for a session, he fills the hour with angry, contemptuous descriptions of the incompetence of his coworkers and the inhuman burdens that result for him.

Soon John begins to hint that it would be in the interest of his health that he quit this job. Mary panics. Will John leave work (and treatment) precipitously? Will he then fall into a dangerous state of depression? And if John quits treatment at this point, how will this affect Mary's training? Will she fail to graduate on time, because she won't be able to complete the analytic hours with John that are part of her requirements?

Eventually things heat up, and John acts out more and more, missing sessions and failing to pay for the treatment. Mary becomes exasperated. And now the tables turn in supervision, as I become something of an advocate for John. Refusing what I see as a reasonable request to change an appointment time, Mary seems to me to be suddenly completely fed up with John and ready to "fire" him as a patient. I find myself trying to slow her down, cautioning her against acting out in a retaliatory, impulsive way.

Mary and I do talk this through, and both the supervision and the treatment continue. Although I do believe that the treatment had impact and helped John develop some insight, in my judgment much work still remained when John decided to terminate. Having met the training requirements,

Mary was entitled to bring John into her private practice. The issue of the fee became unavoidable. It really would be unreasonable to expect Mary to see John in her private practice for three evenings a week at the severely low fee he was paying. I can't say it was that surprising, or even that sad for any of us, when he announced he was going to end the treatment. Our supervision soon ended too. And although the feelings between us were explored, I wondered at the time if we could have done better. But we parted amicably, knowing we would probably have some contact in the professional circles where we both belong.

Sharper Than a Serpent's Tooth

Many years later, I heard of Mary's early retirement. With some mixed feelings about whether or not it was wise to initiate contact with her, I called her. What followed was extremely painful for me. She told me a saga. After John left she worked with several other very challenging, demanding patients. In more than one case, she really "bent over backwards" to meet their needs, only to be rebuffed. Either they left treatment precipitously, with no real explanation, or patient and clinician tortured each other until one or the other ended the treatment somehow. Mary described how she suffered, most especially from their ingratitude for how much she had tried to do for them. My impression was that she just let her practice gradually slide away. It ended, as T. S. Eliot (1930) might say, not with a bang but with a whimper.

As I mentioned earlier, this is a composite, and I am leaving out some details for the purpose of confidentiality. In each case, the therapist left the field at a relatively young age. There is more than one way to construe the reasons. My own belief is that each of these clinicians suffered burnout and then let circumstances persuade them to leave the field.

I remember their passionate commitment, talent, and promise. I feel I failed them, although it is also true that I am not sure exactly how. But I know that I want another chance. And I also know that I won't get one.

What happened? I can express only my version of it. I believe the pain and accumulated rage got to be too much. It became impossible to retain what Epstein (1979) called "good analyst" feelings. Or, we could say, the consequences of excessive therapeutic zeal (Arnold Cooper, 1986) became too great.

Many questions remain for me. But it is clear to me that I feel sorrow for these former colleagues and for the field. No matter what happens next, we have all suffered a severe loss. In a sense, life lost. An investment in training, in a profession, didn't have sufficient returns. It was cashed in.

Shame and sorrow are the two protagonists in this book. Some might see me as shaming Mary too much, and others may see me as trying too hard to protect her by not confronting her sufficiently. Some may see me as not active enough as a supervisor, whereas others may feel I was too engaged (especially in trying to control John's treatment). Depending on one's point of view about good supervision, and good therapy, I can be seen as failing in various ways. But what can't be doubted is that Mary ended her career feeling deeply underappreciated and extremely sad. I think shame and sorrow often play key roles in burnout. There is only so much any of us can take without losing heart. How many times can you bear listening to your voice mail and hearing a patient abruptly terminate? How many times can you wonder what you did (or didn't do) to cause this? How many times can you look in the mirror, questioning whether or not you have the "right stuff" to be an analyst, and still get dressed and ask the next patient in?

How many times can you wonder whether or not too many patients will leave this month for you to pay the rent? After yet another termination and a bout of severe self-questioning, can you still be hopeful with the next new person? Can you tell colleagues why they should send more referrals your way? Can you explain to managed care agents why they should pay for a treatment with you? Can you respond to your patient's next barrage of questions about the worth of your work together?

Beyond this, can we all feel ready for whatever suffering will cross our paths tomorrow? Can we buzz in the next person who just lost his or her parent, partner, child, or good health?

STILL PRACTICING

I am suggesting that therapeutic resilience, or avoiding burnout, requires an emotional capacity to face profound loss and failure without losing heart. We have to willingly enter tragedies and, to some degree, make them our own. And then, we have to open the door to doing it all again and again.

I am still practicing bearing the companionship of shame and sorrow. I have no doubt that they will always be with me. The only question is how well we will all get along.

I have a personal goal. It helps keep me going. When I end my practice, I want to feel I can do it with grace. I want to end in style. My style. This means, to me, that I must be good at facing failure and loss. Whenever I stop practicing, I will have failed some people, to some extent. And by the end I will lose them all. Before I face these final moments, I want to become a really good loser. I practice every day. In this respect, as I already noted in Chapter 9, I follow the poet Elizabeth Bishop's (2010) advice. She tells us to keep losing.

> "One Art"
> Lose something every day. Accept the fluster
> of lost door keys, the hour badly spent.
> The art of losing isn't hard to master ...

Epilogue: Still Practicing

Writing teaches me what I think. When I started working on this book, I understood "still practicing" as a declaration that, after all these years, I am *still* functioning as a therapist. It also signified that, despite having more than four decades of experience in the field, I am still *preparing* to become a better clinician in the future. It was not until most of this book was written that its title took on a third meaning for me.

"Still practicing" expresses my feeling that, at least for me, clinical work is serving a particular *personal* need. Hour after hour, it gives me opportunities to develop a greater ability to bear shame and sorrow. By the time I close my practice, I hope to have adequately honed my capacity to bear my inadequacies and losses with grace.

Every encounter with a patient can be an exercise in humility. Our failures so frequently outnumber our successes. Many hours fill my heart with sadness for the connections I am failing to make. If I can learn to bear this as a clinician, perhaps I will become a better loser in my personal life.

From our earliest training experiences, we practice therapeutic resilience. Whatever happened in the previous hour should not incapacitate me in the next. No matter how inept I felt with my 9 o'clock patient, I need to enter the 10 o'clock hour with enough faith in myself to function. No matter how grievous the loss I had to bear in the 10 o'clock session, I need to recover enough to give my attention to the person who comes at 11. I can't afford to dwell too long in the mutual misery that clouded the 10 o'clock hour.

For me, still practicing has come to mean continuing to learn how to take life's blows and move on. No one explicitly taught me how to do this in my training. But my best teachers, themselves, were masters of this art. Among them, Ralph Crowley, MD, certainly stands out. He was my first analytic supervisor. Ralph exuded kindly humility. He met my hesitations and self-doubts with a steady pursuit of greater understanding. Ralph had a wry sense of humor and a simplicity and directness in his manner. Every hour with him had the feel of a new beginning, in the sense that each supervision session gave us another chance to connect with each other and with the treatment process I was presenting. Ralph was willing to hear anything

I had to say, but he usually had a view of the material that somewhat differed from mine. Generally, he stated his perspective in a matter-of-fact but friendly tone. His attitude told me that differences in point of view are part of the landscape, neither good nor bad. Whatever happens in a treatment session or a supervisory hour has a story to tell. We should listen carefully, with the humility to know we will miss much of it but with all the alertness we can muster. Inevitably, we will lose many of our chances for connection and make a few of them. We should never lose sight of the ground we have gained, because that can give us the strength to face the next hour.

Ralph made it clear that he, himself, was still practicing. He told me stories of his own clinical shortcomings, past and present. When he thought it would be useful for me to read something, I found a copy of it on my chair when I came in for supervision. Ralph spoke in actions, as well as words. His actions told me that my development mattered. Most important, this message never wavered, no matter how things were going in the treatment I was presenting or in our supervisory work. Ralph's steady effort taught me about clinical resilience. You listen for whatever the work can tell you about your fulfilled and missed opportunities. You respond with joy, sadness, impatience, anger, or another emotion. Then you move on. Somehow, you keep practicing.

If life is a story of show-and-tell, Ralph showed (in his actions) the same story he told (in his advice). In other words, he had integrity. I never had the impression that he was immune to shame and sorrow. He was just good at recovering from them. I am still practicing the art of recovery. I believe it is an art, rather than a skill, because I think there are no rules or recipes for it, but it can be modeled. I hope that developing this art in my work will help me with my personal life. My influence, my insight, my reach is always limited. In shame and sorrow I feel moved to protest these limitations. In my work, I am striving to use protest's fury to fight for more life, for myself and those I touch. What is limited in me should motivate me to stretch as far as I can. I would like to end my practice (and all else) as limber as possible. I hope to live all my endings with some of the passionate grace my teachers conveyed.

References

Anouilh, J. (1951). *Antigone*. London: Methuen.

Aristotle. (1984). *The complete works of Aristotle* (Vol. 2) (J. Barnes, Ed.). Princeton, NJ: Princeton University Press.

Aronson, S. (2009). The (un)designated mourner: When the analyst's patient dies. *Contemporary Psychoanalysis, 45,* 545–561.

Auden, W. S. (2010). Musee des Beaux Arts. In K. Young (Ed.), *The art of losing: Poems of grief and healing* (p. 3). New York: Bloomsbury.

Baum, L. F. (1900). *The wonderful wizard of Oz.* Chicago: George M. Hill.

Berman, E. (2002). Others' failures—And one's own. In J. Reppen & M. A. Schulman (Eds.), *Failures in psychoanalytic treatment* (pp. 263–289). Madison, CT: International Universities Press.

Berman, E. (2004). *Impossible training: A relational view of psychoanalytic education.* Hillsdale, NJ: Analytic Press.

Bernstein, S. B. (2008). Writing, rewriting, and working through. *Psychoanalytic Inquiry, 28,* 450–464.

Bishop, E. (2010). One art. In K. Young (Ed.), *The art of losing: Poems of grief and healing* (p. 215). New York: Bloomsbury.

Blechner, M. J. (1997). *Hope and mortality: Psychodynamic approaches to AIDS and HIV.* Hillsdale, NJ: Analytic Press.

Bodnar, S. (1997a). Gidget goes to Sing-Sing: An interpersonal therapeutic approach to HIV positive substance abusers. In M. J. Blechner (Ed.), *Hope and mortality: Psychodynamic approaches to AIDS and HIV* (pp. 97–115). Hillsdale, NJ: Analytic Press.

Bodnar, S. (1997b). Dances with men: The impact of multiple losses in my practice of psychoanalytically informed psychotherapy. In M. J. Blechner (Ed.), *Hope and mortality: Psychodynamic approaches to Aids and HIV* (pp. 221–237). Hillsdale, NJ: Analytic Press.

Bonime, W. (1982). Psychotherapy of the depressed patient. *Contemporary Psychoanalysis, 18,* 173–189.

Bonovitz, C. (2009). Welcoming the voices: Constructing a supervisory attitude in psychoanalytic training. *Contemporary Psychoanalysis, 45,* 415–422.

Bornstein, M. (2004). The problems of narcissism in psychoanalytic organizations: The insularity of power. *Psychoanalytic Inquiry, 24*(1), 71–85.

Bose, J. (1995). Depression. In M. Lionells, J. Fiscalini, C. H. Mann, & D. B. Stern (Eds.), *Handbook of interpersonal psychoanalysis* (pp. 435–469). Hillsdale, NJ: Analytic Press.

Brodbeck, H. (2008). Anxiety in psychoanalytic training from the candidate's point-of-view. *Psychoanalytic Inquiry, 28*(3), 329–344.

Bromberg, P. M. (1979). The schizoid personality: The psychopathology of stability. In L. Saretsky, G. D. Goldman, & D. S. Milman (Eds.), *Integrating ego psychology and object relations theory* (pp. 226–243). Dubuque, IA: Kendall Hunt.

Buechler, S. (1995). Emotion. In M. Lionells, J. Fiscalini, C. H. Mann, & D. B. Stern (Eds.), *Handbook of interpersonal psychoanalysis* (pp. 165–188). Hillsdale, NJ: Analytic Press.

Buechler, S. (1996). Supervision of the treatment of borderline patients. *Contemporary Psychoanalysis, 32*, 67; 86–92.

Buechler, S. (1998). The analyst's experience of loneliness. *Contemporary Psychoanalysis, 34*, 91–115.

Buechler, S. (1999). Searching for a passionate neutrality. *Contemporary Psychoanalysis, 35*, 213–227.

Buechler, S. (2000). Necessary and unnecessary losses: The analyst's mourning. *Contemporary Psychoanalysis, 36*, 77–90.

Buechler, S. (2002a). More simply human than otherwise. *Contemporary Psychoanalysis, 38*, 485–497.

Buechler, S. (2002b). Joy in the analytic encounter. *Contemporary Psychoanalysis, 38*: 613–622.

Buechler, S. (2003). Analytic integrity: A review of *Affect intolerance in patient and analyst. Contemporary Psychoanalysis, 39*, 323–326.

Buechler, S. (2004). *Clinical values: Emotions that guide psychoanalytic treatment.* Hillsdale, NJ: Analytic Press.

Buechler, S. (2006, March 4). *The legacies of shaming psychoanalytic candidates.* Paper presented at the Mt. Sinai Symposium, New York.

Buechler, S. (2008). *Making a difference in patients' lives: Emotional experience in the therapeutic setting.* New York: Routledge.

Buechler, S. (Ed.). (2009). Special issue on the ideal psychoanalytic institute. *Contemporary Psychoanalysis, 45.*

Buechler, S. (2010). Overcoming our own pride in the treatment of narcissistic patients. *International Forum of Psychoanalysis, 19*, 120–124.

Burka, J. (2008). Psychic fallout from breach of confidentiality: A patient/analyst's perspective. *Contemporary Psychoanalysis, 44*, 177–198.

Coltart, N. (1993). *How to survive as a psychotherapist.* London: Sheldon Press.

Coltart, N. (1996). *The baby and the bathwater.* Madison, CT: International Universities Press.

Cooper, Alan. (1969). Problems in the therapy of a patient with masked depression. *Contemporary Psychoanalysis, 5*, 45–57.

Cooper, Arnold. (1986). Some limitations of therapeutic effectiveness: "The burnout syndrome" in psychoanalysis. *Psychoanalytic Quarterly, 55*, 576–598.

Crastnopol, M. (2003). Reply to panel questions. *Psychoanalytic Dialogues, 13*(3), 379–389.

Crastnopol, M. (2009). Institute life beyond graduation. *Contemporary Psychoanalysis, 45*, 358–363.

Davidman, B. (2007). What are we studying? *Bulletin of the Association for Psychoanalytic Medicine*, 41, 77–81.

DeAngelis, T. (2001). Surviving a patient's suicide. *American Psychological Association Monitor*, 32, 70.

Dickens, C. (1837). *The adventures of Oliver Twist*. London: R. Bentley.

Didion, J. (2005). *The year of magical thinking*. New York: Alfred A. Knopf.

Dimen, M. (2011). Lapsus linguae, or a slip of the tongue? A sexual violation in an analytic treatment and its personal and theoretical aftermath. *Contemporary Psychoanalysis*, 47, 35–80.

Dostoevsky, F. (1985). *The double: Two versions* (E. Harden, Trans.). Ann Arbor, MI: Ardis. (Original work published 1846)

Dupont, J. (Ed.). (1988). *The clinical diary of Sándor Ferenczi*. Cambridge, MA: Harvard University Press.

Eidelberg, L. (1968). *Encyclopedia of psychoanalysis*. New York: Free Press.

Eliot, T. S. (1930). *Selected poems*. New York: Harcourt.

English, O. (1976). The emotional stresses of psychotherapeutic practice. *Journal of the American Academy of Psychoanalysis*, 4, 119–210.

Epstein, L. (1979). The therapeutic use of countertransference data with borderline patients. *Contemporary Psychoanalysis*, 15, 248–275.

Epstein, L. (1999). The analyst's "bad analyst" feelings: A counterpart to the process of resolving implosive defenses. *Contemporary Psychoanalysis*, 35, 311–325.

Fiscalini, J. (1985). On supervisory parataxis and dialogue. *Contemporary Psychoanalysis*, 21, 591–608.

Freud, A. (1936). *The ego and the mechanisms of defense*. London: Karnac Books.

Freud, S. (1917/1915). Mourning and melancholia. Standard Edition, 14: 237–258. London: Hogarth Press, 1957.

Freud, S. (1926). Inhibitions, symptoms, and anxiety. Standard Edition, 20: 87–175. London: Hogarth Press, 1959.

Frost, R. (1971). *Robert Frost's poems*. New York: Washington Square Press.

Gabbard, G. O. (1992). Afterword. In R. W. McCleary (Ed.), *Conversing with uncertainty: Practicing psychotherapy in a hospital setting* (pp. 137–150). Hillsdale, NJ: Analytic Press.

Gaines, R. (1997). Detachment and continuity: The two tasks of mourning. *Contemporary Psychoanalysis*, 33, 549–571.

Gogol, N. (1960). The nose. In *The diary of a madman and other stories* (A. R. MacAndrew, Trans.) (pp. 29–56). New York: New American Press.

Guntrip, H. (1969). *Schizoid phenomena, object relations, and the self*. New York: International Universities Press.

Hanson, K. (1997). Reasons for shame, shame against reason. In M. R. Lansky & A. P. Morrison (Eds.), *The widening scope of shame* (pp. 155–191). Hillsdale, NJ: Analytic Press.

Hirsch, I. (2008). *Coasting in the countertransference: Conflicts of self-interest between analyst and patient*. New York: Routledge.

Hoffman, I. Z. (1998). *Ritual and spontaneity in the psychoanalytic process: A dialectical-constructivist view*. Hillsdale, NJ: Analytic Press.

Impert, L. (1999). The body held hostage: The paradox of self-sufficiency. *Contemporary Psychoanalysis*, 35, 647–673.

Issacharoff, A. (1997). A conversation with Dr. Alberta Szalita. *Contemporary Psychoanalysis, 33*, 615–632.

Izard, C. E. (1972). *Patterns of emotion: New analysis of anxiety and depression.* New York: Academic Press.

Izard, C. E. (1977). *Human emotions.* New York: Plenum Press.

Jacobs, T. J. (2008). Discussion of contributions to *Psychoanalytic Inquiry* issue on analytic writing. *Psychoanalytic Inquiry, 28*, 510–518.

James, W. (1890). *The principles of psychology.* New York: Henry Holt.

Kafka, F. (1948). *The penal colony: Stories and short pieces* (W. Muir & E. Muir, Trans). New York: Schocken Books.

Kantrowitz, J. (1996). *The patient's impact on the analyst.* Hillsdale, NJ: Analytic Press.

Kavanaugh, P. B. (2006). On cutting the grass, psychoanalytic education, and the interweave of ideology, power, and knowledge: An historical perspective. I R. Raubolt (Ed.), *Power games: Influence, persuasion, and indoctrination in psychotherapy training* (pp. 119–157). New York: Other Press.

Kernberg, O. F. (1996). Thirty methods to destroy the creativity of psychoanalytic candidates. *International Journal of Psychoanalysis, 77*, 1031–1040.

Kiel, N. (1964). *Universal experience of adolescence.* New York: International Universities Press.

Krystal, H. (1975). Affect tolerance. *Annual of Psychoanalysis, 3*, 179–217.

Langan, R. (2002). Portals. *Contemporary Psychoanalysis, 38*, 477–485.

Lansky, M. R., & Morrison, A. P. (Eds.). (1997). *The widening scope of shame.* Hillsdale, NJ: Analytic Press.

Lerner, A. J., & Loewe, F. (1956). *My fair lady.* Broadway production.

Levenson, E. A. (1982). Follow the fox: An inquiry into the vicissitudes of psychoanalytic supervision. *Contemporary Psychoanalysis, 18*, 1–15.

Levenson, E. A. (2003). On seeing what is said: Visual aids to the psychoanalytic process. *Contemporary Psychoanalysis, 39*, 233–251.

Levin, A. (2005). Patient suicide can exact huge toll on clinicians. *Psychiatric News, 40*, 10.

Levine, H., & Reed, G. S. (Eds.). (2004). Problems of power in psychoanalytic institutions. *Psychoanalytic Inquiry, 24*(1).

Lindsay-Abaire, D. (2006). *Rabbit hole.* Broadway production.

Lionells, M. (2009). Save the baby, not the bathwater. *Contemporary Psychoanalysis, 45*, 311–316.

London, J. (1965). To build a fire. In M. Crane (Ed.), *Fifty great American short stories* (pp. 264–284). New York: Bantam Dell.

Maroda, K. (2005). Legitimate gratification of the analyst's needs. *Contemporary Psychoanalysis, 41*, 371–389.

Maroda, K. (2009). Analytic training and the problem of infantilization and dependency. *Contemporary Psychoanalysis, 45*, 316–322.

Marshall, K. (2008). Treating mourning—Knowing loss. *Contemporary Psychoanalysis, 44*, 219–234.

McCleary, R. W. (1992). *Conversing with uncertainty: Practicing psychotherapy in a hospital setting.* Hillsdale, NJ: Analytic Press.

Michels, R. (2008). Discussion. *Psychoanalytic Inquiry, 28*(3), 395–399.

Miller, A. (1986). Depression and grandiosity as related forms of narcissistic disturbances. In A. P. Morrison (Ed.), *Essential papers on narcissism* (pp. 323–348). New York: New York University Press.

Mitchell, S. A. (1992). Foreword. In R. W. McCleary (Ed.), *Conversing with uncertainty: Practicing psychotherapy in a hospital setting* (pp. xi–xvi). Hillsdale, NJ: Analytic Press.

Mitchell, S. A. (1993). *Hope and dread in psychoanalysis.* New York: Basic Books.

Morrison, A. P., & Stolorow, R. D. (1997). Shame, narcissism, and intersubjectivity. In M. R. Lansky & A. P. Morrison (Eds.), *The widening scope of shame* (pp. 63–89). Hillsdale, NJ: Analytic Press.

Oates, J. C. (2011, February 27). Why we write about grief. *New York Times Week in Review*, p. 4.

Orange, D. M. (2009). A psychoanalytic colloquium. *Contemporary Psychoanalysis, 45*, 353–358.

O'Rourke, M. (2011, February 27). Why we write about grief. *New York Times Week in Review*, p. 4.

Palmer, J. (2008). Forging an analytic identity through clinical writing. *Psychoanalytic Inquiry, 28*, 477–493.

Phillips, A. (1994). *On flirtation.* Cambridge, MA: Harvard University Press.

Piaget, J. (1954). *The construction of reality in the child.* New York: Basic Books.

Raubolt, R. (Ed.). (2006). *Power games: Influence, persuasion, and indoctrination in psychotherapy training.* New York: Other Press.

Reppen, J., & Schulman, M. A. (Eds.). (2002). *Failures in psychoanalytic treatment.* Madison, CT: International Universities Press.

Rilke, R. M. (1934). *Letters to a young poet.* New York: W. W. Norton.

Sartre, J. P. (1956). *Being and nothingness* (H. E. Barnes, Trans.). New York: Philosophical Library.

Schafer, R. (1983). *The analytic attitude.* New York: Basic Books.

Schafer, R. (1984). Supervisory session with discussion. In L. Caligor, P. M. Bromberg, & J. D. Meltzer (Eds.), *Clinical perspectives on the supervision of psychoanalysis and psychotherapy* (pp. 207–231). New York: Plenum Press.

Schmideberg, M. (1947). The treatment of psychopaths and borderline patients. *American Journal of Psychotherapy, 1*, 45–70.

Searles, H. F. (1965). *Collected papers on schizophrenia and related subjects.* Madison, CT: International Universities Press.

Searles, H. F. (1986). The countertransference with the borderline patient. In M. H. Stone (Ed.), *Essential papers on borderline disorders* (pp. 498–527). New York: New York University Press.

Shakespeare, W. (1972). King Lear. In K. Muir (Ed.), *The Arden edition of the works of William Shakespeare* (pp. 1–206). London: Methuen. (Original work published 1633)

Shapiro, S. A. (1997). There but for the grace of ... : Countertransference during the psychotherapy of a young HIV-positive woman. In M. J. Blechner (Ed.), *Hope and mortality: Psychodynamic approaches to AIDS and HIV* (pp. 115–133). Hillsdale, NJ: Analytic Press.

Sherby, L. B. (1989). Love and hate in the treatment of borderline patients. *Contemporary Psychoanalysis, 25*, 574–591.

Silver, A. S. (2002). Thorns in the rose garden: Failures at Chestnut Lodge. In J. Reppen & M. A. Schulman (Eds.), *Failures in psychoanalytic treatment* (pp. 37–63). Madison, CT: International Universities Press.

Solomon, A. (2008). Depression, too, is a thing with feathers. *Contemporary Psychoanalysis, 44*, 509–530.

Spiegel, R. (1967). Anger and acting out: Masks of depression. *American Journal of Psychotherapy, 21*(3), 597–606.

Spiegel, R. (1968). Supervisory collaboration in the treatment strategy for masked depression. *Contemporary Psychoanalysis, 5*, 57–61.

Spiegel, R. (1980). Cognitive aspects of affects and other feeling states with clinical applications. *Journal of the American Academy of Psychoanalysis, 8*, 591–614.

Stern, D. B. (1997). *Unformulated experience: From dissociation to imagination in psychoanalysis*. Hillsdale, NJ: Analytic Press.

Stern, D. B. (2002). Language and the nonverbal as a unity: Discussion of "Where is the action in the 'talking cure'?" *Contemporary Psychoanalysis, 38*, 515–527.

Stern, D. B. (2005). The man who mistook his impact for a hat: Reactions to the interview. *Contemporary Psychoanalysis, 41*, 691–713.

Sullivan, H. S. (1948). The meaning of anxiety in psychiatry and in life. *Psychiatry, 11*, 1–13.

Sullivan, H. S. (1953). *The interpersonal theory of psychiatry*. New York: W. W. Norton.

Sullivan, H. S. (1956). *Clinical studies in psychiatry*. New York: W. W. Norton.

Tomkins, S. S. (1987). Shame. In D. Nathanson (Ed.), *The many faces of shame* (pp. 133–161). New York: Guilford Press.

Untermeyer, L. (1971). An introduction. In *Robert Frost's poems* (pp. 1–14). New York: Washington Square Press.

Vida, J. E. (2002). The indispensable "difficult event." In J. Reppen & M. A. Schulman (Eds.), *Failures in psychoanalytic treatment* (pp. 17–37). Madison, CT: International Universities Press.

Voltaire (1759/2005). *Candide or optimism*. Burton Raffel (Trans.). New Haven: Yale University Press.

Winnicott, D. W. (1949). Hate in the countertransference. *International Journal of Psychoanalysis, 30*, 69–75.

Winnicott, D. W. (1965). *The maturational processes and the facilitating environment*. Madison, CT: International Universities Press.

Winnicott, D. W. (1971). *Playing and reality*. London: Tavistock.

Young, K. (Ed.). (2010). *The art of losing: Poems of grief and healing*. New York: Bloomsbury.

Zeddies, T. J. (2002). Sluggers and analysts: Batting for average with the psychoanalytic unconscious. *Contemporary Psychoanalysis, 38*, 465–477.

Zimmer, H. (1948). *The king and the corpse: Tales of the soul's conquest of evil* (J. Campbell, Ed.). Washington, DC: Bollingen Foundation.

Index

A

Abstraction, 179
Adolescence, 170
Advanced clinical training
    anxiety regarding, 4, 32
    difficult patients; *see* Patients, difficult
    inhibitions during, 32
    inpatient experiences; *see* Inpatient
        experiences
    power, abuses of; *see* Power,
        abuse of, in analytic institutes
    reasons for seeking, 3
    shame during, sources of; *see* Shame
        during clinical training
    traditional, 29
Alcoholics Anonymous, 79, 80, 82, 91
Ambivalence, 20
American Association of Suicidology, 72
Analysts. *See* Clinicians
Antigone, 118
Anxiety, clinicians', 28, 32
    chronic, 137
    discomfort of, 48, 97
    fictional candidate, in, 37
    good-me/bad-me, 97, 98, 99, 127, 130
    inpatient experiences, resulting from,
        61–62, 69
    termination, related to; *see under*
        Termination
Appointment process, training analyst,
    29–30
Attrition, war of, 204, 205
Auden, W. H., 177

B

Bartering, 166
Berman, Emanuel, 29

Bias, interpretation, 30
Bible, 210
Bodnar, Susan, 62–63, 65–66
Borderline dynamics, 125–126
Boredom, 143
Boundary violations, 191–192
Brodbeck, Horst, 28
Buechler, Sandra, 179
Burnout, analyst's, 136, 140–141,
    212–213
    avoiding, 217
    effects of, 216–217
    origins of, 213–216

C

Candide, 138
Case presentations, 28
Chestnut Lodge, 66
Clinical identity
    new *versus* experiences clinicians,
        90–91
    overview, 89–90
    unformulated, 90
Clinical training, advanced. *See*
    Advanced clinical training
Clinicians
    analysis, undergoing, 19–20, 21–23
    challenges faced by, 25–26
    competence of, 25–26
    courage of; *see* Courage, clinicians'
    entitlement, feelings of, 13–14
    humility of, 15
    infantilizing, 43
    limitations on, 164
    qualities of, 6–7, 15
    qualities of, negative, 27

self-esteem; *see* Self-esteem
transitional objects, role as, 9–10
Cognitive losses, 163
Coltart, Nina, 72, 73, 133
Compartmentalization, 113
Confidence, professional, 4, 11–12,
    14–15, 94, 110
Confidentiality, 83, 191, 216
Coping skills, clinicians', 71, 130
Countertransference, 14, 23, 179, 180,
    214
    character issues, 118
    defensiveness, 34
    exploring, 104–105
    paranoia, relationship between, 122
    phases of, 116
    supervisor, in, 41
Courage, clinicians', 31, 32
Criticisms by patients, 160
Crowley, Ralph, 24–25, 219
Curiosity, 28, 179–180, 209

D

Davidman, Ben, 31
Death of a patient, 134–136, 186.
    See also Termination
Defense mechanisms, 44, 59
Defensiveness, 9, 101, 137–138
Depression, 21, 84, 141
Didion, Joan, 177, 178
Difficult patients. *See* Patients, difficult
Disbelief, suspension of, 115
Dissolution, 144
Doolittle, Eliza, 100, 188
Dostoevsky, Fyodor, 48

E

Ego, 90, 190
Elasticity, 201–202
Eliot, T. S., 153
Emotional resilience, 8
Empathy, 8–9, 13, 48, 78
Enactments, 18, 104
Envy, 85
Evaluations
    challenging, 51–52
    impact of, on career, 50–51
    negative, 51
Exhibitionism, 188

F

Failure, 217
    blame regarding, 66–67
    clinicians' feelings regarding, 66,
        67–68, 92–93, 101–102
Fallibility, 167
Financial aspects of clinical training,
    20–21, 164–165
Freezing, 138
Freud, Anna, 11
Freud, Sigmund, 58, 90, 106, 110, 145
Frost, Robert, 152

G

Gabbard, Glen, 70
German Psychoanalytic Association, 28
Grandiosity, 192, 194
Grief, 63–64, 111, 145, 146. *See also*
    Termination
Guilt, 21, 37, 85

H

Harmony, magical, 170
History, patient, 4
Honesty, radical, 204
Hope, false, 115

I

Idealization, 27
Identity, clinical, 23–24, 27
Individuality, 111
Inferiority, feelings of, 147
Infighting, professional, 144, 194–196
Inpatient experiences
    AIDS unit, 62–63
    anxiety feelings regarding, 61–62, 69
    coping skills needed for, 71
    description of, 58–59
    despair, 60, 71
    failure, feelings of regarding, 66–68
    grief, 63–64
    impact of, 59
    long-term effects of, 62
    shock of, 58, 61
    terror, 64–65
    trauma of, 61
Insensitivity, 99
Integration of self, 49

Integrity, 24
Interpretation bias, 30
Intimacy, limits on, 127–128
Issacharoff, Amnon, 16
Izard, Carroll, 64, 99

K

Kafka, Franz, 32, 48
Kernberg, Otto, 27
King Lear, 166–167, 168
Kolloquium, 28–29

L

Levenson, Edgar, 165, 170
Lionells, Marylou, 53
London, Jack, 64, 65
Loneliness, 85, 189
Loss, 171–173, 178. *See also*
        Termination

M

Maroda, Karen, 53
Marriage, 169
McCleary, Rita Wiley, 67, 68–69
Misconduct, 192
Mitchell, Steve, 23, 67–68
Muted affect, 128

N

Narcissism, 11, 12, 17–18, 21, 100, 109,
        123–125
    healing, 190
    opportunities for while teaching, 188
    patient feedback, related to, 26
Need-fear dilemma, 128
Neutrality, passionate, 6, 17
Nonschizoid functioning, 7–8

O

O'Rourke, Meghan, 187
Oates, Joyce Carol, 187
Object-constancy, 133
Obsessive-compulsive defenses, 201
Obsessiveness, 113, 114
Oedipus, 167, 168

P

Panic attacks, 37
Paranoia, 27, 28, 29, 113
    countertransference, relationship
        between, 122
    curiosity, *versus,* 122
    dangers of a paranoid atmosphere,
        120
    description of, 117
    mutual, 117
Patients, difficult
    case examples, 75–77, 79–82, 86–87,
        91
    challenges of, 88–89
    hand-holding, 106
    impulsiveness, 79–82
    new clinicians, 77–78, 91
    overview, 75
Phillips, Adam, 210
Politics, analytic, 144, 194–196
Post-modernism, 110
Post-traumatic stress disorder (PTSD),
        138
Power, abuse of, in analytic institutes
    ideal training, *versus,* 52–53
    potential for, 52
    sexual advances, 69–70
Procrastination, 113
Professional confidence. *See* Confidence,
        professional
Projection, 120, 148
Psychoanalytic work, requirements for,
        9–10

R

Resilience, analytic
    bouncing back from
        defeats/emotional upsets,
        202–208
    humor, use of, 207–208
    overview, 201–202
    types of, 208
Resilience, emotional, 8, 210–211
Rigidity, 27
Rituals, analytic, 168

S

Sartre, Jean-Paul, 114
Schizoid functioning, 7, 8, 127–128,
        129, 130

Schmideberg, Melitta, 165
Searles, Harold, 71
Second-guessing clinical choices, 92
Self-betrayal, 42
Self-censorship, 53
Self-confidence. *See* Confidence,
    professional
Self-confrontation, 18
Self-criticism, 79
Self-disclosure, 204–205
Self-esteem, 3, 15, 53, 78, 99
    impact of assaults on, 107–109
    loss of, 179–180
    overview, 99–100
    secure, 194
    threats to, 71
Self-examination, 4–5
Self-exploration, 53
Self-interest, 173
Self-reliance, 128–129
Shame during clinical training, 21
    difficult patients, related to, 89;
        see also Patients, difficult
    ease of inducing, 109–110
    emotions complicating, 63–64
    fictional candidate faces failure,
        35–41
    inevitability of, 41–42
    inpatient experiences, resulting
        from, 61–62
    knowledge lapses, 109–110
    loss, feelings of, relationship
        between, 146
    negative evaluations, resulting from,
        51
    other fields, *versus* training in,
        42–43, 44
    pain of, 147
    professional *versus* personal shame,
        45–46
    shaming by other colleagues, 193
    sources of, 32, 33–35
    termination, related to, 150
    vulnerability, relationship between,
        40
Silver, Ann-Louise, 66–67
Solomon, Andrew, 90
Sophocles, 167
Soul mates, 173
Speaking on clinical experiences, 189
Suicide, patient, 72–73, 102, 141
Sullivan, Henry Stack, 97, 106

Sympathy, 8, 9
Szalita, Alberta, 16, 17, 18

T

Teaching, 188, 189, 192–193
Termination
    abrupt, 44–50, 92, 114
    anxiety related to, 136–138
    arbitrary, 164–165
    averting, 150
    case example, 175–177
    death, likened to, 133, 134, 136
    Ellen, fictional candidate, 44–50
    emotions regarding, complexity of,
        150
    motives for, 132, 133
    mourning, 135, 136–138, 139–141,
        141–142, 144, 145
    respectful, 174–175
    suspicious, 132, 133
    unfinished business, sense of, 158
Terror, 64–64
Transference, 179, 180
    erotic, 14
    negative, 132
Transformation, 10–11
Transitional space, 180
Transitions, 15–16
Trauma, 90

U

Uncertainty, 12
Unfinished business an analysis, 157, 158

V

Voltaire, 138

W

War of attrition, 204, 205
Werth, Jr., James L., 72
Withholding, 126, 127, 142–143
Writing about clinical experiences,
        183–185, 186–187, 189

Z

Zimmer, Heinrich, 210